STATE WORK

STATE WORK

Public Administration and Mass Intellectuality

Stefano Harney

Duke University Press   Durham and London 2002

© 2002 Duke University Press
All rights reserved
Printed in the United States of America on acid-free paper
Typeset in Scala by Keystone Typesetting, Inc.
Library of Congress Cataloging-in-Publication Data
appear on the last printed page of this book.

This book is dedicated to
Carl Thorpe and Anne-Marie Stewart.
They taught me more about working in government,
and more about justice and laughter,
than I could ever record.

CONTENTS

ACKNOWLEDGMENTS

The idea for this book first developed while I was working with British economist Robin Murray in the New Democratic Government in Ontario during 1994–1995. His ability to combine a scholarly life and a bureaucratic one with such enthusiastic creativity was inspiring. Also in Toronto, I would like to thank Corrado Paina and my brother Nicholas DeMaria Harney for their comradeship and insights. In government and politics in Ontario over the course of four years, I was lucky to work for, at different times, Rosario Marchese, Tony Silipo, Elaine Ziemba, Jeff Rose, and Donato Santeramo. During those four years, I also learned much by working with Elizabeth Price, John Montesano, Nick Bianchi, Shana Wong, Selwyn McSween, Surinder Singh Gill, Wei Fu, Debbie Burke-Benn, Frank Longo, Bill Forward, Dev Ramnarine, Cikiah Thomas, Marilyn Roycroft, and Julius Deutsch. Paul Kwasi Kafele taught me antiracism in theory and practice. I am indebted to everyone at the Ontario Antiracism Secretariat, the Community Economic Development Unit, and former Premier Bob Rae for the chance to experience a social democratic government in action.

This book took final form thanks to a seminar I attended on the state taught by Randy Martin at the Brecht Forum/New York Marxist School in the spring of 1999. I could capture only a fraction of the surplus he generated in that seminar and our many conversations, but he has all my thanks. Also in New York City, my productivity was greatly enhanced by a flow of wisdom and drink from Fred Moten. Errol Louis, Harry Cliadakis, Toby Miller, Michael Gilsenan, and Mario Motti also provided festive insight. I first started writing this book soon after I was appointed assistant professor of sociology at the City University of New York, College of Staten Island in 1998. There I would like to thank my colleagues and my chairperson, Judith Balfe. A junior faculty summer stipend from the Research Foundation of the City University of New York permitted time for research on the *National Performance Review* of the U.S. government in Washington, D.C., and a scholarly incentive leave from CUNY allowed time for final revisions.

I thank also Tony Tinker for his incisive reading as well as Jonathan Pincus, Jonathan D. John, Peter Riggs, Michael Gaouette, and John Harney for their helpful suggestions on sources. At the Brecht Forum, I was welcomed and supported by Liz Mestres, Sam Anderson, Merle Ratner, and Eli Messinger, and at Revolution Books in New York by Smitty and Joan. I would also like to acknowledge the dedication and encouragement of my editor, Raphael Allen, at Duke University Press. Final revisions to the book were made while I was a senior Fulbright scholar at Gadjah Mada University in central Java, Indonesia. There I would like to thank Nelly Paliama at AMINEF, and at UGM, Dr. Djoko Moerdiyanto in Facultas SASTRA and Dr. Purwanto in FISIPOL.

Alice Joseph-Harney, my partner from Trinidad to Java, provided me with her love and genius.

STATE WORK

INTRODUCTION:
HANDS OF A GOVERNMENT MAN

At dusk I await

Imperial edicts from

The Golden Gate. . . .

When I complete my tasks

in this world

I will go fishing

And never return.

—Li Po

When one thinks today of a government worker, it is not likely the poet in his labyrinth who comes to mind. Instead, two images seem to jostle for attention in popular culture. On the one hand, the government man is the gray figure of administrative anonymity.[1] He may cower like a character from a Franz Kafka story, sneak like the body counter in Nikolay Gogol's *Dead Souls,* or be officious like the image of the tax collector in East Asian cinema. But in any case, he is a man without qualities. He is a dull and interchangeable part of a bureaucracy, slinking forth from his colony to be received with the annoyance an insect endures. What qualities he has are given to him by that colony, even if the literary conceit is to break this anonymity. On the other hand, the government worker is the quintessential contemporary man of action. Chow Yun Fat playing a Hong Kong cop or Yaphet Kotto as Inspector Ghiradelli in the U.S. television series *Homocide* come to mind as recent images. Such figures are bound, but just barely, by government bureaucracy as they act, with the drama often in the borders of this contract.

Increasingly in contemporary popular culture, these two images of the government worker come together. When they do, they form the conspiracy genre. This genre's lure is that the most quotidian can hide the most extraordinary, and what could be a more ordinary hiding place than government bureaucracy for such a surprise. Yet the genre itself has changed, too. In the 1960s, it was represented in a film like *The Manchurian Candidate* or a television series such as *The Avengers* as more extraordinary than ordinary. Conspiracy was the fascinating exception to a mundane world. Certainly Steed wore the uniform of the Whitehall bureaucrat in *The Avengers,* but he was clearly a bureaucrat apart. Tipped off by the visual sequence of the opening credits, the viewer knew immediately this was not just another government office. Nonetheless, *The Avengers* introduced an unruliness into their government work, generating "a superfluity of screen images" that threatened to spread beyond their special case. As Toby Miller notes, each episode generated too much meaning, a postmodern condition in which suddenly anything could represent the conspiracy of not being only what it seemed.[2] But for all that, Emma Peel kept things on the plane of the extraordinary. By the 1970s, conspiracy seemed less of a special case: not the lone assassin and the president anymore but a haphazard figure suspended in a vast web not of his own making. The image here was of Robert Redford in *Three Days of the Condor* insisting that he just read books.[3] When his fellow researchers at a CIA think tank are all murdered, Redford goes on the run, and although the film ends by suggesting he might have exposed the conspiracy, there is little sense that his was an isolated case or even a clear one. By the 1980s, the inability to perceive the conspiracy enveloping the hapless bureaucrat is taken to absurdist heights in Terry Gilliam's *Brazil.*[4] Here, the bureaucrat is so baffled by the conspiracy that destroys him he can only fantasize about its destruction as the destruction of the government itself.

By the end of the 1990s, undoubtedly the premier vehicle for conspiracy was the television series the *X-Files.* This series works on the premise that the U.S. government is indeed like the one in *Brazil.* The government worker survives by recognizing this, or in the idiom of the show, knowing that the truth is out there and not in the appearance of government at all. The drama is no longer located in thwarting conspiracy, but in surviving its omnipresence. What was once a distinct if rowdy threat to the order of good government from outside in *The Avengers* was now a generalized condition infecting all of government. Something remains important about the government worker's labor—as a seeker after the truth—but this labor seems detached from the government now. Conspiracy appears to have fulfilled its work. Thus, the conspiracy genre would seem to be a good example of postmodernism understood as the completion of modernism, where the enthusiasm for new programs and plans gives way to the disenchantment that if everything can be made new, nothing can be trusted to be only what it seems. In the images of postmodernity, all government work is disrupted by questions of its meaning and intent. It is worth remembering that Jean-François Lyotard's *The Postmodern Condition* begins as a report he wrote working for the government of Quebec in Canada. Suddenly, the state is keeping strange company. Not even the recent publication of a startling work of cold war nostalgia, *Seeing like a State,* by leading theorist James C. Scott seems capable of restabilizing this wayward object around old dualities.[5] No wonder directors can't make James Bond films anymore.

But there is more going on with the *X-Files* than just the generalization of conspiracy, and with it, the sense that any government worker's drudgery might hide a secret. As conspiracy has become an everyday condition it has merged with the everyday in the rest of society. These FBI agents are forever discovering conspiracy not just in the agency but in sleepy small towns, routine medical exams, or traditional cultures. In these instances, both government and the rest of society act on each other to surface conspiracy. These images of government seem to raise as many questions about the rest of society as about themselves. Where does the conspiracy end if one cannot find the end of the state?

Of course, not all conspiracy images invoke the government, and some narratives of conspiracy are still discrete, with the good guys vanquishing the mischief permanently. And a lot of images of government work just operate out in the open, as one follows police officers or other bands of armed men into situations where however serious the crime, the threat is not to the integrity of government (except perhaps from the brutality of the pursuers). But whether the uniform is blue or gray, for all the disfavor and drudgery, the government worker is easily conjured as an image in present-day society. And something about the government, that rhetorical whipping post for so many politicians and business propagandists, in rich countries and increasingly in poor, can nonetheless grip one in images of a life-and-death struggle for its survival, as if it were suddenly the most important thing in one's life. Most gripping of all seems to be the conspiracy genre, where the ordinary hides a secret, and the more ordinary, the more fantastic the secret.

Fredric Jameson argues that the conspiracy genre in the United States is a political form, a displaced totalizing urge to know that things are connected, even if by a sinister puppet master.[6] Perhaps this is true. These fantasies spun out of government work certainly need investigating. Why are they so abundant? But before asserting that these fantasies are really about something else, such as a totalizing urge or a psychological compensation for the inadequacies of citizenship, perhaps one should consider that government work itself is a richly desiring machine. Perhaps people are generating and experiencing something in government work itself that leads to fantasy and pleasure. Moreover, there may be a couple of advantages to using these images, not as devices for interpretation but rather as markers for investigation into what they cannot speak.

To begin with, it may be possible to avoid a kind of modernist cultural studies still using art and the artist, however decentered at first sight, to stand for a larger set of cultural practices and even social formations, and using readings of these objects in place of more varied investigations. In inspired hands like those of Jameson, this approach can be mesmerizing precisely because he can make the object prismlike. Yet there is also a risk that such readings can be received as high-handed suggestions that others pursue the specifics of the case, both social scientifically and politically; or even that a politics of aesthetics will not translate into an aesthetic of politics, with pleasure remaining behind in the prism. Perhaps by starting at the other end, this book can avoid some of these implications. On the other hand, to discard these images at the outset of an investigation into government work would risk another kind of reductionism, equally counterproductive, for certainly work includes fantasy, if not often pleasure, and fantasy stands in some relation to labor. More specifically, what does it mean that government work seems to produce fantasies for others, when production for others is a compelling definition of labor in the first place?

That government would be a labor of fantasy, a place where desire unfolds, is a strange idea, it is safe to say. For me to claim that government, or for that matter labor, should be attached to desire, will obviously meet with some skepticism across a range of opinions. With the triumphalism of the post–cold war moment, with the retreat from center to right in politics, and with the Left regarding both labor and state as part of a shady past, proposing that it might be worth investigating why so much fantasizing seems to arise out of the experience of government is sure to raise suspicions. It might even produce some snickering among government workers. It is certainly an idea that I would have greeted with exasperation at many moments during my four years as a public sector manager. And yet there are other moments I remember as precisely unexplainably pleasurable. I bring up my own experience at this point not to say it validates this idea, although it definitely motivates this study, but instead to indicate that this idea should not be mistaken for an argument about a mass psychology of power, or order, or domination. I was a midlevel manager without any of these dispositions. Nor, obviously, would a reading of conspiracy films or police dramas as mass psychology be consistent with a treatment of government work in the first instance for how it is daily experienced. But this is not to say that the interest of people in government who do not work in government should go unexplained. So, what is government work and how does it generate so much interest in popular culture at a time, it is almost too apparent to say, when there is so little interest in government among U.S. citizens, with many other developed nations now following suit? The abundance of these fantasies in the face of the citizenry's disengagement with formal political processes demands attention.

Perhaps a phenomenology of government work might soon show that there is something about laboring in the state that becomes laboring on the state and in turn becomes activity for others without bounds, a place of fantasy. Moreover, it may be an activity not only for others but with others, where administered publics are sparked to recognize something of the labor in themselves, a labor that is not a displacement of society but a practice of it, a practice of society on society. In each concrete instance, this labor is experienced not just as the line at the Department of Motor Vehicles and not just as a symbol of a universe of citizenship but also in its contradiction, as this practice of society on society, of which the universe of citizenship is only one public, and not very satisfying, result. And the odd power of this mundane moment on both sides of the wicket comes from what Michael E. Brown and Randy Martin might call the specter of another fetish: that of the society of producers itself.[7] Or so this book will argue. But how to do it? And what would it prove anyway? I think the answers to these two questions are interdependent.

The way to tackle the quotidian world of government work would be to use what is currently the main scholarly tool of the everyday, cultural studies—a tool that given the dimensions of popular imagery involved, would seem especially suitable.[8] Yet when one looks at cultural studies, there is a conspicuous absence of scholarship on government, work, and most especially both.[9] This is no accident. Cultural studies largely developed in reaction to scholarship on work and the state that seemed to ignore the everyday and its generations of difference and meaning. In fact, it was to some extent because those other scholarships appeared to have run their course that cultural studies attracted so much attention. Those scholarships yielded to cultural studies in part because they seemed incapable of addressing the social and political issues of the day, and particularly the rise of new social movements and the growing commodification of knowledge.[10] This is an ironic statement, however, since now it is cultural studies that suddenly seems overwhelmed by the social and political issues of the day. Think of the way capital is currently fleeing its social basis under what is termed globalization, or the way the U.S. government has turned to massive race-class repression in the prison-industrial complex to keep order, or the crushing debt and job subjectivities may have acquired to sustain accumulation. Cultural studies has much to say about the way this is happening. But is it doing it? And even if one takes the broadest notion of cultural studies as including postcolonial, performance, body, and sexuality studies—to name a few of the most productive—does it have enough at its disposal for the task of putting critique in the service of a new kind of politics?

On the other hand, perhaps as cultural studies now knows what it is like to feel the sting of its own limits or the loneliness of trying to go it alone, a more sympathetic revisit of the scholarships it once sought to invigorate though soon superseded with youthful confidence might lead to some insight into its own challenges. At least for a scholarly impulse like cultural studies that interrogates boundaries, it might be worth asking why the boundaries of state and labor seem so impregnable.

The last truly influential theoretical works on the state and labor were written and published at the same time that cultural studies was, in fact, inventing itself in England. This chronology should be a reminder not to be too clever with intellectual histories as well as a clue to mutual dependencies. Nicos Poulantzas published his studies of the state in English-language editions throughout the 1970s.[11] Harry Braverman launched widespread renewed interest in the labor process with the publication in 1974 of his monumental *Labor and Monopoly Capital: The Degradation of Work in the Twentieth Century*.[12] Perhaps only writing from the vantage point of cultural studies would these works even be connected. They were written within differing marxist traditions on different continents, and they inspired separate and often mutually uninterested scholarly courses of investigation in those that followed. Yet for all that, they share an obvious connection in imperatives of the day. Poulantzas, an exiled Greek communist, found himself trying to affect the French Communist Party's approach toward parliamentary democracy—an approach called Eurocommunism. He was concerned that if the state were approached as a unity and not a field of forces, the party would be outmaneuvered. Braverman wanted to account for the weakness of the U.S. labor movement at that moment and, at the same time, show that the movement held the key to combating the government-led co-optations, or outmaneuverings, of the movement's concerns.

Although his book came to be known for his thesis on workers' skills being the main obstacle to capital accumulation, Braverman did not propose accumulation as an objective and ineluctable machine of de-skilling. As Tony Tinker notes, contrary to much of the subsequent labor process literature in England, Braverman's task was in large measure to debunk the U.S. government's reskilling myth, in which education and skills upgrading would bring prosperity to all. In its place, Tinker explains, Braverman proposed a skill polarization and dialectic of de-skilling.[13] Subsequent labor process scholars have focused either on questions of worker subjectivity, in the case of British academics, or more essentialist questions of identity at the point of production politics, in the case of U.S. academics.[14] But as Tinker concludes, both lines of inquiry have neglected Braverman's intervention in the politics of the day. Consequently and ironically, it has been left to technocratic literature to see the breadth of Braverman's thesis, and particularly the mutual insinuation of state and workplace in both subjectivity and politics. Meanwhile, that technocratic literature of course has no interest—for instance, in the hands of Robert Reich—in talking about a critique of capital accumulation, but is happy to use Braverman's insights twenty years on to talk about the skills gaps, the Internet divide, and symbolic workers, none of which respects the factory gates or understands labor and the commodity as narrowly as labor process scholars often seem to. And although the technocratic literature loves the way game theory lets them keep score, they have always been quick to say that rules are made to be broken. By contrast, Braverman has been followed in the United States by those who seek to master code class struggle into a chess match. From a different direction, cultural studies soon asked what do they know of class who only class know.

The great works of Poulantzas have suffered a significantly similar fate. He saw the need for the Left to theorize the state, but it was again the technocratic literature that within a few years, and usually without citing him or citing him only casually and disparagingly, announced that it was "bringing the state back in." Cultural studies saw technocratic scholarly interest in the state and its decision making for what it was: an attempt to disappear new social movements, though it was also an attempt to disappear the labor movement. Timothy Mitchell has made a devastating critique of the technocratic state scholarship.[15] He identifies the two major approaches to the state in postwar U.S. scholarship: the political systems approach and the state-centered one. In the first, he documents the impulse among leading social scientists in the 1940s and 1950s to make their discipline a weapon in the cold war. To do this, U.S. social scientists would go beyond the formal mechanisms of the state to explain the conditions in civil society that permitted the weeds of communism to grow, and in the diagnosis provide the weed killer. This political system was a civil society approach, avant la lettre, and it failed, as Mitchell points out, because it inadvertently discovered that the political could be everywhere—not a useful policy position. On the other hand, although Mitchell does not say so, for all its lack of integrity, it grasped the porous qualities of politics and civil society more firmly than the restoration of civil society advocates in the new cold war seem to.

Mitchell suggests the failure of the political systems approach, together with the obvious interest in the state in the Third World in the 1960s and 1970s as well as the marxist debates, paved the way for the technocratic literature to focus on the state. Yet this technocratic literature, Mitchell concludes,

> defined the state in a variety of ways, most of which took it to be not just distinguishable from society but autonomous from it. To re-establish the elusive line between the two, however, the literature made the state-society distinction correspond to a distinction between subjective and objective, or ideal and real. It did so by reduc-

ing the state to a subjective system of decision making, a narrow conception that failed to fit even the evidence that the state theorists themselves present.[16]

Mitchell spares a third approach to the state revolving around new institutional economics and transaction cost theory writers who manage to combine the functionalist weakness of some certain marxism with the subjectivist weakness of technocratic literature.

Mitchell's critique is so strong he cannot help it ricocheting into the best contemporary state scholarship, what there is of it, on the Left. In the work of Bertell Ollman and Paul Commack, he points out that the connection between the state and the long-term interest of capital is properly taken as key. And by working at the level of the universe of exchange, a crude functionalism is avoided while the state's symbiosis with capital accumulation is plausibly posed. But because he has just exposed the weakness of the subjective-objective separation on which the technocratic state-centered literature relies, he must note that this marxist scholarship also depends on an unacceptably ideological explanation, however sophisticated, to describe the modern state, in which its form is a reflection of the terms of abstraction set up by the universe of exchange under capitalism. Mitchell remarks that this is how Poulantzas came to understand the necessary form of the state when confronted with Michel Foucault's innovative work on power in the late 1970s. Poulantzas argues that what Foucault "describes as discipline—processes of individualization, the modern production of knowledge, and the reorganization of space and time—should be explained as aspects of the way capitalism organizes the relations of production."[17] It is the factory that creates serial, cellular time and space along with distinctions between mental and physical worlds, and these categories in turn are used to build the unit of the nation-state and the idea of modern government as overarching, mental expertise. But in this logic, marxist theories, just like technocratic theories of the state, end up explaining the state form as an ideological projection, either of capitalist relations—as in technocratic terms, even more problematically, it is explained as rationality—or interest group politics.

At this point, Mitchell distinguishes his approach from those based on ideology alone by introducing the concept of state effects, in which he suggests the borders of modern state and economy are produced by "certain novel practices . . . methods of organization, arrangement and representation that operate with the social practices they govern, yet create the effect of an enduring structure apparently external to those practices."[18] Mitchell's advance is to see the state, like capital, as a site for the techniques of production, not just power. And in fact, this returns us to another response in the work of Poulantzas.

The other way Poulantzas developed his conception of relative autonomy, aside from viewing it as the result of affinities of abstraction produced by capitalist social relations, was to talk about the state as a field on which class struggle took place. This has traditionally been understood, by Claus Offe and Bob Jessop for instance, as a more marxist way to explain divisions in the state crucial to interest group interpretations in the technocratic literature. As such, it is portrayed as a struggle over meanings, resources, decisions, and commodifications out in society using the abstractions of capitalist social relations resident in the state. But what if Foucault had led Poulantzas to consider the materiality of this struggle as truly a field of labor? What if Poulantzas meant that the very labor of making the state daily produced its own parallel problems of extraction and abstraction? What if what Mitchell calls state effects were understood as embodied technique in a field of labor? If one sees the state as an ideological construct built on terms thrown up by the universe of exchange, it becomes difficult to reunite that ideology with a materiality of its own, as Mitchell proves. Nevertheless, one could maintain materiality by recognizing the state as labor under capitalist conditions. Such labor produces state effects at the level of a universe of exchange (citizenship, nation-states, education standards); then, too, such state effects as commodities get their power not just from symbolizing this universe of exchange but also from symbolizing the underlying society of producers that makes this universe possible. And because these state effects are so conscious of their symbolic use as markers of equivalency, they constantly if inadvertently draw attention to the mutual interdependencies of labor that make incessant comparison, equivalency, and exchange possible. These interdependencies surface momentarily to suggest the possibility of another kind of fetish.[19] No wonder, then, that the experience of state work leads to dreaming, fantasy, and glimpses of pleasure at odds with the surface of both labor and government.

So perhaps state work is the term for that kind of labor that most knows itself as comparison, equivalency, and exchange in the social realm. And perhaps this self-reflection gives rise to certain fantasizing, even to Steven Seagal playing an Environmental Protection Agency field officer in *Fire Down Below* (WB, 1997) who snaps human limbs to protect water quality. This fantasizing is not the same as emancipatory politics, although I am suggesting it might be part of such a politics of state work and not its substitution. To determine this claim, however, cultural studies is needed. Cultural studies can help take seriously the phenomenon of other dreams offered by the society of producers, and to take their production seriously as politics—but only if cultural studies is willing to recognize the labor out of which these things are coming, and therefore, to take seriously questions of organization of government, labor, and even party, or in short, state work.[20] Perhaps this is exactly what cultural studies needs to do for itself, too. Like the agent who tries to leave the company, sooner or later cultural studies may have to look at these hands, the hands of a government man.

Braverman and Poulantzas looked down at their hands to see what Michael Hardt has called more recently the coming of post–civil society, building on Gilles Deleuze's idea of a society of control. In this phase of real subsumption, of all kinds of labor being born and dying within the history of capitalism, Hardt notes that the old institutional forms of discipline organized by civil society are not really necessary anymore, that new "whatever identities" themselves need capital for their orientation.[21] Both Poulantzas and Braverman may well have seen this coming, and like Hardt, have wanted to find "new potentialities in the form and nature of labor, or creative social practices."[22] If Poulantzas could have viewed the situationists as government dreamers or Braverman the League of Revolutionary Black Workers as fantasizers of labor, might they have gone further or been followed elsewhere? Cultural studies should be ready to ask such questions. What other social rhythms are the society of producers creating as a basis for politics even in the sway of capital's undulations?[23]

The way this subject is investigated might turn out to also answer the question of what can be achieved by doing so. The rhythm of communism may also be its road. And yet, as if the case for looking for socialism in government bureaucracy were not already counterintuitive, looking for socialism in the age of capitalist triumphalism might make the project appear redundant before it gets started. Still, it is precisely those technocratic sciences devoted to becoming state work that look a lot less triumphant than they ought to. A review of the social sciences in the postwar period makes it hard to escape the conclusion that rather than saving capitalism, capitalism saved them. As a result, most social sciences have either abandoned the ambition of earlier generations, however misguided, in favor of pure technique or soul-searching. But whether the disciplinarity is parodic like rational choice modeling or pathetic like social economics, it may be, taking Hardt and Deleuze a little further, the archaic disciplinarity itself that is the best clue to its irrelevance.

Under these circumstances, it might be wise to ask what state work is becoming and why it cannot be captured by these disciplines. As it turns out, there is one such discipline that claims to be about exactly labor in government. Public administration, as I hope this book will show however, has little to say about labor or government, and public administrationists have almost nothing to say about why their subject would be the site of so much popular imagination. This is not accidental. They are haunted by the specter of government as a workplace and the workplace as a government. Thus, on the one hand, the revolt against hyperrationalism in the discipline, and on the other hand, the special pleading for government as a unique environment.[24] This fear in turn leads them to misrecognize the greater threat to the present order in state work they strive to promote: a politics bound neither by government nor workplace and growing up with only the ever expanding interdependencies of state work as its temporary limits.

But if public administration does have its limits, it is at these very limits that cultural studies can test its own ability to go further, engaging labor and government, and through them, state work.

1. YES, MINISTER:
THE RISE AND FALL OF THE ONTARIO
ANTIRACISM SECRETARIAT

It may well be that a thorough analysis of the state would demonstrate its difference from government and define it in relation to the agencies of capital.—Michael E. Brown, *The Production of Society*

If the popular images of conspiracy suggest there is more to government work than meets the eye, and if the muteness of those same images direct the investigator to disciplines that might say more, those disciplines do their part to fan the embers of suspicion. Whatever is lurking in daily government work seems to invite investigation, but such investigation soon takes on the atmosphere of the conspiracy images that prompted it. If there is a socialism hidden in government quotidian, no one, it soon turns out, is going to make it easy to unveil. This is nowhere more evident than in the discipline supposed to be about daily labor in the government.[1]

The discipline of public administration has spent a century distinguishing itself from other bodies of knowledge and practices.[2] Many scholars have worked hard in recent years to justify this separation by building the discipline's theoretical integrity.[3] Yet for all this, public administration is neither about government, a topic left to political science with dire consequences, or labor, a topic once relegated to industrial sociology and then more recently to labor process theory.[4] Asking public administration to explain what in government work generates such popular dreaming therefore yields no answer. But the investigator is left with a good lead: Why is public administration not what it appears to be? Why does it claim to be about government labor when as this book will show, its presence ensures that government and labor will be treated not just elsewhere but separately? Hunches swirl around this lead. Could there be something to hide in the combination of government and labor? Could there be some connection between this separation and several other notorious separations in scholarship? At the same time, such an investigation cannot help but begin quixotically. After all, are not government and labor old windmills on the landscape of globalization? Do not both finance capital and new social movements hurl past these history-bound edifices in a blur? If so, it would be hard to find a more quixotic place to start than the socialist government of Ontario, Canada in the 1990s—and a more quixotic figure than me.

WORKING IN THE GOVERNMENT

In 1992, I had completed my doctoral dissertation on Caribbean nationalism and converted it into a book manuscript as evidence of my labor power. I was living at home in Toronto again after a peripatetic path of graduate training, preparing to compete with a reserve army of academic wageworkers in selling this labor power, when I received an offer of work in the Ontario Ministry of Intergovernmental Affairs.[5] In 1990, the New Democratic Party (NDP) of Ontario had won an unexpected majority in the province's parliament—a province that is the most populous and prosperous in Canada. Most of Canada's welfare state is administered at the provincial level, by a system of civil service based like most in the empire on the Whitehall model.[6] Now this province and its welfare state were in the hands of a party that called itself democratic socialist, even if once in office it would refer to itself as social democratic. The change in signifier was not unimportant but either way it could be argued that it was the most genuinely Left-oriented government to hold an industrial and financial center in North America any time in the last fifty years. The year 1990 was another cold one for parliamentary social democracy around the world and an especially harsh one for the Left in general, with the "collapse of the Soviet Union" already commonly narrated as a "foundational image" in a story about somebody else.[7] In this context, the NDP victory carried a kind of popular front appeal, not least because the party itself offered such repetitions of difference in its daily life. It was good news, and like most good news, it was the goodness and not the news that got most of the attention. If it was not much remarked in the United States, Canada's Left was quick to recognize its own exceptionalism in this moment.

PLEASURES OF THE MONDAY MORNING
MEETING

I spent over three years working for the NDP government. I began as a policy analyst on constitutional issues and finished as a campaign manager for one of the parliamentary candidates in the government's bid for reelection, moving from the civil service to the party proper in this last position. In the middle, I rose as far as manager in the Ontario Ministry of Citizenship and Culture, within the Ontario Antiracism Secretariat, and most of my experience during these three years was as a bureaucrat officially without party affiliation. I had a lot of ambivalence about working for a social democratic government, about working as a manager in a government bureaucracy, and about working generally. It was not so much the limits of social democracy or problems of state power that preoccupied me, however, but the more immediate and everyday experience of my work. I wanted to understand it better, especially its mysterious pleasure.

An account of my experience begins in the countless professional development seminars, retreats, and workshops where I sat thinking about why I was working in government, my preempted career as an academic, and the growing difficulties my friends in the NDP seemed to be having. And I thought about why I was sitting through all those sessions listening and talking about what we were supposed to be doing and how we should arrange ourselves to do it. At the same time, I enjoyed the sessions, even looked forward to them. This entire book comes out of this moment, in a way, sitting enjoying something I felt was completely unsatisfactory. At the superficial level, the sessions were enjoyable because they broke the routine, and unsatisfactory because they used private sector language and models to talk about my work. But if I had stopped the analysis there I would probably have been moved to write a book about labor relations in the state or privatization.[8] This book is not interested in either of those terms as they have been handed down.

Rather, I suspected that my conflicting feelings hinted at a deeper question of what it meant to work for the government and perhaps even what it meant to labor with others in general. I do not mean by this suspicion that I take labor to be a kind of common denominator through which a universal language is possible for an ideal-type organization to emerge. I am speaking instead of a socialized labor that "brings people together without dictating what they do with their togetherness," as

Randy Martin puts it. And since labor is not an identity category but "an activity that confronts its own conditions of production," it must confront them within the categories of difference that constitute social life.[9] That I was able to turn this suspicion to productive use by writing this study I owe completely to my coworkers and not because this is the gracious beginning of a book but because they recognized the specificity of struggle in difference that socialized labor made possible. Although there are many kinds of antiracism, many of my coworkers seemed to be under the impression that this social democratic government was actually interested in the anticapitalist kind. It was lucky for me that they had this impression, even as it may have kept the minister up nights. Something was generated by these workers as they tried to realize antiracism work in the government. That something, I only later suspected, was the state itself. It changed the way I understood our labor as well as the state I experienced through government.

MANAGERS LIKE ME

It also changed what I was looking for when I went in search of books and articles written about working in government to help me understand my condition. As I read public administration, public management, public policy, organizational theory, and related political science literature, my first impressions were that they were oddly uninterested in what it meant to work in government.[10] This is not to say that I was not hailed by this literature. In fact, today especially there is a growing body of work dedicated specifically to my managerial importance, from the reinventing government project to the public management discourse. Mark H. Moore, the leading authority on public management at Harvard's Kennedy School of Government, claims that managers like me should be "seen as explorers who, with others, seek to discover, define, and produce public value." In this view, I was supposed to "look *out* to the value" of what I was producing "as well as down to the efficacy and propriety" of the means of production. I would "engage the politics surrounding [my] organization to help define public value as well as engineer how [my] organization operates."[11] I would be at my best, suggests Ralph P. Hummel, another authority on public bureaucracy, when I "convoke the political community to formulate public values that do not yet exist."[12] To do this, I would have to mix a historical knowledge of the bureaucratic paradigm with postbureaucratic ideas as tools to "deliberate about the relationships between results citizens value and the work done," according to the often-cited book *Breaking through Bureaucracy*.[13] All of these contemporary formulations seemed to be addressing my question.

As early as 1987, British economist Robin Murray placed these formulations in a more theoretical and political context when he began to speak of post-Fordist public bureaucracies where workers would be freed to produce more value as private sector workers had been in some European industries.[14] The politics of Murray's work suggested that value might stay with the government worker, or be hers or his to give in a process of cooperation that could run ahead of capital's efforts to reduce it. Yet unlike Murray's prescient work, the literature on public management hides as much as it unveils, as I will try to show in chapter 4. What is posited as government value and created as the citizenry's values, and the unity of public value supposed to result largely through public managerial initiative, sets up a fetish of struggle. These are the public management scholar's state effects as much as the public manager's. The fetish of struggle for common value within and between the naturalized categories of government and public conceals the production of naturalizing categories like government, state, public, and citizen, where the real struggles take place behind the back of society. The term public value masks a double extraction based on exploitation. People are simultaneously asked to accept a wage and citizenship. Both are a reduction and extraction of what they have produced.[15] For the state worker—and I will show that this category is ever expanding—this double reduction/extraction is thoroughly conflated and simultaneously most conscious of itself as a specific kind of abstraction, named in public management literature as public value. Public value cannot help looking like a lot less than what went into it under these circumstances. Public value to the state worker, who does nothing but put effort into it, can appear pretty shaky—a system of equivalency and exchangeability that comes at an intimately high price. Hence, any crisis of difference in state work is also a crisis of this kind of abstraction, a crisis of capitalism, at its hegemonic base, in its very categories of false promise. It is something to dream about. In this sense, the new public management literature follows the same line as the public administration literature I sought out.

Many public administration writers seemed in general to view themselves as neutral experts trying to improve a system whose meaning was already apparent. As state workers, they seem not to have questioned the price, despite my assertion above about the power their questions could carry. Thus, in Nicholas Henry's leading textbook in the field, *Public Administration and Public Affairs,* he takes the occasion of the seventh reprinting to conclude that "one can learn the techniques of management science, the notions of organization theory, and the intricacies of policy formulation and implementation, but ultimately public administration is a field of thought and practice in which personal ethical choices are made." These choices should serve "the prime directive of management," which "is to look after the system."[16] But if the prime directive is already set as systems maintenance, then ethics seems to be unnecessary, or else it seems to be simply something produced by the system itself. Even *Star Trek*'s crew might balk at this prime directive. Perhaps they encountered enough Alterity to question the notion of a system maintained by ethics. The exemplary state workers of the future *Star Trek* crew operate less as managers of systems, for all their retro-colonial frontier making, than as new subjects of intergalactic cooperation forever constrained by a federation (and an audience) that wants only motion, novelty, and immediate value. Hence, none of our trekking crew can ever hold onto love or friendship beyond the ship. Duty to the federation made the series possible, but this serialization also robbed them of something deeper.

Just like *Star Trek*'s Data or Seven of Nine, I knew it was no longer being human that made government workers valuable, yet there was little exploration of these workers as brain machines embodying state practices. That would require asking what government was, how it was different from or the same as the state, and where it began and ended, not just out there but in us. My experience was that people did not act in many instances like these borders were commonly agreed on, or even knowable in them or out there. In his essay comparing public and private management, Graham T. Allison takes up the famous formulation of one of the field's pioneers, Wallace Sayre, who helped set up Cornell University's groundbreaking School of Business and Public Administration. Allison reports that Sayre then "left for Columbia with this aphorism: public and private management are fundamentally alike in all unimportant respects." In his public managerialist update of this theme, Sayre does not seem to be troubled by the century-long pervasiveness of management techniques across public and private sectors. He takes it as his task to distinguish for a new generation two kinds of management on the naturalized terrain of state and economy.[17] I wanted a literature that would start at the other end with the subjectivities that produced such distinctions.

Instead, I ran into accounts of subjects made up of the prime directive. Barbara Koremenos and Laurence Lynn Jr., for example, asked me to consider game theoretical models as a way to understand my work as a manager in government. Lynn is the discipline's leading advocate for a renewed positivism. The authors contended that game theory could give some rigor to the growing web of network analysis in public administration.[18] But by this point in my preliminary readings, I did not want to understand only how we labored; I also wanted to understand why there was so much emphasis on such explanations. A social theory like game theory that could give an account of my reasons for action, but not an account of its own was already disappointing.[19] I realized at the end of my cursory tour that I would need public administration because my experiences raised questions and did not provide answers, but my relationship to this discourse would have to be one of suspicion. I will come back to it again in this book, building a history of it as well as a history of suspicion around it.

If public administration was going to be a coy witness, I realized that I had better get my questions straight. I suggested in the introduction that Michael E. Brown and Randy Martin imagine for us a fetish of the society of producers worth dreaming about. But how to wake up in this dream? How to glimpse the state as it transforms labor into work, and in the shimmer of that image, catch the society of producers making the state? One line of questioning that might help draws on a collection of Italian workerist theorists whose ideas of labor long ago made an exodus from the workplace proper. This is the operaismo and autonomia tradition in politics, a tradition that as Michael Hardt says, "builds on Marx's claim that capital reacts to the struggles of the working class; the working class is active and capital reactive." These struggles—born in Brown and Martin's terms by the interdependencies the society of producers create and begin to advance even as they are required to abandon them by capital— "precede and prefigure the successive restructuration of capital."[20] Using them will mean a strategy of reframing government work, involving what Kathi Weeks calls "the immanent, creative, and strategic dimensions" of the "ontology of labor and the modes of subjectivity to which it gives rise."[21] But in the government, these laboring practices are at the same time signifying ones—that is, they are already a struggle over the general intellect, as Antonio Negri uses the term.[22] This is to say, I could see that my work and that of my colleagues had a real effect on us and others, even though sometimes all we seemed to be doing was talking and acting as if antiracism mattered. Conventional public management writers would not use a term like signifying and do not often use one like laboring, but their telling elision of value as both a moral and an economic category in the phrase public value is a recognition of the way the state must increasingly operate at the level of the real abstraction in the production process, and in its own state labor process, to help ensure private accumulation through a price-making market. In other words, our state work was cultural work, linguistic work, and the work of pleasure. Signification became material in it at the same time that labor became immaterial. Perhaps this is true everywhere today, but was especially clear in our government work.

Studying government work, then, is studying the way "language is itself put to work," as Paolo Virno says.[23] What I am calling state work is involved in a process by which one "might account for the complete fusion between culture and production," and the continuing appropriation of surplus value from this deeper level of social cooperation. State work, this study will argue, is at once the domination of the general intellect by capital and the place to find the trail of a mass intellectuality that is the basis for social cooperation within capital's governmentality. In stronger terms, wresting control of this new level of social cooperation is the possibility labeled here mass intellectuality.[24] It seems possible to look at what we wanted to do in government and how that became state work as a way of glimpsing a larger process of antagonism in the control of the general intellect through and in state work for the purpose of capitalist appropriation. How we tried to fight racism and produced anew the state would be only half the story. Because the discipline we *learned* as well as experienced is now embodied in us in cooperative production skills that threaten to socialize the political in ways that would disperse the state entirely. This book is a product of this cooperation and at least a trace of the threat.

In this first chapter, I am going to explore some of these experiences in the civil service and the questions they led to by way of a brief history of the agency in which I worked, and an ethnographic look at some of our efforts. I am especially going to recount our efforts at creating an anti-racism policy for the government and the cultural politics that emerged around the idea of antiracism as policy. Then, in the "*Showboat* crisis," I will explore the way that state work has become an attempt to organize the "raw material" of what Maurizio Lazzarato calls immaterial labor. That raw material was subjectivity, and it was organized as once material labor was organized for capital—to create value in the production process. But the production of subjectivity has escaped any close relationship to organizational forms, and social movements have other ideas about this subjectivity. As we labored on this crisis, we saw our work make a public sphere for an exchange of politics, yet we also sensed the appropriation that made this politics possible. These experiences not only raised a number of questions that public administration seemed to leave unaddressed but also pointed back to the question of our labor. At this new level of productive subjectivity, labor seemed more invisible than ever, and yet in state work it seemed still to show its face, however fleetingly. In the next chapter, this visibility reemerges in a discussion about the organization of our labor within state work. I will outline our training in popular education, in reengineering, and our work with a community economic development unit in the government—a unit that was designed to explore the nature of state work. From there, I try to answer some of the questions that my experiences raised, reengaging the limits of the mainstream literatures on these subjects as a way to go forward.

My specific experience in government came to an abrupt halt with the defeat of the NDP in their reelection bid in 1995. Of all the areas of administration that fell under the control of the next elected party, the Thatcherite Ontario Progressive Conservative Party, none was smashed as quickly and surely as the Ontario Antiracism Secretariat and related Employment Equity Commission. This destruction was partly to fulfill a race-baiting campaign promise and partly the revenge of the civil service itself on a threatening professional development. But this dismantling of government agencies did not dismantle the enlarged social world created by antiracism. We made immaterial labor a matter not of the intellect but subjectivity in our antiracism state work. The immaterial labor of subjectification goes on, and for it to produce Ontario's wealth, subjectivities must constantly be produced and consumed, and as important, they must become the other, as Marx pointed out about production and consumption.[25] Parliamentary political parties are only techniques of trying to channel such sociality, albeit no less real for being in this position. That the abundance we produced is still so much with us in the double sense of its persistence and character as subjectivity is what I came to see as the value of our labor beyond this defeat. How we could continue to constitute this value for ourselves is the question that motivates this look at state work.

EMPLOTTING A CONTEMPORARY HISTORY
OF THE NDP

The Ontario N D P came to power in the fall of 1990 in a surprise election. It was a surprise both because it was called unexpectedly and early by a confident centrist party, the Ontario Liberals, who enjoyed a huge majority at the time, and because the N D P won that election for the first time in the history of Ontario, forming a majority government. The N D P had a long history of ruling in the country's western provinces and of pioneering advances in the welfare state, including what became national health insurance, based on what is called a single-payer system, so dreaded south of the border. But the N D P's coming to power in Ontario, with a budget the size of New York City's and an economy as big as that of New Zealand, was a shock to the establishment's system. The N D P had its roots in a sometimes uneasy mix of farm-based populism and heavy industry trade unionism. Into this mix came first an urban intelligentsia centered around the universities, school boards, and local issues, especially development concerns. In the 1970s, a discernible immigrant Left began to swell these ranks, most notably radical Italian intellectuals who joined a mass immigration of Italian laborers, the largest such postwar immigration in a province remade by this phenomenon. These laborers generally supported the Liberal Party, as did many other newer immigrants. It had been the party in power federally for much of the initial period of immigration of Italians, Portuguese, Greeks, and Slavs during the 1960s and 1970s, and more important, the party in power as these groups led citizenship drives in their communities. But a considerable number of Italian laborers moved into N D P politics through the trade unions and because of the presence of a group of charismatic Italian N D P members of the provincial Parliament in the 1970s. (It is less clear that the strength of Left politics in Italy did anything for these laborers other than reduce their susceptibility to anticommunist ideology.) These Italian NDPers were joined in the 1970s and increasingly in the 1980s by progressive intellectuals from throughout the British Commonwealth who came in the working-class immigrations that began en masse only after Canada repealed racist immigration laws in 1965, a good fifteen years after European mass migration began. These Commonwealth intellectuals from the Caribbean, Indian subcontinent, and Indian diaspora in Africa were often British educated, and brought not only a background in Labor Party politics but also the newer ideologies of postcolonialism, feminism, and especially antiracism.

With such diversity, the provincial NDP was much more a "movement organization" than a party structure, and in many ways this was its strength and the reason for the gross underestimation by its rivals.[26] (The *Toronto Sun*—a right-wing, Rupert Murdoch–style tabloid—screamed, "What Have We Done?" on its cover the morning after the election.) But as might be anticipated, the transition to government for such a party was fraught with difficulty and full of sudden pressures. It had, in fact, previously been part of a coalition government with the Liberal Party in the mid-1980s—a coalition that had ended thirty years of machine politics by the Progressive Conservative Party in the province. But as a junior partner, the NDP was not forced to reshape itself in the image of a governing structure and was able to retain its collective momentum.

In October of 1990, the NDP reacted to its election and the task of forming a government by throwing a party. It opened the doors of the Ontario legislature to the public for the evening. I went with my mother and brother to the party. In the cavernous main hall, a Peruvian pipe band I knew from the subway played for a jubilant crowd. The new premier, Bob Rae, unaccompanied by any security, was wandering through the crowd shaking hands and embracing friends. And a building I had known as a bastion of Waspish preserve looked literally taken over by the city's residents. Within weeks, this high point of hope for change was followed by an editorial in a major daily by the new premier titled "Why I Am a Socialist."[27] The title of the Throne Speech, in effect the plan of proposed action for the new government, was the "People's Agenda." The speech was coupled with a second celebration during the swearing in of the premier and cabinet ministers, and it reflected the party's diversity as it laid out ambitious goals for labor law reform, an environmental bill of rights, and employment equity legislation, to name only a few from the long list. The agenda also included Keynesian-style public works projects to pull Ontario out of the recession it was just then beginning to suffer from an ill-conceived and ill-executed free trade agreement between Canada and the United States—one that Canadian businesses had wanted so badly they were willing to accept almost any set of terms.

The premier had been one of several leaders in the radical student movements at the University of Toronto in the late 1960s and early 1970s. He had briefly been my father's student. My father, Robert F. Harney, was an immigration historian at the university, and as a kid I had met Rae occasionally in the 1970s when he became first a labor lawyer and later a federal member of Parliament in the NDPS always small third party contingent in Ottawa. In 1990, his new ministers in government included trade unionists, feminist and educational activists, and career NDP politicians. Many of the new ministers, and especially their staffs, were more familiar with being arrested or at least shut out of Parliament than in playing host to people off the street in that building. In the excitement of this agenda and these role reversals, however, were also some of the seeds of the NDP's frustration. How much these frustrations can be separated from the concerted assault on the new government by the corporate press and Bay Street financial class remains an open question. But this history starts both from how I became aware of these seeds and how I want to resist either the defeatism of blaming these pressures or finding in social democracy certain internal contradictions. The NDP's time in office might well confirm that both these factors help explain the demise of its social democratic experiment. Neither factor is politically interesting, though. Nor are the critiques of them necessarily generative of a new politics. To see in the NDP's demise a failure to seize control or to implement a model is to make certain assumptions about government and state, and party and labor, which I will want to interrogate. Perhaps more intriguing is that even in its sharp turn to the Right, Ontario still experienced an expansion in the language of politics, and indeed an expansion in concerted collective protest that was a legacy of the way the NDP helped reproduce a richer Ontario society at a moment of capital flight, as that capital abandoned the social base of its wealth. The argument could be made that the NDP left the province a far more self-reflective and self-aware collectivity than it found it, and produced more far-reaching questions about what future this mass intellectuality might like to make out of Ontario's present. Today, if the future remains at the back of Ontario with the reelection of the Conservative government, it nonetheless retains the threat of being next. All that such an anachronistic Conservative government can do at present is to make lines in the sand dividing public and private—divisions more problematic than ever for a society of such expansive state work.[28]

In the aftermath of the election of the NDP, the Ontario establishment did overcome its shock and division in these first few months of what seemed very much like a world turned upside down to go on to mount a four-year assault on the government from editorial rooms and financial trading houses. Interestingly, traditional heavy industry warmed to the government and its generous investment and training programs. But in general, the government was under siege from within six months of its coming to power and remained so until well after the next election day four and a half years later when a victorious tabloid press continued to drive truckloads of rock salt into NDP wounds. This was the world into which was born the Ontario Antiracism Secretariat, the child of a majority government that was written off as an unfortunate accident in Ontario's power game.

THE ANTIRACISM SOCIAL MOVEMENT

As the site of antiracism ideology for the government, the Ontario Antiracism Secretariat became the symbol of the antiracism social movement, a loose collection of people in motion who were connected to community organizations and the NDP. They formed advisory groups to the minister, and following the *Stephen Lewis Report on Race Relations*, a cabinet roundtable together with six ministers.[29] The NDP had always been able to accommodate social movements like the antiracism one in its status as an opposition force. In government this became more difficult. Civil servants were, in some cases, blamed for the slow pace or limited voice of antiracism in the government's agenda. For instance, the black community would blame the cautious approach of civil servants in failing to denounce what they saw as a degrading production of the musical play *Showboat* in a public performance hall in a Toronto suburb.[30] Community dissatisfaction with the secretariat's unwillingness to act as a high-profile spokesagent on racist incidents and conditions accumulated until they ruptured during the NDP's reelection campaign. At a time when the crypto-racist campaign of the Right was gathering steam and attracting press coverage in April 1995, one black activist and university professor stated at a press conference that the NDP government had done nothing for black people. It was a painful charge both for the government and the black community, who were previously and subsequently discounted by the party as reliable allies in elections. (Indeed, more sustained efforts were made with the Chinese, South Asian, and Italian communities during the election. Party officials cited the supposed lack of trustworthiness of the black leadership and its inability to pull the vote on election day as reasons for de-emphasizing that community's support, thereby reversing cause and effect.)

The Ontario Antiracism Secretariat ultimately pleased neither the social movement that sought its support against the government nor the party that sought its loyalty against much of the rest of the bureaucracy. The reasons for these difficulties might be said to stem from problems both with making social change in government and over what antiracism represented as social change. But it could also be maintained that these two problems were articulated in confusing ways. The more social change began to define itself, the more it was forced to define government action, our labor, and therefore become more self-critical. This was difficult in a world where to be self-critical, self-reflective, provoked uneasiness or impatience. That world was one in which politics and government were taken as known, and only the question of what was socially just had to be worked out. Fortunately, in working out that issue, many antiracism workers in the secretariat, both careerists and interlopers, reached some radical conclusions that threw the question of the politics of their labor in the state into sharp relief—to my benefit, and I hope perhaps for anyone interested in the state and its relation to the agencies of capital. Dealing out that concern internally in the secretariat repeatedly began with emplotting a history of the term antiracism.

EMPLOTTING ANTIRACISM

Antiracism in Ontario began in opposition to two other not always distinct approaches to combating and analyzing issues of race and cultural diversity: race relations and multiculturalism. Multiculturalism appeared in Canadian public life in the mid-1970s, and for a decade was a dominant ethos, especially in metropolitan life. Canadian Prime Minister Pierre Trudeau set the tone for the term when he declared in the

House of Commons that Canada had two official languages and no official culture.[31] He was reacting to the considerable demographic and political power of the postwar immigrant boom, first from southern and Eastern Europe, and then from the Third World. He was slyly encouraging Francophone Third World immigration to Quebec to preserve its linguistic difference. He was also reflecting an urban reality, where by 1980, half of Toronto's population was born outside of Canada. By 1990, Vancouver had topped that percentage. Multiculturalism became government policy and Gramscian common sense. People used multiculturalism to describe their circumstances and those of their nation. This multiculturalism, despite the weight of its numbers, did not of course encounter a preexisting homogeneity either in immigrant life or that of the First Nations.[32] Nevertheless, the new concept was now operationalized by government funding around two public imperatives: the preservation of cultural diversity born of immigration, and the sharing and educating necessary to maintain public support and understanding for such an ethos. As the 1980s saw the increasing immigration of non-European peoples to Canada, race relations came to exist as a complementary term to multiculturalism, meaning essentially that as citizens we had to try harder to understand each other now that some of us were more alien. Race relations in government also began to speak about access issues as well as ending discrimination and stereotyping.

By the mid-1980s and into 1990 with the election of the NDP government, antiracism was in ascendancy. Antiracism took a harder line. It maintained that discrimination against visible minorities was embedded in institutions and systems, and their practices and cultures. It also emphasized that discrimination and racism could be unintentional—that is, have no singular, human agent, yet create class and race beneficiaries. This is not an unfamiliar history to readers in England, Australia, and elsewhere, though it is perhaps to those in the United States who have recently engaged the multiculturalism term. U.S. multiculturalism is sometimes closer to Canadian antiracism in its recognition of systemic roots and unacknowledged group privileges. Despite the capture of the term, like antiracism in Canada, U.S. multiculturalism continues to exceed its uses.[33]

Still, it should not go unremarked that in a year when the Ontario government put nearly $12 million into antiracism—1991—Paul Gilroy published an article in England called "End of Antiracism," and Etienne

Balibar was lecturing about the appropriation of the term by the far Right in continental Europe.[34] As the NDP government fell in 1995, similar warnings were issued about U.S. efforts in a collection titled *Mapping Multiculturalism*.[35] In Ontario, the limits and vulnerabilities of a social movement fighting the malicious effects of racial differentiation under capitalism escaped none of these concerns, but neither was that movement halted by the idea that it should know its place in civil society. In fact, it thought however briefly to make the whole intercourse of human affairs in its image and taught something about the categories of social science in the process. Moreover, its resolute movement into government acknowledged that civil society was a source both of racism and antiracism. Rather than see the movement as safe in civil society and threatened by government, Ontario's antiracism movement perceived itself as threatened in civil society and attempted to use the apparatus of government to counter that threat. It was not a lack of a movement that limited this apparatus but the fact that this movement existed with the conflicts and reproductions of a capitalist civil society that constrained it. At the same time, this constraint led to theorizing the state as what was produced by the combined labor in government and civil society. In this sense, as I hope to show, Ontario antiracism had already anticipated the problems that Gilroy and Balibar observed, and rejected the U.S. hegemonic categories of a democratic civil society, delimited state, and corporate economy. The vulnerability of these movements was both a condition of their being movements in a capitalist civil society and the incentive to use government to change the reproduction of these differentiations.

EMPLOTTING THE AGENCY PROVOCATEUR

Ontario has had for decades a Human Rights Code. A human rights commission investigated individual complaints of violations of the code, and a human rights tribunal judged such cases. A small race relations unit in the commission dealt with racial bias mostly through education and funding of community initiatives. The commission itself was an arm's-length agency of the Ontario government with the commissioners picked by the political party in power, but subsequently enjoying autonomous stature. In practice, the commission was an outlet for progressives in all parties, appointed there as a place they could exercise an impulse for justice. But the commission's rulings rarely extended beyond the individualized cases concerned. The New Democrats had often promised that if elected, they would create a special agency to fight racism, especially what they termed systemic racism. The motivation for this promise came from two places: first, from within the N DP—those school board administrations where activists from the English-speaking African and Indian diasporas had found positions of some power and began pushing the antiracism methodology they had learned (or perhaps better to say, taught) in Local Education Authorities (LEAS) and at the Greater London Council (GLC) in England—and second, from mostly outside the party as it increasingly defined itself—from graduates of the antifascist youth movements who battled small though infamous packs of skinheads and neo-Nazis holed up in Toronto's Anglo-working-class East End.

Some career civil servants saw the justness and others the career enhancement opportunities in attaching themselves and their departments to antiracism efforts, as they did with the N DP government's other major piece of equality work, employment equity. Employment equity required both the government and large private sector firms to hire according to the demographics of their surrounding region, submit timetables and plans for becoming more diverse, and remove barriers to employment for racial minorities, the disabled, aboriginal peoples, and women. Both antiracism and employment equity in 1992 were just beginning to see the shadow of the rightist media's big guns. They would, in the end, become the central symbols of the right wing's crypto-racist election campaign of disinformation in 1995.

In 1991, the N DP government created the Ontario Antiracism Secretariat, pumping up the old race relations unit and establishing a top civil service position to head the agency. Shortly afterward, in May 1992, multiracial crowds of youth smashed windows and turned over cars following a peaceful rally to protest the apparently unjustified killing by police of a black suspect. The government appointed its senior statesperson and former party leader, Stephen Lewis, to report on the incident and its causes. He recommended changes in education curriculum, community economic development, a review of the justice system to root out institutional racism, and boosting the Ontario Antiracism Secretariat.

By the end of 1992, the secretariat had over fifty staff. Its senior officials were present on all important cabinet and interministerial committees. An antiracism policy was in the works for the government, to replace the platitudes of the old race relations policy. The secretariat was at the height of its powers. It operated a million dollar youth placement program with community agencies, and gave away several million a year in small grants to community groups wishing to engage in antiracism programming and education. It created glossy public education materials along with workbooks for organizational change in other ministries and agencies. The secretariat had branch offices in eight cities and towns in Ontario. There were also moments when the antiracism ideology did hold some revolutionary content. Indeed, it was articulated in several secretariat publications as a philosophy of praxis dedicated to dismantling unjust power systems and opening up institutions to grassroots participation. Throughout 1992 and 1993, as the government struggled to win the battle of ideas over antiracism, several ministers and senior officials spoke publicly of antiracism as the dismantling not only of barriers but of the power structures that excluded racial minorities.

But this short, happy life came to an end by 1994. Antiracism became synonymous with the weakest kind of reform. Ideas like the economic benefit of diversity raised their ugly head. Both politicians and civil servants began looking to the next election and beyond, seeing only oblivion for the NDP. In the campaign of 1995, Mike Harris—former golf pro and failed small businessperson, and future premier—accused the NDP of dividing the province along racial lines and trampling the rights of businesses to hire the best-qualified candidates. Despite his call for returning Ontario to a meritocracy, he defeated the Oxford-educated Rae that spring and his government moved immediately to erase the secretariat in one of its first acts. In the process, he and his government treated both the employment equity commissioner and head of the secretariat like the police force treated youth of color, literally ushering them out of their offices in the company of security—a shameful display.

In many ways, there is nothing left of either the secretariat or the NDP's regime. The NDP has returned to third-party status, and is once again represented in the legislature by a few Italian and feminist members in Toronto along with some labor-based candidates scattered where industries make this possible in the North and Southwest of the province. Its labor and environmental legislation, equity and antiracism work, social housing, rent control, industrial strategy, and aboriginal rights programs were struck from the books in the first year. The secretariat saw well over half of its staff made redundant and what were left of its career civil servants dispersed into other departments. Projects were halted in midfunding, the antiracism organizational contracts with other ministries and agencies were junked, and the cabinet committee on antiracism eliminated.

It might be hard to understand how such a history, combining a move toward the market and its dictates, with a crushing defeat at the hands of a bigoted new Right, could be much of a case study for a book partly about the possibilities of understanding Left participation in social democratic governance through the ontology of labor in government. Nor is it clear from this history how such a case would occasion the kind of critical rethinking of Left organizational frameworks that could turn the term once again from a biographical to a social description. Yet when workers in the secretariat began to labor on antiracism, they presumed that government could be used to deal with this question. As it became obvious that it could not, they caused a reassessment of government's relation to the state, and more specifically, labor's relation to administration and management (that is, reproduction). In other words, these experiences hinted that acting as if social democracy could accommodate the Left—in this case, antiracists—may be a precondition for discovering what in fact is possible for the Left. Antiracism policy and practice became contradictory in this work not because it was opposed by social democracy but rather because it was confronted with the limits of organizational understanding under which this kind of ideology operated. To put it another way, it was the orthodox conception of state and labor, of governing, that revealed itself in the secretariat's progress, just as an orthodox understanding of governmentality revealed itself in the progress of the Community Economic Development Unit, as we will see in the next chapter.

WOODROW WILSON SAID

Another way of naming this orthodox understanding of state and labor, of governing, is to call it public administration. In the United States, public administration is a 100-year-old discipline that takes as its object what Woodrow Wilson called "the running of the Constitution." In Canada, England, and Australia, the running has received more attention than the Constitution since much of the traditions and ideals of governance reside in the civil service rather than a founding document. This is even more the case in continental Europe. Much of the formerly colonized world is administered in ways that bear the mark of its colonizers, mixed with indigenous and socialist impulses in many instances. China and Russia witnessed a more thorough rethinking, even where that has now been superseded by the residual capitalist impulse. I will be focusing mostly here on the United States, Canada, and to a lesser extent England. In all cases, however, the crucial difference established between the making and running of a polity served to distinguish this object and eventually to allow for an autonomy from the discipline most closely associated with the study of making polities, political science. It also overcame a rival attempt, in Germany, to base administration on law rather than on a law of its own.

In the United States, the first president of the American Political Science Association, Frank J. Goodnow, was a founder of the study of public administration. He specifically made what he called the distinction between politics and administration, pointing out in a seminal book alleged to cause "considerable controversy among political scientists at the time" that "all of government is divisible into the making of law and policy, which Goodnow designated as politics, and the execution of the will of the state, which is the general content of administration."[36] His work helped establish the Bureau of Municipal Research in New York City and led to the development of a separate field. For nearly a century since then, public administration has taken a kind of state labor as its object and province. Symmetrically, the current president of the American Political Science Association, Matthew Holden, published an award-winning book in 1996 titled *Continuity and Disruption: Essays in Public Administration*. In the second chapter, "Why and How Political Science Surrendered the Study of Public Administration," he laments the fact that his colleagues have "surrendered the intellectual initiative in studying public administration and surrendered the opportunity and challenge to bring its [political science's] perceptions to bear on important public problems. In consequence, intellectual dominance moved largely outside the discipline, to work on organizational theory, bureaucracy, and management."[37]

This shift from political science proper is exemplified by Leonard D. White, the first author of a textbook on public administration in the United States, the first nation in which a public administration textbook appeared (in 1926). The United States was also the first place to see its social science departments reorganize their labor into specific business and public administration schools (University of Michigan's Master's

Program in Municipal Administration in 1914; the Maxwell School of Citizenship and Public Affairs at Syracuse University in 1924), and the first place to create new institutions for the intellectual production of public administration (City Manager's Association in 1914; Brookings Institute in 1916).[38] In an essay in 1936, White develops a definition of what he calls "the principles" of public administration. He rejects a notion of principles based on truth and instead opts for one based on "action." White states that "in our view, principle must be understood to mean a hypothesis so adequately tested by observation and/or experiment that it may intelligently be put forward as a guide to action, or as a means of understanding." He distinguishes this hypothesizing from a "series of great figures" who "came to personal convictions as to principles," including John Stuart Mill and Alexander Hamilton. By contrast, public administration principles were really tested.[39]

At the disciplinary level, this made much more room for Frederick Taylor's *Principles of Scientific Management* and the Hawthorn experiments of Elton Mayo than for John Stuart Mill. It established an instrumentalist, empiricist, and pragmatic framework for the field that has never been broken. In the end of his essay, White predicted the triumph of this approach with this ominous survey of his world:

> It is significant to remember that it was Lenin who favored the introduction of scientific management—an invention of an American engineer—into the Russian state enterprises. It is significant to recall that the symbol of success widely memorialized in Fascist Italy is the prompt running of the trains. It is significant to realize that, despite the Nazification of the German public service, the National Socialist dictator is welding a stronger national bureaucracy than any which Germany has yet possessed. Nor is it without significance that doubts for the success of the New Deal in America largely turn on the issue of administrative competence. . . . [P]rinciples of public administration may well mark the twentieth century as the first in which this phase of government emerged from the twilight into the consciousness of society.[40]

I only have room here for a historical sketch of public administration to set the stage for an engagement with its current manifestations, but it is worth noting that a year earlier, Max Horkheimer's 1935 essay called "On the Problem of Truth" maintained that "pragmatism overlooks the fact that the same theory can be an annihilating force for other interests in the degree [to] which it heightens the activity of the progressive forces and makes it more effective."[41] Such critical thinking does not mark the history of public administration (nor for that matter, U.S. political science despite Holden's revisionism), whether sketched or scrutinized. Nor does it take hold after a half century of catastrophe aided by instrumentalist theory in the hands of capitalist factory owners or fascist dictators.

In that same essay, Horkheimer, echoing most of the Frankfurt school at the time, insisted that "understanding becomes metaphysical as soon as it absolutizes its function of preserving and expanding existing knowledge, of confirming, organizing and drawing conclusions from it, or the results of that function as the existence and progress of truth."[42] To characterize postwar public administration as metaphysical in the main is both accurate and misleading—misleading because the discourse rarely attains a philosophical level, and accurate because even the introduction of political and thus philosophical problems rarely questions the existence and progress of truth based on function. Even at the end of the 1960s in the United States with the birth of what became known as the New Public Administration or the claims to voice made by feminism in the 1970s, the discourse retained the truths of its role as crafter of better versions of what was already taken to be there.

So, for instance, Rosabeth Kanter's work on private sector bureaucracy, which comes to inspire work in the public sector too, introduces the problem of power that feminists helped bring to the fore in new ways. She posits an accountability without power common for women in positions of responsibility who do not have the networks, experience, and trust of the organization, and who therefore develop attributes of the powerlessness, leading in part to the subjectivity of the "mean and bossy woman boss."[43] But in her model, patriarchy is something that comes from outside the organization and manifests itself in the organization as powerlessness. This precludes not only the role of the organization, whether corporation or government agency, in the reproduction of that patriarchy but more important here, it starts from an impulse to improve the organization against these dysfunctions rather than to take the dysfunctions as logical manifestations of the organization. A similar limit occurs in the New Public Administration in which the bureaucrat is encouraged to take the side of the powerless in delivering services.[44] As with taking the side of the poor in the language of Christian base communities, these initiatives retain an imperative to save the church that redirects the contrary impulse of social justice and certainly of socialism. Thus does Frierean popular education become a conversion experience for teachers and students who open their eyes into a reborn faith. Such a commitment also circumscribes the inquiry of New Public Administration, as perhaps it could be argued it did for much of the New Left as witnessed today by the restored faith of so many of its protagonists. Even contemporary versions of critical public administration, as we will see in the next chapter, retain this desire to be saved.

Nor could it be said of either the New Left today or public administration that this is just a matter of pragmatics, of the desire to be helpful so common to the social sciences in the United States. A book as admittedly useless as James Q. Wilson's frequently cited *Bureaucracy* ("Though what follows is not very theoretical, neither is it very practical. If you read this book, you will not learn very much—if anything—about how to run a government agency") can be set beside the most recent offering by those who would be most useful, such as Marc Holzer and Kathe Callahan, whose 1998 book is so willing it features their "comprehensive public sector productivity improvement" flowchart as its cover art.[45] The basic affinity of public administration with business studies comes not from the pragmatic but fundamentally from the ideological aspects they share. The conversation between public administration and business studies, as we will see in chapters 3 through 5, is compromised throughout its history, starting with Frederick Taylor's testimony to the U.S. Congress up to Al Gore's reinventing government programs, by this misunderstanding. Focusing on differences and similarities in goals, structures, incentives, and outside pressures, these conversations always miss the common commitment to the naturalness of their objects.

In science, it is still often said that what is natural can be known and exists without or despite human activity. Technology, in this view, becomes simply what people are able to do with what they come to know. The science of public administration, even when it is calling itself an art, takes government as natural in this way and human labor as incidental to its existence. This is what Wilson really means when he says that his book is not theoretical, and what Holzer and Callahan presume as they set out to labor on that object. For public administration, as for business studies and most orthodox political science, the government agency and the firm are the universal forms of human life that White observed. All that is left to do is to ensure they are infused with the proper values as well as appropriate levels of abilities and power. This may not seem a profound point but it has great bearing on the ability of these fields to think about experience—something that is supposedly at the heart of the social sciences. These fields were often of limited use in helping me understand my experience, and yet they claimed to represent the parameters of that experience; indeed, many acted and structured the actions of others as if those parameters existed in the Ontario civil service, giving them a certain reality.

It is necessary to say that interests exist in this maintenance of the natural object. Martin Albrow recognized "what importance theoretical formulations have in the process of organizational change" and "that organizational science was part of organizational life" in the early 1970s.[46] Frank Fischer wrote more recently and directly that "during the past two decades an increasing number of writers have turned their attention to the ideological role of the social sciences," allowing him "to put the issue bluntly: organizational psychology emerged to facilitate the bureaucratic processes of twentieth-century corporate capitalism."[47] Yet it may not be sufficient to discover these interests unless one is able to do more than expose them. In other words, if a critique of these interests is a trap into proposing other versions of the same object motivated by other interests, then the critique may be self-defeating. Andrew Ross perceives similar limits in the intellectual movement dubbed the sociology of scientific knowledge. Detailing ethnographically the way science comes to us through culture and society can limit itself, Ross argues, if it comes to imply a politics of better conditions for science rather than the transformation of science into a fully socialized knowledge. Ross suggests a politics of science for the people in which they participate in something still called science, but no longer easily contained within an ethnographic frame. Ross's version of socialism in this conception of "science for the people" is different from the one I want to invoke, however.[48] Although his impulse to interrogate the object called science helps, one might want less to socialize the techniques of administration and symbolization that produce the state effect than to develop from this critique a space where one thinks about the deployment of such administration and symbolization. Just as science for the people risks taking too literally Marx's notion of fishing in the morning and doing string theory in the afternoon, taking over administration (like taking over physics) cannot really be a substitute for taking it on. Politics for the people might mean specialization in service of politics as even better than specialism in the service of generalization.

That is why it is important to me not just to point out the effects and limits of public administration, or even to explain them, but to use them to reject the organization as the right unit of study for looking at human organization. Neither labor nor self-critical awareness of that labor can really emerge so long as the organization represents the locus of its logic, and this I will suggest is as true for socialist impulses as for capitalist necessities. Neither can one be content with an older systems theory that only exchanges organizational structures like the state for practices that nonetheless took place in the aid and within the boundaries of an already given system called society.[49] Foucault's work has begun to open up the possibility of an organizational theory without an organization or society, especially in the recent work of Alan McKinlay and Ken Starkey.[50] But this influence has yet to reach public administration in this form.[51] Nor has the study of labor escaped the boundaries of the firm in other literatures. In the critical juncture of marxist political economy with accounting and management techniques and principles, Tony Tinker and others have developed a brief against the boundary of the firm, or state, as the proper starting point for analyzing the way the social relations of capitalism are reproduced and enriched. Yet one might begin by opening up public administration to its own labor by looking beyond the government at the way state work is trying to complete the socialization of politics and politicization of the social, in Negri's phrasing. Against this looming subsumption, public administration grows more shrill in insisting on the fiction of public and private, and our labor grows more obvious.

None of this is to say that the ideas of public administration did not underpin the world we in the secretariat found ourselves in. Public administration became material in the Canadian civil service. These ideas shaped the forms our efforts took in the antiracism policy. They also supported the forms our organization and reflection took in the re-engineering sessions. But in each case, they proved unable to contain us. Therefore, to tell that story, I cannot rely on public administration but instead record these observations in a kind of ethnography because what can be left of such protocols when neither unit nor recorder will hold steady to observe them—the necessary results of undertaking ethnography in the state today.

I might begin by recognizing in my own project some of the conditions of self-criticism I found lacking in much public administration literature. The idea of doing an ethnography of a state agency is much like the notion of working for a social democratic government when you are not a social democrat. One should only do it if one is hoping something more, or less, will emerge. And the risk always remains that one enacts precisely what one believes does not exist. On the one hand, ethnography implies an object, a unit of study, and perhaps a compelling commonality that is also compelling as a difference. On the other hand, ethnography publicizes what was once private through the labor of representation. Yet at the same time, it could be said to privatize what is public. The ethnographer in a sense takes possession as he or she represents, even marking his or her boundaries as a means of instituting property rights. To say something in this book about my experience as a civil servant in a newly created agency of the government of Ontario is to enter into all of these ethnographic relations. I published a brief account of the last days of this agency under the NDP government in 1995 in a journal a couple of years later. In it, I accept through the act of representation my dual role as a trained academic and civil servant, and thereby lay claim to the territory of the agency as if assigned somehow to continue to work on it by the academic division of labor. In the process I also created some, perhaps unknowable, amount of publicity for the agency through the act of making it mine. But beyond these effects, through this representation I identified myself with a social democratic government, the approach of ethnography, and an epistemology of the state.

The state presents itself as object in this epistemology.[52] It presents itself as evidence of the public and private rather than as the social arrangement that tries to ensure those categories. The state is like ethnography in its active publicizing of the social, and through its division of labor, the privatization of those publics. As understood from both historical sociology and Foucault, this act of publicity is an act of the state's own birth, but even in this moment of publicness, the private emerges in the act of control. Differentiation becomes the grounds for the private, while the act of asserting the commonality of the public becomes the grounds for differentiation. The rise of the agency I study here required the publicity of elections, recognition of the state in general, and authority to recognize populations in general before its specialty could be born. Once born, custody battles began. Property rights were claimed. And the agency's relations to the whole now emerged in a discourse of exchange. Was it worth funding? Who was benefiting? What else could the civil servants be doing instead? Who should decide its future? All these questions were asked and answers attempted based on some notion of comparative value that was only possible once the agency was separated and differentiated. This might be the case with the idea of a social democratic state generally. The idea of the social democratic state is not possible without the idea of the undivided social from which it emerges but neither can it avoid the fate of that social under capitalism. Yet before leaping forward to these kind of conclusions, these last points may again recall ethnography.

Ethnography concerns itself with difference—often making its choices based on borders of difference. That it has also made states and state power in this process remains the fundamental condition of its birth in colonialism. An ethnography directed at the state starts with a notion of differentiation between state and society, or state and economy, just as the ethnographies that made states and state power. An epistemology of a state agency continues with a notion of differentiation between one unit of the state and another. The people it studies are themselves concerned with these differentiations. They make them through their labor, and thus the ethnographer of the state (and perhaps all ethnographers) share in the labor of their object. For me, this was both literal and theoretical (and perhaps again it always is). I worked for, supervised, and worked with other state workers to create the agency and reproduce it, and with it, ideas of the public and private as well as the differentiations through which we know both. But I am aware that I labor still in this way, representing yet again this earlier labor. One reason this study begins as an ethnography of a state agency and ends as an investigation of labor in the state is that my own labor in the double sense escaped the agency itself, living on beyond it now, and straining past it then. On the other hand, I can be accused of not doing a proper ethnography just as I was accused of not working properly for a social democratic government. Politics got in the way of propriety when I worked for the Ontario civil service as it gets in the way now of ethnographic propriety as I represent that experience.

But I cannot help at the outset acknowledging the categories under which this labor takes place. The question becomes, Is this epistemology reached through an ethnography of the state or does an ethnography of the state lead to this epistemology? This latter view might capture Pierre Bourdieu's answer in *The State Nobility*, where he sees the functionaries as describing their way into an effect of state.[53] I suppose that despite these considerations, my hope is that they can instead be shown to destabilize each other. In the second chapter, I will try to explore how this approach might help address what it means to work in a social democratic government without being a social democrat. This shift to an analysis that asks what it means to labor in the state from an account of agency starts here in this first chapter, however, at the beginning of my doubled labor.

I saw the agency initially through my labor in making it for the first time. I was already aware of this labor as more than just state labor, or so I thought until I explored state labor more. My previous training as an academic in both sociology and anthropology, and therefore even in the labor of representing the agency—in the first instance, as the education and publications coordinator—led me to seek other representations of the kind of labor I was doing. I sought not ethnographies of state agencies but accounts of state work from within the academic disciplines that had privatized this public sector: public administration along with organizational and management theory. As I discovered, these accounts were privatizing in a double sense—and in the process, called conventional explanations of privatization into question—laying claim to the state, and advocating that the state redraw the boundaries between the public and private. But in my first labors, imagined now to be more full of my current labors than they probably were, I was looking for ways to understand what I was being asked to do, what I was experiencing in this workplace, and how I might gain enough control of that labor to feel that I could connect it to my sense of political direction.

As I worked as a civil servant, I did not work actively or systematically as an academic until near the end of my term in government. I will leave until the third chapter an account of this more systematic academic labor and my engagement with academic literature on the state. In the present chapter, I will introduce such literature as it was introduced to me, bit by bit, and often out of the context of disciplinary history. Of course, the present account is not now innocent of that disciplinary history, or more generally, of the ethnographic authority that can be constructed through time and space. The workers I write about can and do speak for themselves eloquently, then and now. Again and again, they pointed out the contradictions in state and labor that form the ethnographic text.

My work in the state, whatever either of those terms may hold in what follows, did not begin in the agency I will describe here, nor did it end in the project I will describe in the next chapter. For that matter, it was not contained, even in the most conventional sense of that word, during the periods I worked in the agency and on the project. It was not contained even according to some of my conventional civil servant colleagues because of my putative connections to the political party that created both the agency and project. By extension, the charge was that it was not contained (but neither then was theirs) because the agency and project themselves made sense only as extensions of other, more explicitly political work in the party and the political offices of the sitting ministers. These charges were not untrue, although I found it difficult to accept the terms of those distinctions then, as I do now, for reasons that should become clear. It is also true that my work was not contained because I began my employment in the civil service as a policy analyst in another ministry and ended my employment, at least in part, as an employee of the NDP, managing a parliamentary campaign.

THE ANTIRACISM POLICY

The antiracism policy was the secretariat's first obligation both to the NDP and the community members who made up the antiracism advisory group. With the growth of the secretariat in size and responsibility, education and development inside the agency became equally important. The NDP placed the mandate of antiracism almost entirely in the hands of career civil servants who had never known an NDP regime. They then hired from the outside an agency chief, at the rank of assistant deputy minister. Being in a Westminster-style civil service, even this appointment was made by career civil servants. If in the end someone with Left sympathies was hired, this had more to do with the politics of antiracism than with the party. I and a few other of these civil servants had more or less direct ties to the NDP or Left movements that had occasion to consider themselves working in or with the NDP, and we were more or less not truly careerist in our positions in the civil service.

The first charge of the agency was to create a government-wide antiracism policy to replace the old race relations "prayer" on the walls of each ministry. The mid-1980s was a period of great expansion in the discourse of policy in North America generally. The secretariat developed initially by augmenting its policy staff, and expanding into organizational change and education activities. For the traditional frontline civil servants who were incorporated into this new agency, this emphasis was unsettling. Of course, part of this unease was a fear of the new combined with a defensiveness. Frontline staff prided themselves on knowing the communities with which they worked. Policy and organizational change seemed a step removed from service to those communities. Problems arose in what was called policy development and implementation. First, many of the civil servants, including workers of color, were skeptical of the change in ideology and worried that their expertise as multiculturalists or race relations specialists would be undermined by this new, aggressive approach. Second, many of the civil servants, again including most of the workers of color, had strong ties to centrist and right-wing parties. These ties tended to be with progressive elements, either the so-called Red Tories or Left Liberals. In any case, they stood to gain more as agents for these parties than agent provocateurs for the NDP, especially as they accepted the popular wisdom that the NDP would be a one-term government. The third problem was that senior political officials were assigned to oversee the agency from the offices of the cabinet, premier, and minister of citizenship, but they were denied day-to-day access or influence. The new head of the agency was equally impatient with the policy, wanting a clear statement about systemic racism that would give the secretariat the power to be heard in other ministries, agencies, and boards around the government. That an antiracism policy became central to the mandate of the secretariat, failed ever to be adopted by the cabinet, and became so contentious in the secretariat and the movement, first sent me to read about policy more comprehensively. In the secretariat, the very idea of policy seemed unstable.

Public policy, policy studies, and policy implementation took hold in the United States and Canada in the 1970s, and steadily gained ground in the 1980s.[54] There are two obvious causes. Although public administration as a discipline had long asked itself about the connection between administration and politics, the movements of the 1960s forced an urgency into this question. Administration would have to be justified, and policy was the form of speech for this justification. Administrators would have to be political, and policy was the place where they could be.

Workers, too, began to reflect on the administration of their own conditions of labor—a reflection also contained in policy. The famous Winnowbrook conference was the culmination of this political pressure, even if it had in mind to be the beginning.[55] It was cut short in the mid-1970s by the forces of reaction, ironically enlisting many unwittingly. Implementation studies were originally produced by those unwitting administrators. Focusing on the difficulty of moving from politics to policy to the delivery of programs, these studies highlighted policy from the other side looking back. Instead of being concerned with how administration could be articulated by policy, they explored how policy could be articulated by administration. They were instrumentalist with a vengeance, and a politics that might have been predicted by Horkheimer, where pragmatism became of equal use to a stronger enemy, accompanied this turn. But implementation studies needed policy as a foil, even if policy was often now shorn of its earlier politics. Policy was still king in the public administration literature in the crisis period of the 1970s and into the 1980s until public management, with the regicidal evidence of implementation, pushed it aside in the late 1980s. This emplotment of public administration was always a matter of contention, and the Winnowbrook initiatives did not entirely evaporate, reappearing in worker humanism and quality-of-life circles—before these too fell victim to the other, harsher strategies of pushing the relative surplus, like total-quality management and reengineering. This last had already swept through private industry and was knocking on government's door in 1992, most visibly as part of the reinventing framework adopted by Gore in the Clinton administration's early days.

IN THE POLICY SHOP

A closer look at the antiracism policy may help clarify something of the limits of that ill-fated policy discourse. Shortly after the assistant deputy minister for antiracism, Anne-Marie Stewart, was hired in 1991, she began a reorganization of the newly designated Ontario Antiracism secretariat out of the old race relations unit and to develop an antiracism policy for the new government. Stewart was a Trinidadian with high-level managerial experience in both Canada and Trinidad. She had been a senior administrator at the Toronto Board of Education as well as an executive at Trinidad's national airline. She had developed a model of antiracism training, and had clear and consistent views on antiracism. What Stewart encountered as she attempted this reorganization were traditional divisions between policy and program work in the agency. In the ministry, policy work consisted mostly of handling human rights cases and commenting when asked on other government initiatives. Program work consisted of acting as liaison with one or more ethnically defined communities, or sometimes with all ethnic communities in a region. Program staff would dispense small grants to organizations within these communities and create briefing notes for the minister or premier should either be planning to visit a community organization. Stewart's reorganization was strategically designed to disrupt these old divisions and make the secretariat "more proactive." As part of this reorganization, I was transferred to the agency to manage its public education and publications program, and a colleague of mine from intergovernmental affairs, Paul Kwasi Kafele, was transferred to create and run youth programming. Kafele was an experienced antiracism worker who at a young age had been appointed executive director of the Jamaican Canadian Association before coming to work for intergovernmental affairs. Selwyn McSween was also transferred to head the efforts to develop an antiracism policy. All of us came to the secretariat in a short span and at the management level. Together with the reconfiguration of the secretariat into two units emphasizing organizational change and education, these rapid transformations unsettled the civil servants who had spent a number of years in the ministry working in traditional ways.

The reconfiguration was said to be transitional, while the organization grew, and the antiracism policy was developed and approved. This gave the assistant deputy minister the necessary powers to make change, but also reinforced an atmosphere of uncertainty. The minister of citizenship, Elaine Ziemba, had publicly promised an antiracism policy. At first, the secretariat staff worked with the idea that the minister would bring the policy forward to a regular cabinet committee for approval. It would then become the policy of all provincial ministries and agencies, although not a mandatory policy for what was called the broader public sector: school boards, hospitals, police forces, and municipalities. The broader public sector in Ontario receives sufficient provincial funding for such policies to be implemented, yet the scale of the effort and perhaps the politics of the policy served to limit the government's objectives as the antiracism policy developed. Nonetheless, it was a mark of the party's commitment to antiracism and related initiatives that the minister, from an ethnically Polish and Ukrainian riding that would not interpret these policies as directly beneficial, forcefully saw through employment equity legislation and regulations, and presided over the expansion in size and influence within the ministry of the secretariat.

But the antiracism policy was not forthcoming. Instead of a policy, what the government got was a set of practices in education, organizational change, and community development. The drafts of the policy itself were repeatedly returned to the secretariat for more revision or consultation with other ministries, especially once the policy had to be submitted to the Antiracism Cabinet Committee. In the interim, the secretariat staff published antiracism booklets, developed antiracism audits of other ministries, and entered into dialogue with community organizations about what antiracism meant, and consequently how the agency and those communities should work together. The energy and creativity of antiracism thinking and action went increasingly into these activities, and thus away from the policy and its development process. Moreover, secretariat staff increasingly came to feel that the policy was no more than a license to do the work in which they were already engaged. My own understanding of antiracism and the resulting way that I worked grew from conversations with other workers, in particular the assistant deputy minister and the youth coordinator. What did it mean that the antiracism policy could fail, while so much antiracism work went on nonetheless? It partly meant that space was made available by the party and assistant deputy minister regardless of the state of the policy. As well, it meant that the antiracism social movement did not stop and start with policy formulation in the government.

But policy also did not seem to be necessary as a way to talk about antiracism. It did not serve, in other words, as the politics of administration. Why was this conception of policy not endorsed by the secretariat staff? The answer lies in these explorations of antiracism practice and its origins. By the time the secretariat was prepared to deliver the antiracism policy, the NDP government was under sustained assault from media and big business. And having set a high standard of propriety to contrast with the previous government, the premier now found himself having to dismiss a series of ministers who came under attack for mostly nonvenal actions that nevertheless were seized on by the press. In the bureaucracy, clashes between NDP officials in the ministers' offices and both senior and junior civil servants became commonplace. In response, the premier's office began a process of centralization, concentrating power in the hands of the premier and his staff, and with a select few ministers running new superministries. From the perspective of the premier and his staff, this action was necessary both because of the extraordinary assault by a hostile press, the big business community, and among senior civil servants with barely covert loyalties to other parties, but also to cut down on the perceived indiscipline in the party as a whole, among backbenchers, and among ministers' staffs further from the center of power.[56] This concentration of power coincided with the streamlining of the government's agenda and renewed efforts at so-called fiscal responsibility. Employment equity, the government's promise of affirmative action in large firms and the broader public sector, remained within this tightened orbit. Antiracism did not. This is one way of explaining the slowdown in the approval of the policy and its eventual abandonment. But it is only a descriptive explanation. How antiracism landed outside this orbit requires a deeper look at why this tightened orbit was created. Looking at antiracism labor can help here.

UNRULY PRACTICES

In a publication called *A Guide to Key Antiracism Terms and Concepts*, the secretariat came to define antiracism by saying it was "a process which acknowledges the existence of systemic racism and through policies and practices seeks actively to (1) identify, (2) challenge, (3) reduce racism in all its various forms wherever they exist." In a companion document, *On Antiracism and the Ontario Antiracism Secretariat*, the assistant deputy minister lays out a model for antiracism organizational change: "Within any organization, there are three distinct sets of factors which influence the way it works. One set has to do with dominant beliefs and values, another has to do with the organizations systems (practices, procedures, rules, policies, etc.); the third has to do with people's behaviours and their experiences with the organization." In the same publication, she commits the secretariat to "putting racial minority communities at the very centre of the Secretariat's business" and to developing "closer links with communities on whose behalf it advocates, as well as to the establishment of effective channels of access to government for those communities."[57] These documents were handsomely designed and printed in large quantities for distribution in these communities, and they were widely sought and apparently used, especially the book of definitions. It is possible to argue that our understanding of antiracism was undertheorized, but I think equally important to assert it was not untheorized—important for two reasons. First, because this theorization took place in spite of the policy, not as a result of it, and second, because this theorization took place in the body of the antiracism movement itself. What propelled this theorization was what propelled the movement, and its production in the government resembled its production in the party. What was seen as the inability of that movement to translate itself from part of a party to the government can also be seen as the theoretically informed practice of that movement with regard to organization generally.

The key lay in the way antiracism was produced, in its labor. The antiracism movement was part of the NDP in that it fought the artificial scarcity of identity use for others. The movement identified the production of race for the use of others as a surplus. This surplus of race could exhaust racism, but it could also supersede itself in that process, offering people the opportunity to produce for their needs in a new way, and in turn, engendering new ways to produce those needs. This understanding left little room for a party that used the idea of organization to limit actions, practices, and identities below what was self-generating in this antiracism pursuit. Indeed, the party had been subject to this kind of critique and opened by the surplus of identity offered to people through the movement. Such a surplus now had little need to use the government as a set of responsibilities and limits. Throughout the party and now the government, the unruliness taken to be symptomatic of an inability to take responsible action in government could also be represented as continuing social movement practice in the party. This practice involved the presentation of the movement as the excess available for use in society, thereby leading beyond the social democratic map of distributed sufficiency. These movements showed that people could work all day and despite having value taken away in the operation of capital, could produce still more value for others. They were movements precisely because they sought organizational form for this surplus, and by doing so, offered not only the prospect of surplus use but vehicles for obtaining such value in society. Like other movements clustered around and through the NDP, antiracism had in mind to exceed the party as it was constituted and applied the same thinking to the idea of government. In both cases it could be said that in antiracism, the search for the state, or what Antonio Gramsci called an autonomous state life, required the use of a social democracy party or social democratic government to develop state practices.[58] These state practices superseded the NDP government. They did so through the insistence that the production of race was not bound by government or scarce in the market but instead represented a social surplus more accurately understood as what could be available to society through the intense productivity of identity engendered by capitalism. In this way, the production of race is also a way out of government or economy and into society in general as a practice. The production of race, of identity in general, is a labor seeking its form. In that search, it is used by government, used by the market, and understood by the entwined disciplines that attend these entwined objects. But it seeks more. This became clear to me as we sought more for antiracism.

An ethnographic story may serve to illustrate, though of course not prove, this labor of insisting on the bounty of race and its availability. The management group of the secretariat, nine of us, embarked on a series of discussions as the failure of the antiracism policy was imminent and antiracism programming replaced the development cycle of this policy.[59] In one of the first meetings, the assistant deputy minister proclaimed provocatively that she never believed there was such a thing as policy anyway. I had just that morning listened to a friend who often tutored me about the civil service—Carl Thorpe, a retired senior manager in the Ministry of Culture—tell me about the ebb and flow of policy and program units, and the rise and fall of fortunes connected to these tides. In the staff meeting, we took up the bait of the assistant deputy minister's statement. We contended that charging us with writing a policy was designed to limit our work. Others argued, on the contrary, that it was the license we sought to do our work. It was Kafele who finally asked what our work in fact was. Gradually, we developed two ideas. First was the notion of bringing racial minority communities to the heart of our daily work and then to the heart of the government's daily work. Second was the idea that we had to fight the racism that prevented this from happening through the identification and reduction of barriers thrown up by ideology or structured practices. The reduction of racism was through the production of race. But that alone was not enough. Our labor had to reflect a use of race, and that meant we had to produce ourselves as raced for use. We expressed this strategy by talking about the secretariat. It had brought us together, but it should not determine our work, we said. Our task had to be to re-create ourselves as we came to understand antiracism.

What we were teaching in other ministries, then, was a practice of taking up identity in others for the pleasure and value of that diversity, and by so doing, remaking oneself as a relation of identities, including race. In other words, it was not the reduction of race or identities to a standard without privilege (the defect in some current U.S. thinking on race privilege).[60] It was the extension of identities as labors of self-creation that we sought. When we finally returned to the policy, it appeared hardly worth discussion. If it did indeed exist at all, it seemed now to exist only as something we did in the act of this collective self-creation that would have to be returned to our discarded pile as our work proceeded. It was neither limit nor license, but a marker in one place where such labor was unfolding, capable neither of capturing self-transformation nor the societal wealth that informed this transformation and escaped its governmental grasp. We rarely spoke of the policy again in management meetings and, aside from a moment when we experienced the affront of its rejection once again at a Cabinet Committee on Antiracism session, felt we had surpassed it. The labor of these meetings changed our agency in the antiracism movement. We had identified our labor as having no ends, but only the means of difference. Or it might be said that bringing communities to the center of our work and breaking down barriers to that invitation was a way of insisting on difference as the collapse of means and ends.

In the public administration literature, in policy literature, at the time of these meetings or now, there is little to support or explain these experiences. So in Matthew Holden's recent attempt to bring public administration back into the fold of U.S. political science he calls for a "political theory of administration—specifically to explain 'turbulence in the environment of operating administration.' " He notes in a chapter on administration and what he labels plural societies that although "ethnic difference is crucial to administrative practice virtually everywhere in the world, it is essentially absent from administration theory."[61] The object of his pursuit is "integration," and administration is the vehicle. If one could learn how to administrate fairly despite the existence of difference, one could come to minimize and presumably end or at least trivialize such difference, severing it from power relations. Aside from the question of how this pluralist-integrationist approach brings anything different in the way of political theory to a field already imbued at least from the time of E. Pendleton Herring with this dynamic, Holden's essay fails to see anything of use in identity and anything of identity in use. But he is certainly correct to say that the questions of identity and difference are rarely addressed in public administration discourse.

Feminist interventions in public administration offer an exception. Camilla Stivers, drawing on Wendy Brown, calls for a freedom of the administrative state that is "embodied" and recognizes that "living things cannot overcome themselves, but must engage with the materials of existence to draw forth possibilities rather than to try to impose form on them."[62] She suggests that ideas of neutral expertise, the ideal public servant, and administrative discretion as well as the administrative state all require a feminist critique that will acknowledge the historical dependency of liberal democracy on an unpaid private sphere based on the labor of nurturing and cooperating, however diversely this was practiced. It might therefore be said that expertise, the expert, and the study of the expert's actions have all been constructed in a public sphere with a dirty secret.

THE PHANTOM ADMINISTRATIVE STATE

Stivers also rightly critiques Dwight Waldo's administrative state concept as serving as an instruction manual for maintaining such a public sphere.[63] But here is where one might make a distinction in order to understand the production of race against racism differently. If such production were merely an effect of the public sphere, then a kind of multiculturalist sphere might be advocated in its stead, where such dependency were acknowledged and accounted for. This is the position implicit in Stivers's work and also, for instance, in Nancy Fraser's attempt to renovate a flawed Habermasian sphere.[64] But this is an effort to put the feminine into circulation, to find its equivalencies in a sphere of exchange, through the famed communicative act. The workers in the secretariat along with the people mobilized in the antiracism social movements who moved in and out of contact with them insisted instead on the production of difference, and saw the work of the movement as the attempt to secure conditions for this production and use of difference. It may be no accident, then, that forms that could not contain difference fully—whether parties, governments, or governmental agencies—were useful to the movement, but like the idea of the public sphere, had to be forms of organization that could not contain antiracism or any other associational principles emerging out of the social basis created by capitalism.[65]

One way of understanding why these forms could not contain difference is to see them as arrangements for the production of difference—arrangements that had to be created, that were themselves labored moments made to direct other labor. The experience of the secretariat with the *Showboat* controversy made our state work more obvious, and with it, shed some light on the limits imposed by accepting the position Bruce Robbins characterizes as the "unacceptable and necessary" public sphere.[66] The city of North York in metropolitan Toronto was to christen its newly built and publicly funded theater, since named the Ford Center for the Performing Arts, with a revival of this Jerome Kern musical. The controversial theater entrepreneur Garth Drabinsky was the prime force behind this new production, which was designed to move on to New York after its opening run in Toronto. News that the play had been chosen caused immediate controversy in the African Canadian community—made up overwhelmingly in Toronto of immigrants from the Caribbean and Horn of Africa. These protesters called on the secretariat to issue a statement condemning the choice and work to have it canceled. Protesters contended that the play, based on the book by Edna Ferber, was demeaning to people of African descent and especially to young people, who would see only subservient images of themselves in the musical, and that it was an imperialist insult in this new Canadian public theater.

It is sometimes argued, including in the volume edited by Robbins, that the public sphere is a flawed (but necessary) conception of politics because it excludes workers, women, and people of color, and was a product of the European bourgeoisie's lingering revolution. Different solutions are posed to this problem: multiple public spheres, performative spheres, or a democratized state or media that can ensure inclusion. Or more rarely, a solution is rejected altogether because the public/private split at its base is regarded as a fatally flawed way to try to conduct politics, destined always to include and exclude. But the marxist response to this debate that publicity is itself a product of capital and the divisions of labor that sustain it, cannot without elaboration explain its persistence and attraction to people. Presumably, such publicity is enforced by the state in this view. But in seeking a broader understanding of the state, and the question of consent in its labor, it seems reasonable to ask how and why people produce versions of themselves for the use of others. Politics does have to begin with this labor as well as come to engage it. In this view, politics could not be something people do once they have the space to do it in, whether public sphere or soviet. It must instead already be bound up with a whole world of production, with creative subjectivities at work. It seems no less possible to talk about the appropriation of politics, therefore, than of labor producing anything else for the use of others under capitalism. One of the gains of the Italian workerist tradition over, for instance, the Habermasian notion of the communicative act is to see the growing capitalist necessity of appropriating communication, abstractions, immaterial labor, in short subjectivity itself, and its effort to force this social life into exchangeability. Following this line of reasoning, it might be suggested that a public sphere is then most commonly this appropriation of the abstraction of politics produced by workers.[67] That public sphere might be one that appropriates the politics produced by women in domestic labor and Africans in the slave trade in its classical formulation in the seventeenth century. Or that sphere might be one that appropriates all the politics produced by the antiracism movements of the twentieth century to use for its own purpose, mixing it with the values of social movements past and present that form the dead labor of appropriated spheres past.

In the secretariat, the case of *Showboat* found us confronted with the increased production of race we had helped create, but it was distorted for private profit taking. Both sides claimed antiracism. The producers brought in Henry Louis Gates Jr. to lecture on the historical significance of the play as an appeal to racial reconciliation in the United States. The protesters looked to the secretariat that their advancing work had helped to build to counter this assertion. But the only reason the play could exist as a revived and more "antiracist" version of the Broadway classic was because of the work of antiracism movements, just as was the case for the first version. The labor that produced the sphere that permitted this work and its defense is thereby appropriated in a view of the public sphere that does not see it as a labored effect. Public spheres are always appropriations because they are always abstractions. Yet those whose labor produce them, each time with more sophistication and intensity, lose control over this abstraction precisely to the degree this is denied. Moreover, a recognition of this labor would make the place of politics so constitutive of society that the notion of sphere would undoubtedly wither.

The phrase "recognition of labor" is, nevertheless, a naive one. Subjectification, that which might recognize, is itself conditioned by a labor whose production of politics, of identities for use by others in understanding this condition, is being appropriated. Labor was always able to resist and sometimes imagine these real conditions because not all this abstraction can be appropriated from the brain of its maker. But now in state work, and in immaterial labor generally, something new can be glimpsed in this historical development. This is the other gain of the Italian workerist tradition over Left-liberal versions of a public sphere. In the case of immaterial labor, appropriation is coming from the brain—a process both infinitely more lucrative in the human capacities it exploits, and infinitely more difficult for the operation of appropriation and the convertibility to exchange. More politics is produced, more escapes, and the possibility of mass intellectuality becomes a real abstraction finally. In this *Showboat* controversy, for instance, we as state workers labored on a field built by the antiracism movement and deriving value from productions of race in the play as well as around its staging. The very ground of its staging required these layers of production for it to realize value, and with each new level of production its potential value increased. At the same time, its value grew steadily more contested by the same producers of race who also produced a politics that was increasingly difficult to appropriate and represent fully without opening the recognition of labor on which this appropriation depends. A Left-liberal reaction to this controversy in the public sphere might suggest other rival spheres, or critique the racism or money that permits this sphere to dominate. This could not account for the generation of a more robust politics, however, except as resistance or a response to deprivation. Nor could it explain the mixture of pain and pleasure attending the task of producing new versions of race and antiracism only to see them stand away and confront us as something alien.

EVERY COOK CAN GOVERN

In the end the show went on—with picketing protesters kept well away—and it was a success, moving to New York. But the argument that won the day was that too much was invested in the musical, that it was too important economically to be canceled or allowed to fail. A play about race was defended on economic grounds. This was a twist on an argument that insists race be ignored because the economic was so important, and not so much a twist as a new combination. Value was to come directly out of subjectivity. For those of us in the secretariat involved with the community negotiations and meetings with Garth Drabinsky's LiveEnt entertainment group, we had come full circle to mainstream's public management's unexamined use of the term "public value." That such value can indeed be understood in both senses is not the insight of public management, though. In fact, for public administration in general it seems that publicity, and the ethics and politics that attend it, is labor only for state workers who must prepare and maintain the sphere. That the state labor of each of us in the secretariat was appropriated much as the labor of countless others in the antiracism movement might cause us to question public administration's view of public value. If public value is itself an appropriation of the politics of others, it cannot at the same time be the collective realization of politics. In other words, if its first ethical meaning is to be maintained, its second meaning of social wealth would have to extend to the wealth of politics produced by subjectivities in all labor. But under such a condition, the notions of public and the state become irrelevant. Yet we were not irrelevant. Instead, we remained essential to producing public value in this crisis. By containing antiracism labor as state work, our work could be understood as a technique of appropriation in which the use of produced politics, real abstractions, is guaranteed according to the ability to appropriate it. It could be understood against the assertion of a technique of organization in which use of that abstraction would be according to need as well. If this technique of appropriation is successful—and in the secretariat, it was clear this was an open question—it can produce the effect of the state in the sense Timothy Mitchell suggests.[68]

But it can also be noted that the way capitalist society produces abstraction, bound up with appropriation, now leads to a vulnerability. Such abstraction leads to public spheres and states as ideological effects, and studying state labor can explain how. Nonetheless, with the emergence of immaterial labor as the source of wealth creation, the battle is joined. The antagonism that the capitalist production process produces is carried now to the level of real abstraction. Ideological effects like the state, citizenship, or the economy are now directly antagonistic to the labor that produces them since they are effects of appropriated abstraction. Earlier marxist theorists like Poulantzas and Bertell Ollman, who tried to answer the question of how capitalism produced a specific state form, described that state as an effect of the social relations of production. Today, it is not the relations of production that produce the state; Mitchell's notion of the process of abstraction in capitalism might instead be extended. It appears that the forces of production themselves now directly produce the state effect. To reverse this contention: the labor that produces the state effect now occurs directly in the forces of production, directly in the wealth-creating process. To ask "How does this happen?" is to imply a stability to this new development. This remains for history to prove. At the moment, this new era of mass intellectuality reveals only instability—an instability measured by the fragility of state work.

But what can be made of this assertion theoretically or politically? In a pamphlet written by C. L. R. James for workers in Detroit on Athenian democracy, he offers an interpretation of that democracy in which politics was not the decision making about the labor of society but that labor itself.[69] James describes the Greek theater as the prototype for this kind of politics—a politics that led to abstractions for the use of all. By contrast today, state work must increasingly operate in labor itself to produce the effect of a decision making separate and above labor, a specialized abstraction. But because that operation is in immaterial labor, in the labor of real abstraction, it makes the state's processes apparent and the effect unconvincing. It points to a new level of inseparability between labor and politics at the level of this real abstraction, as it imperils any act of appropriation that would keep them separate for the purposes of profit taking or state making. James's hope for his Caribbean was precisely that politics would become the central labor of these city-states. It was to be a mass labor that did not direct other kinds of labor but arose directly from it. Its organizational forms would come out of the full complexity of labor in general and its production would be the purpose of all labor. This is why James took Greek theater as the highest form of politics, produced as it was out of labor yet for itself.

2. REENGINEERING IMMATERIAL G-MEN

The improvement of the quality of life, starting from the reorganization of the time of our lives, must be worked out and designed through a political mediation among women.—Alisa Del Re, "Women and Welfare: Where is Jocasta?"

My experiences with policy analysis and in the *Showboat* crisis made me aware that the techniques I was using as a public manager were producing state effects, images of a state that hid our labor in endless conversion to comparison and decision, policy and law. Because we made the public and private everyday, we were both uniquely aware of this discipline and deeply embedded in it. And since this work was not just a reflection of capitalist relations but a generator of them, we felt intimately the loss that is the private and the degradation that is the public. But we also felt the strange pull of these logics, the way they fit easily with, as Michael E. Brown puts it,

> those other aspects of culture and language that are laden with the logic of exchange, the putative privacy of purpose that is analogous to the privacy of property, the incessant comparisons by individuals of one another according to general standards of "performance" and the other strictly organizational/managerial matters that presume the possible exchangeability of individuals as things, and the uses of type-names or credentials indelibly to mark persons, places, things, and events, as cases, instances of genre, or legitimate encumbents to a claim of official license."[1]

It was a biopolitics that went well with our Italian suits.

Yet if we were not careful in the secretariat, our acts of administration would convince us that this abstraction called the state was more than the sum of its parts, and indeed these effects might persuade us that the abstraction alone gave meaning to those parts. Once we were convinced, it would be easy to see the discipline of public administration itself as a natural response to that abstraction and not itself a set of state effects. With a clearer eye, though, I was beginning to recognize that public administration discourse was really itself a labor that ended up understanding itself in part through the state object it creates and in part through the "academic capitalism" in which it was embedded, as Sheila Slaughter and Larry L. Leslie call it.[2] In both ways, it offered its effects as ideals in place of its own labor and other potentials. I would certainly have to heed Bourdieu's warning that public administration was a way that "the state becomes the thing that speaks itself through those who would speak of it."[3]

But embedded in these practices, we found it easier said than done. Thus, not only did we see that antiracism policy emerged out of antiracism practices even though the formal policy had been shelved but also that this state effect came to act on the secretariat demanding a public sphere as its echo chamber in the *Showboat* crisis. The danger arose from the intimacy of these effects. Our daily work produced us as subjectivities who were liable to think of the state as an organizing principle for our lives.[4] In this condition we were both alone, but also had company. We were alone because we worked amid such an intense fog of state effects in the civil service. We in fact had company, though, in two important ways.

First, one might speculate that neither the discipline of public administration nor our daily work produce state effects. Is the recent and popular film *The Matrix*, for instance, about the state, or has one already made the state anew by bringing up or watching this film? State effects produced through what might be called the realization of citizenship may be less intense than our state work, but they may be state work nonetheless. The labor of watching the television show *COPS* (not to speak of making it) is full of the techniques of spectacle that bring people together to imagine the state as the collective form of their social life, as I suggested in the introduction. That this abstracted social life takes on a life of its own is tragic due to its inadequacy as an imaginative form. When one watches a police officer hail a citizen, to turn Louis Althusser's phrase, it is not surprising that one should come to believe in the law but it is necessary to see the labor that created this drama in the first place if one is to have anything more than the rule of law. Because we wanted to realize antiracism, to reimagine social relations where new kinds of abstract life would be possible, we sensed the anemia of state effects in our very labor. But we also had no clear place to turn, no other space free of the state. We couldn't, in short, go to the movies when things got tough. The more the circulation and realization of the state was disarticulated, the more movies escaped their own labor and that of the moviegoers, meant the more the state got away again, returning to its hideout in the government. Yet having the state close at hand was a way to keep capitalism nearby, and a way in turn to think of socialism from the differences of capitalism, instead of simply as different from capitalism. As Alisa Del Re argues in her refinement of workerism with feminism, discussed to conclude this chapter, it is precisely what I am labeling state work that must be brought with us in exodus in order truly to be left behind through the new mediation of difference.

But the second similarity we had with others also complicated our attempts to elaborate our labor beyond the bounds of the state. With this understanding of state effects that I was producing as a public manager, I started to be more aware of other truth effects. If we could not find refuge in the movies, nor could we could find it in the antiracism social movement or a Left party now without also asking some questions. Does the social movement or party not also produce such truth effects, in the most extreme cases of success leading to the naturalization of civil society as the true state of humanity, on both the Left and Right?[5] Has civil society not been de-historicized, as Michael Hardt has shown, and reconstituted as a mirror abstraction of state and economy, supposedly with its own ethos, language, and labor?[6] If so, how could those of us in the secretariat think of the antiracism social movement or the NDP without falling into the trap of forgetting that civil society might also be that which speaks itself through those who would speak of it?

MOVEMENT ORGANIZATION

A better account of how the state gets made might benefit from a better account of how a Left party gets made, and thus, how labor and truth effects create the domain of civil society and thereby contribute to the borders of the state. For help with this I turn to Michael E. Brown's depiction of the U.S. Communist Party as a "movement organization," where "the ambiguous or unrecorded experiences of ordinary people participating in social movements are no less important for understanding political organization" than formal party decisions and personalities.[7] Brown shows the way an approach to historiography that credits people in history with an equivalent intelligence, ambivalence, and complexity to those who seek to understand that history can elaborate historical experience, even helping to enact a scholarly approach that recognizes its own limits by always insisting on more from its subject than history can capture. If parties and nongovernmental organizations also hide experience behind the effects of form, then the way these categories of society get produced is not that different from the way the state gets produced, and perhaps then they are also not as separate as, for instance, the World Bank currently likes to suggest.

What is gained here by understanding the party as a movement organization, a place of experience, is not the notion that the party is informal—a trite observation about complex organizations—but that it does not revolve around decisions about its own ontology at all. The organization, the party, is instead a limited and largely unsatisfactory representation of evolving associational labor. Informality cannot save this image. The image is as fleeting as a decision in the minutes of a meeting now lost to history. What endures is the communism that throws up the party in its process of self-discovery. So, too, the capitalist corporation or land-grant university is held together neither by formality nor informality (whether called strategy, professionalism, or bounded rationality), but by coerced and congealed labor, differing largely from the experience of the U.S. Communist Party only in the degree to which labor is aware of itself as labor. In this sense, the U.S. Communist Party and Shell Oil are separated only by the opportunities for labor to experience itself critically. The more that labor is encouraged to speak about its product or restricted to that language, the more the product comes to resemble the form and the real form escapes, marked only, as Marx said, by the residue that is that product.[8] This is so for oil workers, professors, or Communist Party members. Organization traced by its product under capitalism will be as impoverished as that product, itself only residue. Of course, organizational studies is necessarily an example of this. Keeping in mind the idea of movement organization might help, then, to remember that useful labor and the difference it generates should not be so easily sacrificed to the organizational residue of government, party, or movement.

In Ontario, as that party, that movement organization, moved into government, the temptation returned to focus on decisions and policies—that is, to account for it as a government or state. In other words, to privilege a separated ideological explanation over an examination of the practical embodiment of this movement. Its victories and failures, personnel and interpersonal conflicts, and its relationship to an electorate, press, or social class came to dominate discussion.[9] As this movement organization took power, it gave the appearance of filling the state and emptying the government. We often spoke of the NDP government and what the state or province could do after the free trade agreement or with the federal system. The persistent "disidentification," to borrow Jose Esteban Munoz's term, of the antiracism movement with the party had its continuation in the disidentification of the party with the government.[10] If such disidentification must necessarily want more of something else, not just less of an offered identity, this process let loose in government might yield new insight. But often the discursive pull of political power led to the masking of these practices in favor of a measurable, linear, and reliable narrative of progress in government. This pull operated as much for the leadership of the party as the press. The result was both a government that was taken to be the NDP and a state that was taken to be the NDP government. Government was empty of both party and extraparty practice, and the state was reduced to this new ideological force. To go to work for the government in this context, was to understand oneself also in this both empty and full way. Workers in the Ontario Antiracism Secretariat were now the full representation of antiracism and empty vessels of our will to implement it, supposedly bound only by the constraints of pluralist politics. A look at labor in the government, however, exposes the poverty of this view.[11]

This might be done by extending the movement organization analysis to the state, through the party in government. In theoretical terms, this might be understood as exploring the deployment of the state by civil society, following Gramsci. Or it might be understood as how the production of immaterial labor remakes the state, following Hardt and Negri.[12] In any case, renewed attention to the ambiguous or unrecorded experience of the government worker offers a way to retain and expand a view of the state as a kind of movement organization itself. Such a view may help explain how the government worker can come "to promote the circulation of its deliberative practices within the contexts of its political practices, though the difficulties of this will and must always encourage resistance to it."[13] Perhaps an attention to the actual subjectivities produced in government can help the state worker become more self-reflective in this work, and to concentrate on what was self-creating, joyful, and useful about the movement as well as movement organization labor that brought us to government, or that brings any such Left movement or party to (some of) the formal techniques of state.

Many of us had worked in the party or antiracism movement and now found ourselves trying to understand the experience of state work. In our daily labor, we sensed that the return to the movement that so often occurred in argument and strategy was less a matter of reminding ourselves of our principles or roots than it was a logical outcome of movement politics. The practices of antiracism required the restless production of race, something a state agency could not hope to contain. The question of what we were producing, then, and who we were becoming, seemed to require a knowledge of our practical quotidian activity.

The importance of understanding our labor was brought home to us most clearly by the attempts to address the organization of our work. In the course of three years at the secretariat, we experienced and helped create three dialogues about the organization of our work, or what in managerialist terms was always referred to as organizational change or change management. We were to experience this change, but were also ourselves to become change agents, in the same vocabulary. In the first year, we contracted with the Doris Marshall Institute for Education and Action, an organization born of the schools movement in North America and revitalized by the Cuban and Central American solidarity movements. The institute employed with us the *Naming the Moment* project, which was actually produced by a larger movement of people around the Jesuit Centre for Social Faith and Justice in Toronto.[14] These sessions reflected in the first place the tension between the managerialist notion of change and that of the social movement. The institute's presence in our agency and others was a prominent continuation of movement organization politics into the government. But it was not the only continuation of such practices, as our next two experiences proved. A managerialist approach replaced the institute with sessions only for management workers at the secretariat in the next year. These reengineering exercises captured what was at the time the most current language of managerialism in the United States. Still, these exercises and retreats also raised questions about the boundaries of our work and the object of organization itself. Then in 1994, I had the chance, together with the six workers I managed, to join another experiment in organization. This was the developmental administration project of the Community Economic Development Unit of the Ministry of Economic Development and Trade. In this unit and its work, movement organization reemerged in ways that offer lessons for the future.

At the time, I turned to the public administration literature to help me understand these experiences in organization and ambiguous practices of mobilization that continued in government. I had already seen our work disciplined by this discourse in the divide between policy and program. Public administration addresses this as a split between theory and practice, or politics and administration, or it tries to resolve it internally as human resource or public management. And public administration, informed in part by organizational theory, did address me as someone who had to have my government work organized. But that address was consistently useful only as a limit beyond which seemed to lie a better account of our experiences.

NAMING THE MOMENT

With the encouragement of several of us who had recently come to the secretariat, the assistant deputy minister sought and received approval for funding to contract with the Doris Marshall Institute to train the newly expanded secretariat on antiracism concepts and practices. A series of all-day, all-staff workshops took place in the first half of 1993 based on the *Naming the Moment* project, a broad community training program inspired by both the popular education models of Paolo Friere and political analysis of Gramsci. Very early in our experience in the secretariat, therefore, leftist political analysis was brought to bear on our organization. It might be worth noting how rare this phenomenon was and acknowledging it as an exceptional case from which to speak about public administration or working in government. It would be deceptive to suggest that this kind of engagement was happening throughout the government or with all government workers. Rather, it might be better thought of as the kind of "moment" the subsequent training sought to identify.

This is not to say that versions of it were not happening in Ontario at this time as the Ministries of Labor, Education, Housing, and Food and Agriculture, to name a few, engaged social movement organizations in sustained dialogue. In many cases, these engagements significantly troubled the border between social movement and government as well as the workers who labored in parts of these ministries. There was often the chance to see how a knowledge of government produced a power that not only disciplined these movements but showed the way that discipline might be used to produce new state arrangements—constituent arrangements that permitted social movements to remain mobilized in new forms of organization.[15] If this idea seems abstract or wistful, it also looked obvious at moments when it was not new interests that were presented to the government but new ways of understanding interest itself as enforced scarcity and competition in housing, education, or land. In the case of the secretariat, of course, it was a chance to end the notion of interest in identity and cultural forms in favor of the social surplus.[16] We wanted more for others as a condition of our interest.[17]

Roughly thirty workers joined the training sessions. Another ten support staff were included on a rotating basis after discussion about the split between professional and clerical. The sessions were conducted by Jojo Geronimo and Marlene Hammer, with Geronimo continuing after Hammer had left for other commitments. Geronimo was a veteran of the Filipino Left and an extraordinary educator. The training was designed to cover the four phases of the *Naming the Moment* popular education model. Each phase was to take a full day. The phases were: identifying ourselves and our interests, naming the issues/struggles, assessing the forces, and planning for action. In the first session, a "social tree" was used to discuss who the workers of the secretariat were. The tree itself was then critiqued as a model. A series of "historical time lines" about race and antiracism formed the focus of the issues and struggles in the second session. In the third session, "forces with us," "uncommitted," and "forces against us" lists were created about antiracism work. In the final session, we used a "free space" model that connected constraints on action with possibilities of action. The sessions were to continue with work on how to integrate these analyses into daily work in the agency, but the contract with the institute was phased out in favor of training sessions for management workers the following spring of 1994. Budget constraints, a more cautious political leadership in the party, and the concern of senior career bureaucrats with the ideology of the sessions probably combined to produce this shift. But the sessions did yield some glimpses of our practices.

As the context for the secretariat was elaborated through these exercises, the importance of the antiracism social movement for organizing the events, conditions, and actions of the people in the room became paramount. When the tree was made, time line completed, and lists divided, it was clear that the antiracism movement gave coherence to the sessions. Worker after worker referred to "our work" in ways that made it clear that the work was not a government job but a commitment to social justice preceding and exceeding the form of that commitment. In so doing, the movement replaced the secretariat as the common origin—that is, the reason we were all in the room had more to do with this movement than this agency. Moreover, in the plans of action, more of the workers envisioned the future in terms of this movement than they did in terms of the secretariat. The secretariat was also situated as an instance within the identity of many workers, and the skills and abilities gathered by the secretariat had their origins before and outside the secretariat, and looked to future development beyond the secretariat. In other words, the Doris Marshall Institute was not merely an emissary of a movement that now spoke to government workers but a reminder of the historical and critical process that created government labor, that created the state. The state thus became a moment in antiracism. It became an organizational form for the movement not for itself, much less for the policy or position of antiracism. These sessions at first did not seem exceptional for all these identifications. After all, many of the workers both old and new to the secretariat came from communities of color and had embarked on careers in the government within some form of social equity work. But if the question of antiracism labor is considered, something more might emerge.

The secretariat would not be the first government agency to face workers who did not identify with the agency or see themselves through it. This predicament, if it is one, may not apply in some core ministries with career civil servants steeped in the Whitehall-based culture still very much alive in Ontario but it certainly would be one familiar to many outer ministries whose workers might identify with "clients." Lawyers who work for the solicitor general, scientists who work for the minister of food and agriculture, or former union officials who work for the minister of labor might all exhibit some of the same ways of talking about themselves. But when those workers come from social movements, and any of the just named might, they tend to see their labor differently. The antiracism workers saw their labor as collective, and the secretariat was only temporarily what had collected it. They saw their labor as critical of government, even while in it. They looked for a future not of regulation or growth but change through their labor. Thus, the potential was there in the secretariat for the state to appear not as a solid-state synonym of the government but as a set of regulated and self-regulated social arrangements that might be re-created by a social movement. It appeared that the antiracism workers had a basis for resisting arrangements in the state that went beyond issues of working conditions, yet also beyond issues of loyalty to a public.

In many comments, workers insisted that the secretariat had to be arranged so as to facilitate antiracism labor—a labor, moreover, that was admittedly not to be contained within the government nor destined to understand and measure itself through the government. Many of these sentiments took the practical form of complaints and suggestions concerning issues of measurement, reporting, management of people and time, and responsibilities. Many workers expressed the view that antiracism social change had to operate according to the rules of the movement, communities, and workers, and not of the bureaucratic structure as it was presently constituted. But many of these workers were career bureaucrats, and these sentiments might therefore be understood not as naive or wishful antigovernment rhetoric but as a kind of refusal of the discipline of the line. A Fordist government model made little sense to workers as we began to experience what might be called the mass intellectuality of antiracism labor in these all-day *Naming the Moment* sessions. Government machinery—the Fordist line of reporting, paperwork, departments, and hierarchy—was rejected by these antiracism workers, to borrow again from Negri, but it could be rejected precisely because these workers planned to carry its elements within them into new labor on antiracism.

There was thus a price for this confidence. The difficulty of developing this knowledge without coming to exercise a power that confirmed the presence of government rather than that of the social movement became clear in the next training exercises. More fantastically, we might say we were unleashed by these first training sessions as brain machines into the antiracism movement, either capable now of engendering new state arrangements in the service of a development of an antiracist society or using these embodied productive instruments to hold the antiracism movement in the inertia of government policy and program.[18]

The ministry stepped in to try to ensure the latter case. The use of the government in search of better antiracism labor created a kind of fascination with the techniques of government. The term reengineering harks back to the scientism of scientific management—in many ways reincorporating the techniques of human relations, organizational theory, and industrial psychology back into a worldview of the forces of production—but now instead of a unity of human and machine, there is the drive for unity of machine in human.[19] The antiracism workers felt able to produce state arrangements directly from their brains into antiracism labor, the state line having been so thoroughly internalized. Perhaps, then, we were surprisingly susceptible to this new promise of reengineering—a promise that spoke to us as laboring subjects in a cyborgian language. It touched the machined state in us. It spoke as all dominant management ideologies in their times to our level of development. Of course, what it gave it also wanted back and more. As we sat in our first session with the outside management consultant we had much to doubt, but also something that gave us pleasure in this new discourse.

REENGINEERING

Reengineering promised no more products and no assembly line. We would not be judged by the one above us according to the number of reports filed or grants given. Its language of obliteration sounded as much like Marshall Berman as Coopers Lybrand. Reengineering promised to sweep away everything in its path, and we heard this as the death knell of that Fordist state line we saw as so anachronistic and confining to our labor. In its place no more outputs but outcomes, not through structures but processes. The hopes for change, the view of government as a temporary organization for the antiracism movement, were echoed in this introduction and drew us in. Yet to invoke Berman is also to hint at the results of this training engagement. It was not to a society of producers that reengineering spoke but the individual deracinated by the machine inside. If it tried to teach us to hate this brain machine and long for the illusion of a lost humanism, it also sparked resistance in us as we came to see it try to lay claim to our social abilities. I am jumping ahead, though. First, our encounter with reengineering should be summarized. Whatever the underlying reasons in the secretariat for the shift from one training paradigm to another, some of the pressure was government wide. The NDP leadership was convinced by the second year of its mandate that it had to demonstrate it could run a government efficiently. As a deep recession caused by the ill-conceived free trade agreement with the United States began to take hold, government funding was indeed scarcer, whatever the consequences of adopting this unexamined concept of efficiency. We were told that the government wanted restructured and realigned ministries that continued to deliver the important services (and new NDP programs), but more efficiently and effectively. Ministries were to be flatter and leaner. The call for de-layering was the only indication of the NDP leadership's interest in reporting relationships or the level of workplace democracy. Little else about how a government ought to be structured for a party with socialist leanings was evident. Special units in the government did concern themselves with bureaucratic reform issues. The Premier's Council, a think tank inside the bureaucracy controlled by the premier's office, circulated disembodied passages from prominent management gurus like Peter Drucker and prominent neoliberal Democrats in the United States like Robert Reich. A two-page excerpt from Michael Porter on national competitiveness would pass mysteriously across our desk with a cover note from a deputy minister none of us knew recommending it as reading. The only thought given to our labor in the party in any formal forum seemed to be about labor-management questions. Thus, we had not been presented with a model of the state under the NDP or of our labor but had developed dangerous ideas of our own about state work through our training in the *Naming the Moment* sessions—an irony for an NDP leadership concerned with the discipline of its bureaucracy. Reengineering, on the other hand, had definite ideas about labor and strong underlying notions about the state, too.

The reengineering consultant, used to working in the private sector, was humble about his contract with a government agency even as he was firm about the correctness of the method. He began our intensive sessions on reengineering by giving the eight assembled managers the standard definition from the Michael Hammer and James Champy's book, *Reengineering the Corporation:* "the fundamental rethinking and

radical redesign of business processes to achieve dramatic improvements in critical, contemporary measures of performance, such as cost,
quality, service, and speed."[20] A good deal of supporting articles were
distributed with this definition, including one by Jon R. Katzenbach and
Douglas K. Smith about their work on the use of teams, and another by
Rosabeth Kantner on her exploration of the new manager who works by
inspiring others and building entrepreneurial projects instead of gaining
authority through hierarchy.[21] Having introduced the concept of reengineering, we moved on to its technique. The consultant had us develop both a vision and mission statement for the secretariat. For this, he
distributed excerpts from Peter Drucker's work.[22] One statement read:
"Organizations are special-purpose institutions. They are effective because they concentrate on one task"; and another: "Only a clear, focused,
and common mission can hold the organization together." Yet another
maintained that "the organization must be single-minded, otherwise its
members become confused" and start "to define results in terms of their
specialty, imposing their own values on the organization." We immediately interpreted this introduction in light of the understanding of our
labor that we had begun to develop in the *Naming the Moment* training.
Indeed, the secretariat should be a special-purpose institution that does
some things well. It should be an organization among organizations, we
reasoned. And with reengineering, the social movement might make
the secretariat truly dedicated, single-minded even, in the pursuit of
antiracism.

Initially, the management team (as we were now known) was also
excited about the prospective of becoming better in areas such as cost,
quality, speed, and service. Much of this sounded like the answer to the
government's new insistence that savings should be found while "customer service" simultaneously improved. In developing a mission statement and organizational purpose, the managers used the draft policy
goals, such as "providing barrier-free services to newcomers," or "to
provide leadership and serve as a catalyst to eliminate systemic racism
in society."

Next, the managers were asked to design a reengineering process that
would help the agency become better at fulfilling this organizational
purpose. The consultant introduced this section by providing Drucker's
quotations again and distributing some writing in the field of leadership
theory. In an article by James Champy and Donald Arnoudse in *Insights*

Quarterly, called "The Leadership Challenge of Reengineering," we saw combined two popular topics in managerialist discourse. This article specifically confronted the recent soft leadership theory and called for a return to more authoritative leadership to meet the reengineering challenge. Noting that he was working with managers, the consultant drew attention to such points in this article as, "In the short term, reengineering must be more top-down driven than quality improvement"—a reference to the total-quality-management discourse it was fast replacing.[23] Together with Drucker's comments on workers not "imposing their own values" and an organization being "single-minded," these prompts led to lively discussions among the managers. Several objected to the idea of a top-down process or to the workers not imposing their own values since the single-mindedness of antiracism was coming, in their view, from frontline workers. They failed to understand the connection between the mission statement exercise and this new exercise in the reengineering process. The consultant characterized reengineering as the only radical organizational change method, and one that could ask the fundamental question of what government business should be. It seemed to the managers that the general intellect of the movement was better placed to guide this work. In fact, that government business was now so much embodied in state labor that any moment of exclusion was a moment lost, not made more efficient.

Other managers thus brought up the need for the immediate involvement of workers and later the communities served by the agency in the conversation about the change-process design itself. The working managers, as one manager termed herself, began to assert that both the process and outcome should be concerned with enhanced participation, decision making about programs, and definition making of core concepts like racism and community development. The consultant was polite and empathetic in fielding these objections, but he insisted that reengineering was such a radical process that managers had to control it at the outset to avoid panic, demoralization, and resistance from workers. As for the community, like customers in the private sector, they will be built into the outcomes and assessment process, providing input at the consumption end of the loop not the production end. The consultant argued that given the full power of consumers in this system, communities would in fact be more empowered than under the current system. He pointed to a recent editorial in the nation's leading newspaper by the just-retired senior civil servant of the federal government, the former clerk of the Privy Council, Paul Tellier. In the article, Tellier praised himself for starting a massive reengineering process, called Civil Service 2000, just before leaving office. He cited four principles in this process: customer focus, relevancy, removing duplication, and assessing the value of the work. None of these addressed worker participation. But these managers and workers were themselves consumers, customers of antiracism. They questioned the intervention of hierarchy into a labor process where the management function of bringing together services with customers was already bound up in the laborer, residing in him or her just as the state line now did.

It was not much further into the process, at a third two-day retreat in the cottage country north of Toronto, that a second split developed based again on the absence of a strong definition of the *product* of state activity. Managers were asked to enumerate the services that the secretariat delivered. They were then asked to distinguish between the delivery and outcomes of services in order to set up criteria for measuring success. A distinction was drawn between the delivery of a certain number of grants and the outcomes and results of the grant-supported projects. A parallel to the private sector was introduced to help managers comprehend this distinction. The number of cars coming off the line was not an outcome, only an output. An increase in market share, a reduction in labor conflict, or a link to a new product line was an outcome. The distinction between outputs and outcomes was accepted as a helpful one by managers. Managers were concerned that they should be seen to be aware of the social efficacy of their programs and efforts. But the definition of outcomes for the secretariat's case in particular caused some dissension. All agreed that one outcome was greater strength and self-sufficiency for community organizations. There was sharper disagreement, though, on whether the lack of self-sufficiency should be equated with failure to reach an outcome or objective. The private sector consultant interjected that the government had a limited budget like any corporation and could not be in the business of supporting groups indefinitely. Senior managers also asserted that in order to cut costs in the ministry, the growth in self-sufficiency of community groups supported by ministry programs should be a strong measurement of success. Groups must be encouraged to support themselves through internal fund-raising and private sector support. Here the obvious preference for a neoliberal state, at least in the area of social programs, surfaced from the private sector consultant. Several "working" managers objected, stating that some groups might always be dependent on government resources for various reasons including racism, and that at any rate, they were unconvinced that government was not the best way to redistribute money into these communities on an ongoing basis, rather than simply supplying seed money. This position was incomprehensible to the private sector consultant, but interestingly, it also met with strong disapproval from several senior managers. But again for many managers, we were the outcomes and we carried around in us the outputs. Against the expansion of control of labor proposed by reengineering that relied on the articulation of production, circulation, and realization, we began to think of the expansions now possible for an instated labor based on the disarticulation produced by an intensified socialization.

HALF MAN, HALF STATE?

To carry around with us these outputs is to say that the state tool has always been linguistic, always been the report and application. These were forms that had to be imposed on a population and a government workforce, imposed as demography and accounting. But no longer. Now we wished to produce demography and accounting of our own accord. The production of identities met the accounting for those identities in outcomes. If we had gradually become half man, half state through re-engineering, we would shortly see that in practice, it might be more accurate to say this was "the becoming woman of state labor." Negri says of the phrase "becoming woman of labor" that

> it is no longer possible to imagine the production of wealth and knowledge except through the production of subjectivity. And thus the general reproduction of vital processes. Women have been central in this. . . . I say the feminization of labor is an absolutely extraordinary affirmation. The feminization of labor because precisely reproduction, precisely the processes of production and communication, because affective investments, the investments of education and the material reproduction of brains, have all become more essential.[24]

Our cooperation born of state work would now shift from the production desired by capital to the reproduction of desire for difference—a fancy way to say we knew it was our work that made the state, we knew our work was feminine, we knew the state in us gave us powerful visions of affirmation. Our final exploration in organization made this clear.

While managers retreated to reengineer throughout the years of 1994–1995, community organizations, emboldened by the NDP government's Community Economic Development (CED) program, were working with ministry frontline staff on a bewildering variety of innovative projects. And the NDP was receiving direct credit for these innovations. Ministry frontline staff were transforming themselves into multiskilled, flexible state workers, and previously marginalized communities were making great inroads into a massive government program. Most of those marginalized communities credited the NDP with opening up the government's resources and making frontline staff available in a developmental process led by the communities. These communities included emerging immigrant communities—starting to become political forces in the province—progressive union locals who had otherwise grown disillusioned with the NDP, and women's groups, to name only a few. Together, they represented a grassroots network spanning the province. They were newly energized by the CED program and newly impressed with their local NDP members of Parliament. In 1994, I brought my staff to work with this program, and we experienced another kind of organizational practice.

POST-FORDIST STATE PRACTICES?

To reconstruct an ethnographic moment in this history, after the re-engineering training sessions, I came across an argument by Perry Anderson in a series of lectures gathered in the volume *In the Tracks of Historical Materialism*. Here, Anderson points to an absence of what he calls the strategic dimension of marxism in the late twentieth century, found so abundantly in the era of Rosa Luxemburg and Vladimir Lenin. Anderson notes that this missing strategic direction is all the more striking when placed beside the real achievements in the theory of marxism in the postwar period. He refers in the lectures specifically to marxist theories on organizing, revolution, political tactics, and the state. This observation seemed more true than ever to me in the fall of 1994, just as I was discovering an exception. The notion of post-Fordism was taking hold in intellectual circles in the beginning of the 1990s, and a strategic experiment in "post-Fordist government" was taking hold in Ontario. I wondered if it might answer the questions I had about my labor in the state better. And I shortly found that it did help me understand my labor, not so much because post-Fordism became a convincing description of the world but because the practices under its flag expanded our labor so greatly.

NEW TIMES IN ONTARIO

The opportunity to work under this banner came with the appointment of British economist Robin Murray, two years into the term of the NDP government. Murray had authored an influential piece in a special issue of *Marxism Today* in 1988. In "Life without Henry," he contends that the Left has to learn from the efforts of the private sector to move toward a more flexible, specialized, and small-batch production model, and adapt those lessons both to the state and party.[25] He calls this the post-Fordist state. He had experimented with such lessons at the Greater London Council, and would again in Ontario. Since that publication, the idea of the post-Fordist state, and of post-Fordism more generally, has been hotly debated in international leftist circles.[26] I had little knowledge of this debate at the time, but I came to understand something about it through our work with Murray. I especially came to recognize that Fordism as a system of consumption, family life, and citizenship, as developed by Michel Aglietta in the 1970s, might yield to the production and reproduction of difference already at the heart of our antiracism state work.[27] The intensity of that state work provided me with a sense that post-Fordism had as much to do with the deepening stakes of capitalism than with its amelioration. Murray was clear that the politics of post-Fordism could not be measured with studies of how much workers were contributing to production but in how much reproduction was contributing to workers. What we could do with that wealth of difference became a common pursuit.

Murray was appointed as a special adviser with assistant deputy minister status in the Ontario Ministry of Economic Development and Trade. He headed a specific project for which a special unit was created within a new program called jobsOntario Community Action (jOCA)—a program that arose out of the movement organization dynamic of the party and government. It was a CED program involving a government-led investment program in small, cooperatively owned businesses and services.

But joca also expanded to mean all of the educational work necessary to create the conditions for community economic development. In addition to government funding, an important component of the program was the freeing of people's own money in communities, through alternative credit systems and alternative delivery of other government programs. The immodest aim was to give communities a measure of control over their money and economy. The issue of credit in particular linked the small-scale struggles of each community to the larger one of the province's bond rating.

As the NDP government faced the coming recession, it devised a Keynesian program of ambitious public works spending, some of which it would have to scale back in the coming years, but much of which eased the recession and created lasting wealth in the province. But the cabinet of the NDP government, fully half of whom were women, debated the infrastructure as well as jobs programs undertaken by the government and a consensus emerged that many core constituents of the NDP remained untouched by the programs. This debate was partly an electoral one. The argument ran that no matter one's philosophy about the value of reinvesting in roads and union-run technology upgrades, if women, people of color, environmental groups, community-based service organizations, and indeed students and intellectuals were not feeling the immediate effects of the program, then the NDP had no base but the unions, maintained some cabinet members, on which to rely when the opposition turned up the heat. The issue was not electoral politics alone, however. The movements of feminism, ecology, antiracism, and community autonomy seemed to have vanished in the macroeconomic battle.

The attempt to address this imbalance came in joca, a $300 million (Canadian) program. At the politico-electoral level, this CED program was designed to put public investment dollars directly into the hands of core NDP constituents, like grassroots women's groups, the environmental community, ethno-racial organizations, and advocacy groups. Many of these groups were not benefiting directly from the public works projects, nor even from more inventive worker buyouts and pension fund reforms. In the new CED program, these groups suddenly were to be treated as full partners in an economic program, not just social and cultural programs, and that meant in economics ministries rather than just social and cultural ones. But it would be a mistake here to fall into the trap of what Pierre Bourdieu has recently depicted as the "left hand

and the right hand of the state."[28] In fact, what we would come to see happening in jOCA was the movement organization bringing a new productivity to capital through the state, resulting in what we might call the reproduction of certain antagonism at an even higher level. What was represented through the NDP, and these cabinet ministers, was a richness of productive possibilities within the realms of affective and reproductive life—realms that were being drawn into directly profit-making circles by the state labor of jOCA. This required a reorganization of state labor as surely as its opposite, privatization, is at base a reorganization of state labor for this purpose. This is where we as government workers fit in, our brains carrying forms and applications that no longer need to be completed, and our bodies carrying our brains into a more sensuous search. And the experience helped me find another way to understand changing state forms. To think that the "left hand" of the state was not also the "right hand" was to ask something of social democracy it does not have the capacity to deliver.

ORGANIZING CED LABOR

Although theorists like Bob Jessop have gone the opposite way, asking nothing of the state in the face of their reading of a post-Fordist globalization that has become the latest excuse for reducing the state to the government, they do pay attention to changes in labor as a way of trying to read a pure class struggle.[29] For instance, at the heart of many accounts of post-Fordist production across national scenes is an attention to how decisions are made at the point of production.[30] In the jOCA program, decisions about government action, its form and product, were designed to be made by both frontline workers and communities. The program, in a sense, provided for its own flexibility. It carried a dominating description of how it was to be interpreted and implemented. The program was alleged to foster developmental projects. Indeed, jOCA itself was said to be in a constant and unending state of self-development. This descriptor prevented any kind of closure in the program; what was eligible in the program, and what was defined in the program as a community, as economics, all became questions never answered for the last time. Moreover, the program explicitly called for communities and frontline staff to work on these definitions, and it recognized their qualifications for doing so. Similarly, with an individual developmental project, no one could say how much labor was necessary from a field-worker, though one could calculate how much had been given. These qualities served to undermine traditional managerial authority, but also to disturb some traditional community leadership. Such indeterminacy inspired some field-workers to question the need for a traditional structure of management as well as the traditional divisions between community and state, just as they were doing in antiracism state labor. The indeterminacy of community led to challenges and reconfigurations at the grassroots level, as previously marginalized groups took advantage of the fluidity to assert their identity and link to the state. For instance, groups like Low-Income Families Together asserted themselves as a community despite their geographic separation. They then began to redefine the program, and with it the field-worker's role and thus the form of the state in these programs.

Murray seemed to grasp immediately in Toronto's diversity the potential for small-scale specialty products along with differentiated cultural and artistic ones. His *New Times* orientation helped him interact with and activate myriad grassroots groups within the movement of the party.[31] He quickly gathered others around him from inside and outside the government who shared this vision. The efforts of Murray's unit were designed to be catalytic in a program that extended to an unprecedented six ministries and involved hundreds of state workers. The unit served a similar developmental purpose across the government as the program was designed to serve communities. Workers in the unit not only collaborated with communities but with workers from other ministries, thereby helping them to define the program and their work within it. They were encouraged to highlight post-Fordist conditions, which included: abiding multicultural and multiracial identities, and especially a healthy polyglotism; a rich and disorganized small business culture tied to tightly packed neighborhoods following a public transportation grid; a lack of racial residential segregation; and a surrounding fertile belt from Niagara Falls to the Holland Marshes north of Toronto. (Toronto's rate of independently owned retail and service businesses is twice that of most U.S. cities of a similar size.)

All of these conditions, together with a history of rural populism (out of which the predecessor to the NDP had emerged) made the language and practice of CED possible and powerful. Among the projects undertaken by Murray and his CED secretariat were ones to assist black artists in developing collective bids for public arts projects, including on the massive new subway extensions proposed by the N D P; a project to foster an independent aboriginal popular music production company and distribution house to capitalize on the growing interest in the art form inside the aboriginal communities and beyond (this was linked to an ambitious network of aboriginal radio stations, itself linking sometimes remote communities throughout Ontario, a province larger than Texas); a project to create Good Food Boxes, containers of raw fruit and vegetables delivered to households in social housing complexes each month; another to create a culture magazine and arts entrepreneurship organization for Italian Canadian youth, who numbered 150,000 in Toronto and were largely caught between cultures; a program called Network Community Shopping Co-op, creating a kind of caravan of minority small merchants who set up at events, pooling resources and political clout to negotiate access to events throughout the city; and a local money project, called the Local Employment and Trading Systems, in which skills are bartered and green dollars are accepted outside a dollar economy. All of them took advantage of the new tastes developing in Toronto as a result of recent, worldwide mass immigration combined with a high level of economic and consumer expansion. But they also used a variety of nonmarket appeals (some of which, we now recognize, have been co-opted by multinationals). These included appeals to consumers to support "clean clothes"—those clothes made by a co-op of workers making a decent wage—African Canadian businesses, and environmental concerns, to name only a few. These political appeals were combined with nationalistic and "one-of-a-kind-ism" appeals. Together with the niches and links that small firms can find with government help, this strategy produced a flowering of small manufacturing and service activity just off the screen of corporate producers and retailers.[32]

Eventually, JOCA began funding larger community center projects. Many of these centers included a number of microenterprises, restaurants, publishing houses, and sports facilities. In these centers and among the dozens of smaller C E D projects, the workers in my antiracism unit, in the special C E D unit, and across the involved ministries began to spend more time away from ministries in community locations, instead bringing community organizers into ministry offices not for formal consultation but collaboration. Not surprisingly, these workers began to see their relationship to managers, the civil service, the party, and these communities very differently. They wanted more autonomy for themselves and more authority for the community organizers. They cited the developmental nature of joca and started to think of themselves in a similar developmental language. Some workers suggested that the education programs that laid the groundwork for ced should not have to lead to direct projects. Other proposed that these programs, many of them looking like the kind of popular education projects that the Doris Marshall Institute had conducted with the secretariat, should be open to government workers or conducted for them, returning full circle to *Naming the Moment*. Ministry divisions and hierarchies were the main casualties of this new thinking by frontline staff, whose presentations to management committees making decisions on funding exhibited a kind of free space of association that made managers and traditional specialists uneasy.

But the effects on our own sense of ourselves were equally important. As the government and community increasingly had no bounded physical space for us, we also saw that our projects often had no bounded creative spaces. We made the program, and with it, produced useful versions of community or state work. Our emphasis on new forms of production, however—on decentralization, de-layering, flexibility, multi-skilling and teamwork—applied to government work with communities helped us to see our work as having instances of government in it, and to redefine state work more expansively as something that was happening between us and the communities with which we worked. This observation of ourselves might square with some understandings of post-Fordist subjectivity as more contingent and based on multiple cultural readings of how value might be realized. But left at this level, it is easy to see the way post-Fordist discourse could be so available to so many different kinds of politics, and easy to understand why such a reading of post-Fordism by the critics of the *New Times* group could lead to such discomfort with the strategy.

We might instead observe the way public administration has maintained an ability to talk about government in a post-Fordist context. In particular, the reinventing government discourse has absorbed much of the strategy of flexible labor while at the same time maintaining a strong sense of what the state can and cannot be. The discourse of public administration thus avoids the perception we had that flexibility was leading inevitably toward a more complex relationship between the state and society. This is possible for public administration, and reinvention especially, because it maintains the ideology that state work is involved with circulation not production. Circulation of goods and services, of regulations and information, grows more complex with post-Fordism, and hence the need for flexibility. Yet the state's role, as Gore likes to remind us, is to add value through this circulation, not to ensure the capacity for value itself and the condition of its appropriation. A strong version of this view would substitute the circulation of power for these other terms.[33] But at this level, we still remain with Bourdieu in a debate about neoliberal versus social democratic understandings of state labor. The question then becomes where the state redistributes its ability to add value, to business or to health, education, and welfare. From this view arises the idea that a social democratic government can choose to throw its power here behind trade unions or there behind the banking industry.

It is unfortunately necessary to take a more sinister, but also more revolutionary view of the matter. We did not understand ourselves to be reinventing government, nor to be providing a kind of state approval for certain economic activities through new techniques of government to communities instead of corporations. We believed we were producing new kinds of value through a process of recognizing an ever expanding possibility of needs in Toronto (what was referred to as the production of interest earlier). Even the educational programs were aimed at identifying new needs. At the same time, we discussed the possibility of new forms of education, health, and security services being instigated through communities. In other words, this was both a new and an old story, what we might call post-Fordist social reproduction. We were involved in trying to re-create a social base for labor through our labor, but we were also involved in expanding that social base in directions and dimensions not previously organized. Hardt and Negri, I would discover later, were speaking of this social phenomenon when reinterpreting the movements of the 1960s and 1970s, especially in advanced capitalist countries, saying that "the various forms of social contestation and experimentation all centered on a refusal to value the kind of fixed program of material production typical of the disciplinary regime, its mass factories, and its nuclear family structure. . . . [T]his massive transvaluation of the values of social production and production of new subjectivities opened the way for a powerful transformation of labor power."[34] Our refusal of public administration created new needs and desires for a laboring of publics, for a public administration without the state. We could not realize this, but at moments we saw it.

What was new, then, in our state work seemed to be our attention to the use value of Toronto's multiculturalism, itself a state-conditioned discourse since the 1970s in Canada. Our labor broadened and deepened multiculturalism by organizing it through the term communities—something we as state workers could not have achieved without the urge to singularity and development among community organizers. As the needs of communities were articulated, we articulated them with the price-making market. What was embodied in these communities, family strategies and affections, expressive and creative representations of the city, and learning and language techniques were, of course, the capacities of producers to reproduce. By bringing them forward as needs, we cheapened them by giving them exchange value even as we enriched our understanding of the sources of wealth. Women, people of color, the poor, linguistic communities, and all those involved in the arts and social justice work, offered an image of the fully complex character of labor, responsible as it is for keeping society together in the face of capitalist appropriation facilitated by reorganizing the state. This reversal permits us finally to talk about a society of producers using the state for purposes other than soothing the ravages of capitalist profit taking. It offered each of us, including all of us participating in those identities, the prospect of transforming ourselves from half men, half state to what, as discussed earlier, Negri calls the becoming woman of labor. It allowed us to imagine a state transformed such that its effects came to stand for the cooperation of reproduction, a fetish of communism not government, or civil society, or economy. When we insisted that our work and program could look different in every singularity, our insistence became the cooperation that refused the poverty of the state fetish. Each time I met a youth group putting out a magazine or a women's group working on women's health, I offered my work as the end of the state and beginning of something more with them, and I came to expect the same.

Some current thinking has it that the study of culture as a site of politics should be balanced by the study of subjectivities in the workplace. Lawrence Grossberg makes this point as does Bruce Robbins in their essays in the collection *Disciplinarity and Dissent in Cultural Studies*.[35] By extension, the call to study cultural policy asks one to balance the study of culture with an understanding (and embrace) of the state's governmentality.[36] In our focus on state work, on the becoming woman of this labor in particular, it seems possible to say that the notion of balance splits something that is whole. There may be methodological or even political reasons to create these splits, but for my purposes it seems important to insist on the singularity of the common that state work draws to our attention. State work suggests that cultural studies might take on political economy more directly. Rather than culture succumbing to capital, state work contends that the opposite has happened. Each time we discovered the source of wealth in a neighborhood program, we also discovered that capital could do nothing to increase this wealth. This was a wealth of social differentiation in reproduction. It could add to capital, but capital could not add to it. This is not to say that capital investment is unable to make money from these hothouses of culture but that it is now dependent on this social life as once dispossessed labor was dependent on capital. Our state work was a welfare for capitalism, not of it. Again, this was not a matter of how the state directs investment, as in Bourdieu's conceptualization, but something altogether more fundamental. Capital's reliance no longer on labor but the wealth potentialities of social reproduction re-creates state work, makes the private public and the public private. I might now recognize this change in relation to the agencies of capital, but at the time I recognized it first, perhaps necessarily first, in our labor. It was our daily production of difference that held value, not our reduction of difference in our state work. This is what disturbed our state work, made it more than a conversion process, a process of loss. As for us, so too for communities and our common projects. The investments that led to wealth needed the difference rather than sameness of labor in these communities, and most of all, it needed reproductive labor in the broadest sense of the social development of bodies and brains. But capital could not achieve this because its investment pounded sameness out of this wealth. It had to wait, dependent, for human beings to create in the acts of social reproduction the wealth it needed. Our state work was the same. Government would have to wait for us. Public administration would now be dependent on us.[37]

Not Bourdieu, then, but Althusser provides the starting point for grasping state work through public administration discourse, and for seeing that despite appearances, it is public administration that was in the grip of our work and not the other way around. To recall how Althusser understood Marx's critique of political economy, public administration gave itself the state, while pretending that the state was given to it.[38] I have said that this operation is not limited under capitalism to public administration. What Timothy Mitchell refers to as "the powerful, apparently metaphysical effect of practices that make such structures appear to exist," is a social operation of the widest scope.[39] But state effects are perhaps the most obvious and public administration perhaps the most visible way to approach the capitalist appropriation of political abstraction, especially at a conjuncture in which all appropriation is coming to look like the appropriation of abstraction and all abstraction is coming to look cultural, subsuming the economic under social life. The resulting tension between a system of appropriation based on incessant comparison, as Michael E. Brown reminds us, and the production of difference that characterizes social life even as it becomes wealth making, is the occasion for state work, but also for a politics of liberation.

ENGENDERING ABSTRACTION

But if the political reason for choosing to focus on public administration is its obviousness, its clumsiness, its contingency in the process of effects under capitalism, the philosophical reason is also important. If it is true that in state work one can see the becoming woman of labor, one should also approach this position with care. The position should especially not be emptied of the complexity given it precisely by capitalism. This is to say, neither philosophy nor the process of abstraction should be rid of the same complexity. To do so would be to reinstate a philosophy of exchange in the line of flight. In other words, it would be to make of Negri's concept of exodus a naive utopia. To illustrate this philosophical problem, I want to close this chapter with attention to Alisa Del Re's reading of the "perverse process" of the "socialization of reproduction operated by the welfare system" that "socialized this labor as feminine," reproducing an irreducibly complex condition of difference in the general process of socialization under capitalism.[40] And I want to place this difference in conjunction with a look at the most marxist film of the last decade, *The Matrix*. By taking film and television seriously in this study of the state, I am not suggesting the metaphoric importance of these media or even the affinity of their technology to our state formation. Instead, it might be interesting to see them as instances of the way audiences come together to produce state effects themselves, as it might be worth considering them for what they cannot say. The two considerations are perhaps one— the making of public and private, and what these cannot tell of their own making. Among the opportunities and obligations of viewing is to experience the state by bringing the experience of state effects to the dark room. Whatever is partial and unsatisfying about these effects is overcome by producing this problem in common against which both people and nation, on the one hand, and a more comprehensive verb of people/ nation—the state—can be worked by the audience. That this, too, reduces itself again to effect might have less to do with the magic of movies than the bad faith of the activation.

Del Re maintains that moves toward socialism that do not take into account the differentiations reproduced by capital cannot hope to institute a politics of difference capable of overcoming a world in which abstraction is based on the commodity. Thus, she notes the proposals for a reduced workweek, both historically and in contemporary versions like that of André Gorz, always begin within the field of differentiation of wage labor and unpaid labor, and always accept wage labor as the basis for an abstraction of a new politics. This leads, as Del Re asserts, to "a utopia" that "would be founded on the exploitation of women and their unpaid labor of reproduction."[41] Since wage labor, through the feminizing welfare state, is itself guaranteed through the underpaid or unpaid labor of women, any such reduction in wage labor would not produce the same effect for women and men. Indeed, reducing wage labor to increase the time available for the activities of social reproduction might have the perverse effect of giving women lower wages and increasing the expectation of unpaid reproductive labor as voluntary time comes to replace meager welfare state assistance. All of this flows from thinking socialism can be an easy equivalent to capitalism. It is instead necessary to keep capitalism much closer at hand to be reminded of its complexity and wary of its deception of simplicity, operating through the abstraction of the commodity.

Del Re recounts an alternative that does just this, beginning from difference not facile sameness. In 1990, the president of the Italian Senate introduced what was known popularly as the "Bill on Time," produced "on the initiative of the women's section of what was then the Italian Communist Party and is now the Democratic Party of the Left." This bill was designed to overcome the sexual division of labor by producing an alternative model of development for society by taking as its "point of departure the question of time and scheduling," and thus restructuring the city and space. Beginning with "the centrality of the reproduction of individuals, and therefore the subordination of the workplace and the market to it, is the founding element of this 'universality' proposed by women."[42] With difference as principle now, such a universality could be expected to be continuously reuniversalized.

By contrast, if the idea of exodus is rid of difference, it becomes either a tactic of radical democracy or a solution to the problem of alienation (or both). But these kinds of new politics are a trap. In either case, the constitutive elements of this new politics are not only impoverished compared to the social development capitalism offers but still strewn with the land mines of this differentiated development and an abstraction process based on the commodity such that only a politics of difference, with the complexity it entails, could possibly move toward socialism. A constitutive politics of exodus would instead have to keep capitalism near enough to benefit from its antagonisms—that is, to see the transformative power of its differences. This is the philosophical point or a reason to focus on laboring in the state, where the subjectivity of half man–half state exemplifies difference and forces the founding of a "subjectivity of liberation" on its own grounds—grounds from which to see a new horizon. It then becomes possible to say that the becoming woman of labor position is only useful if it is understood to be uneven, differentiated, and irreducibly socially complex. The constitution of a break must be formed on these grounds.

This is what happens in *The Matrix*. Unlike most science fiction and fantasy tales of struggles against domination, this film understands the social movement—in this case and many others, the free colony—as only a moment in a more constitutive battle for socialism. It can show up only as a moment of difference, with the place of socialism appearing as another site of difference at every turn from what it is presumed to be in the figure of the matrix, a highly complex virtual reality implanted in the brains of people to cover a more sinister reality in which machines are the masters of people. The virtual reality world, looking like our world, is conflictual just like the hidden struggle, and at moments as the characters in the film move between levels, the conflicts are united. But the only progress that is made for liberation occurs in and through the level of abstraction represented by the matrix. Our hero, played by Keanu Reeves, who himself exhibits a level of abstraction in his acting and facial expressions fitting to the complexity of his situation, must have his brain plugged back into the matrix from liberated territory. Once inside, it becomes clear that liberated territory depends on and is a moment of this battle in the matrix. If he dies in there, he dies in the territory, and with him the hopes of the territory. Yet he does not die. Rather, he imagines that he can master the matrix only by becoming fully a part of it. He faces state agents who are half men, half machine. He finally overcomes them by flying into one, inhabiting his body and then exploding out of him, becoming that half man, half machine, internalizing the complexity of the matrix in his being. His exodus is a breaking apart from the inside that imagines the horizon of liberation. Reeves becomes the new communist man.

But if anyone else at the WorldWide Cinema on Forty-eighth Street in Manhattan at 1 P.M. on a Monday was thinking of communism as they watched *The Matrix*, it did not amount to much when the movie let out. We shared only the state work of imagining government to let the fantasy work its magic—that and the commerce of WorldWide. It occurred to me once again coming out into the daylight that films like this could only stand in place for what we did not yet share, even as they hint at why it might be fun to share it.

3. REINVENTING STATOLATRY:
FROM NICOS POULANTZAS TO AL GORE

Intense pleasure in skill, machine skill, ceases to be a sin, but an aspect of embodiment. The machine is us, our processes, an aspect of our embodiment.—Donna Haraway, "A Cyborg Manifesto"

I want to pull back now from our experiences in government to look more consistently at how others have explained such experiences—to see what can be gained from such accounts and what can be done at their limits. I will focus on public administration's "particular practices and techniques," which "have continually reproduced the ghost-like abstraction of the state."[1] In fact, I focus on public administration and public management through the rest of the book not because it sufficiently describes our experiences but because it is the dominant description of state work, or at least government labor. I have said that state work might be understood as that labor which most knows itself as comparison, unitization, and exchange. One would expect, then, that the commentary on such work would be acutely aware of these operations. But as I will show, labor is consistently absent as a world-making activity in public administration, and in its absence, the state has a metaphysics of presence even stronger in this discourse than in our daily work.

Indeed, despite the presence of the state object as fetish or foil in much contemporary theory, it is surprisingly difficult to find any extensive discussions of state workers outside the field of public administration, and even rarer to find an interest in the ontology of their labor. In this chapter, I want to begin by establishing the necessity of dealing with public administration. It is necessary by default, but it is also necessary to account for that default. From where does this disciplinary cordon sanitaire come? For most of the past decade, reinventing government has been the official policy of the federal bureaucracy in the United States. Its influence has spread to Canada and through the academic-practitioner field of development administration to much of the globe.[2] It has become the dominant way to speak about state labor in the Anglophone world. In what follows, I am going to explore this discursive formation in its practical embodiment in the state worker in the United States. Reinvention asks something new of this state worker, and as such, it is one way to study the struggling state effects of our post-Fordist moment. In his or her daily work, the reinvented state worker calls on the public to complete the state effect. Such collaborative state effects—occurring as they do now in the details of programs and policies, and requiring rather than authorizing publicity—can be said to be part of what Gilles Deleuze has called the society of control. Producing state effects directly in the subjectivity of labor has its risks, however. This is especially true when such subjectivities are increasingly becoming direct sources of wealth, as Negri has suggested. The risk is that the politics of production and that of representation will become fused, as indeed they are being in wealth creation. What will be left of the state effect in such a future? I cannot say, but I can trace its tendencies in reinvention.

IN SCHOLARSHIP

In a collection titled *A Different Kind of State?* Hilary Wainwright asserts that "a democratic society is one in which all members are able to develop and express their capacities to the full in the running of that society." Therefore, "one of the tasks of a democratic state is to create conditions for this."[3] She proposes autonomous centers of local power as an answer. Her essay appears in a volume that was published shortly after the NDP came to power in Ontario in 1990, bringing scholars and activists together to discuss the reform of public administration and state. Wainwright shares with all the contributors a sense of urgency for that government and the Left in general to deal with the crisis of the Fordist welfare state. This volume was somewhat unusual and laudable in this respect. As well, it is generally unfashionable to talk about state reform on many parts of the Left in North America.

But the volume also shares with public administration discourse certain basic assumptions. First of all, the authors write under the assumption that democratization must mean making the state simpler structurally—something that orthodox public administration also wants, although often as much for "efficiency" as democratization. Thus, Gregory Albo's article in the volume lays out a plan for countering "the marketization of the state" with a democratization of its structures. He calls for shifting power away from the center, leveling hierarchy, more consumer rights for users, developing self-management capacities, and continuing redistribution by the state.[4] Democracy here seems to require simplicity of structure, thereby facilitating better participation. This is another constant theme of the volume. Leo Panitch, for instance, wants "to encourage and facilitate the organization of communities of identity and interest," which "the process of participation can then harness in democratic decision-making" to the "core of the state."[5] It is through better representation, in both senses of the word, that democratization of the state is to occur in this view. Such representation can stem the power of the bureaucrats by forcing them to take account of the people receiving the services. Almost all the essays in the volume maintain this distinction between state and private sector workers, largely through the distinction of producers of services versus consumers of services. This separation of production and circulation runs throughout the volume. David Langille summarized the contributions by distinguishing state workers from "popular sectors"—a conceit that risks reifying the state every bit as much as Robert Reich's populism.[6] In fairness, the volume was designed, like most public administration, to be helpful to government, and in this case to a reformist social democratic government. There is, moreover, hints in some of the essays of a more radical rethinking of the notions of public and private as well as the state effect that is its most persuasive phenomenon. This radicalism is in Robin Murray's essay, particularly in its confidence in the possibility of producing a new kind of state, not just a democratized one.

Murray's work also differs from most of the essays in actually seeing state workers, who in the rest of the volume appear only as the bureaucracy. But in general, this volume follows Left modes of conceptualizing the state worker only in aggregate, the state as the rightful guarantor of the public, the public as a natural way to pursue liberatory politics. Might this perspective benefit from an examination of the state worker, and thus of state work? The naturalized state, bureaucracy, public, and representative politics that flow from this conceit might be disturbed by this closer view. Yet a search of the scholarship, Left, Right, and Center, uncovers an attention to the state worker only from those following the prime directive of system maintenance, even when that is couched in the radicalism of reinventing government. To the extent that these questions arose at all in public administration discourse, it was only in the context of clarifying orders—how broad were the powers of public administration in making the state work, and by extension, what was its brief in the task of making state workers work? In fact, the discussion of ethics and governance were ultimately about these clarifications. For all its strangeness, however, public administration was the only discipline to address labor in the state. Of course, it virtually never addressed the state from the perspective of labor—that is, from the position of that world-making activity where such questions as the reasons for this work would inevitably arise. To address the state from this perspective would have had the direct effect of voicing labor as labor in the state and of calling the state into question as an object—not just as an ideological object of constitutional construction based on contract and sovereignty but a material object made by these practical embodiments.

Even the marxist scholarship was not occupied with state labor, but I did find something, from a past that has taken on a distance far greater than its years.[7] In 1978, Poulantzas concluded that "the essential problem of the democratic road to socialism, of democratic socialism, must be posed in a different way: how is it possible radically to transform the state?" Poulantzas was writing in the same issue of *New Left Review* in which Althusser advised the French Communist Party on strategy in light of its recent electoral defeat, adding to the effect of distance considerably. Poulantzas wanted to transform the state "in such a manner that the extension and deepening of political freedoms and the institutions of representative democracy (which were also a conquest of the popular masses) are combined with the unfurling of direct democracy and the mushrooming of self-management bodies."[8] How is it possible radically to transform the state? Twenty years later, this issue of *New Left Review* seemed to me truly like a document from another time and place—that republic of work whose future Poulantzas and Althusser thought they saw in the present.

Poulantzas warned in his argument against the impulse to "quarantine the state within its own domain and thus halt the spread of the disease . . . to place oneself outside the state, leaving that radical and eternal evil more or less as it is and disregarding the problem of its transformation."[9] He noted that because social democracy and Stalinism were both essentially statist, the Left in his day placed direct democracy and autonomous workers' councils in opposition to them. This was the source of the problem, according to Poulantzas. He believed that one of the seeds of Lenin's strategy, allowing Stalinism to grow, was exactly this exclusive emphasis on direct democracy and workers' councils. By contrast, Poulantzas insisted that to see the state as either a separate site of struggle or as something to be destroyed piece by piece from outside was, in fact, to let it persist and develop until eventually it could challenge and destroy the other site of power, as it did with the Soviets. Poulantzas called instead for a strengthening of political freedoms through an articulation of struggles in the state to gain control of the state, and struggles outside the state to maintain autonomous movements of direct and council democracy. He contended that some political freedoms required a deepening of the institutions of representative democracy, but that this could only be achieved in articulation with other kinds of freedoms best pursued through direct and council forms. And he had a negative assertion for the importance of seeing struggles in and through the state. If such struggles were not joined, to whom were the coercive and surveillance powers of the state left, and what were the consequences of this abandonment?

Yet a quarantining of the state is exactly what one senses from many of those interested in the transformation of society in North America today. Many of the impulses of the new social movement literature and civil society literature it has spawned are to quarantine the state.[10] The work of prominent political theorists like Wendy Brown, the rehabilitation of Hannah Arendt and Isiah Berlin, and the anarchism of Noam Chomsky, all in very different ways can be read as quarantining the state. Of course, some of these thinkers criticize the work of adversaries addressing the state in ways they find untenable, and they write against the dissimulations and abuses of conventional state representations. It is not my intention to prove that there is insufficient attention to the state in the United States. In fact, I believe it would be easier to say that contemporary U.S. theorists are state obsessed. More interesting is the question of the object of their obsession, and the way its objectness shields its labor.

Is it possible to speak of a state as something against which one might write or act, as Wendy Brown does in criticizing Patricia Williams and

Francis Fox Piven, or as Arturo Escobar does in criticizing dependency theorists?[11] Is it possible to conceive of transformative politics as something that grows and matures outside of some state object? I want to suggest that it is the forming of the state as object that permits this kind of quarantining and omits a consideration of its labor—a consideration that might in turn open up the object. Despite Althusser's insistence that marxism only laments its lack of theory of the state yet does not produce one, this object formation stands in contrast to marxist notions of the state form as advanced from Gramsci to Negri.[12] In such notions, it seems to me that the necessity to struggle for the transformation of the state comes precisely from the impossibility of any other strategy, which is at the same time the possibility that the state will be subsumed by society and real abstraction produced for the society of producers. Working in the state led me quite separately to the suspicion that the state object is an ideological representation of my labor, and not necessarily the one that I would prefer. Although a mechanical reading of relative autonomy can yield the same kind of state object, these strategic writings of Poulantzas point precisely to this kind of fluid and dynamic conception of state life. A look at the state form today in North America precludes thinking of the state as an object that could be quarantined, and indeed such thinking reinforces the ideological construction of the state by public administration theorists and misses the ongoing relation to the agency of capital at the heart of the state in contemporary life—an agency made materially manifest in state labor. I hope an examination of state work can lead back to the question of what exactly it is that needs to be transformed twenty years after Poulantzas laid out his strategy. That is, what form does North American state life take today, and how can this form be transformed?

IN EFFECT

After Poulantzas is silence on this question, broken only rarely. In 1981, after the election of the Socialist Party in France, Foucault called for the development of a "governmental logic of the Left."[13] But as influential as Foucault has been, few have taken up this particular suggestion. And those who have, like Leo Panitch and his coauthors, have not operated at the level of what Foucault would consider logic. Perhaps in the United States, since no social democratic, labor, or communist party has held significant office in the last fifty years, thinking about the state on the Left has had to find other sites of practice. Perhaps the one helpful exception and intersection is found in the critical accounting school of the last twenty years, especially its marxist wing. In many ways, it seems the heir of labor process theory transferred to the subjectivities produced not just by management techniques but through them.[14] The work of Tony Tinker and Marilyn Neimark provides a dialectical argument about the changes in capitalist accounting practices, thereby providing a way to see economy effects being produced and, because these techniques are being brought to the center of government, a guide to finding practices that produce state effects now, too.[15] By contrast, the otherwise beneficial efforts in mostly British critical management theory, also derived from labor process theory, break down around the state. Phrases like "the noncapitalist nature of some public sector organizations" are all-too-common ways to draw static boundaries, and the state consistently appears social democratically as something to be preserved rather than transformed.[16] In this approach, critical management theorists agree with much of the U.S. Left scholarship that in turn seems to share with public administration the belief that they know what the state is, and differ with them only in how much they dislike what they know. This may, however, to some extent have freed theorists in the United States who cared to consider the state.

In a chapter on the relation between dance technique and the state, for instance, Randy Martin suggests that the terms of consent, the assent to be ruled by law, result from the terms of technique. The kind and quality of participation that populations find themselves enacting thereby enacts consent. The state, then, is present in technique long after it has left the scene of the body. Following this line of inquiry may help to explain why people hold onto the state, and to the idea of being citizens, when many seem to gain little from the loyalty. Perhaps it is nestled in their bodies through technique, making them think it is necessary for their well-being. But what about technique in a state worker—that is, what about public administration? Could attention to it help resurface that technique and see that it is there for one to develop?[17]

Hardt draws on European sites of state struggle to argue that rather than getting either the autonomous state life Gramsci had hoped to found in the transformation of civil society or the disciplinarity Foucault saw in civil society during the period of the founding of the modern state, there is instead what Deleuze called a society of control. This society, Hardt says, represents the real subsumption of labor under capital as a generalized condition and, quoting Mario Tronti, capital's attempt to withdraw from class relations altogether.[18] Perhaps keeping one eye on the labor of the state in the society of control and another on the reach for socialism the state makes visible in technique, one can begin to "resurface" an order repressed in the dominant state discourse and make a politics of it. If capital is indeed attempting to leave labor behind in bond markets, bailouts, and blue chips, state work may in this double sense be the best way to make something of this subsumption. The irony is that in order to realize this subsumption, to leave behind labor, capital must give the population new techniques on which such a consent will be built—techniques that form the general intellect. Public administration, especially as reinvention and public management, assists in this training, and yet this is a dangerous training for capital to hand labor, dangerous still more for workers to be training workers in such control.

EXODUS IN THE *X-FILES*

Attention to the state worker in this way may be an atypical gaze for the Left in the United States. But it is common enough outside these knowledge-production circles. Beyond public administration, much of contemporary popular political discourse revolves around the state worker and what she or he should or should not be doing, and whether she or he is capable of doing anything at all. This discourse is joined by an attack on the lack of work in specific publics that the state worker is thought to have created: welfare recipients and unionized workers. In some sites of labor, though, the state worker rivals even the welfare recipient as the demon of nonproductivity. The health care debate was perhaps the broadest discussion of the role of the state in the United States in recent years with the exception of the more covert ones on the war on drugs, crime, and immigration. The latter has led to the Immigration and Naturalization Service (INS) becoming the largest agency in the federal government. There is no question here of state worker competence that would impede growth. But the former was destabilized and eventually recapitalized by the argument that state workers could not possibly administer health care. In the case of the INS, state workers were judged capable of the work; the opposite conclusion was reached in relation to health care. Yet these debates rarely disaggregate the state worker enough for one to see the labor itself. The state workers counting ballots by hand in the recent U.S. presidential election, though mostly volunteers, represent a target of attack on both competence and trustworthiness. Strangely, the visibility of their labor on the television news each night made them more difficult, not easier to attack.

On the other hand, in the images of popular culture based on state work one almost always sees nothing but labor. Marx warned against seeing human beings only as workers, yet it is remarkable how much work subsumes the state worker in popular culture. In fact, one can see in these images the way direct labor in the state disappears and labor becomes a social act, part of a circuitry of social production as Deleuze called it. One may also sense the order this circuitry represents and the politics to which it remains susceptible. Because it is not that work is consuming people in these imaginations of popular culture but that human beings and popular culture seem to have consumed work, producing wealth directly from the labor of representing themselves and being represented. Rather than looking at these dramas as metaphor, then, I would like to scrutinize them for the way they portray work. And rather than asking these dramas to explain this portrait, I will turn to public administration to do so.

What Toby Miller terms "population imageries" of the state worker are available across the spectral dial.[19] The imageries of the state worker, perhaps the most dominant imageries of labor on television, are those of law and order. In fact, understanding these imageries as labor highlights how much representation of people working actually exists in the popular media today.[20] Popular police detective series like *NYPD Blue* and *Homicide*, docudramas like *COPS* and *America's Most Wanted,* and the court and law dramas such as *Law and Order* and *The Practice* play beside the state security force of the future, *Star Trek*. For now, the *X-Files* is perhaps the most cultish and symptomatic of all the population imageries.

There are a couple of ways to understand the labor of state workers in the *X-Files*. This series follows the exploits of two Federal Bureau of Investigation (FBI) agents assigned to cases that appear to have no rational, scientific, and therefore legalistic resolution, cases known as X-Files. The first thing to say about their work, then, is that it is by definition endless, without the possibility of techno-rational closure. The resulting tension exists in every plot as they struggle within an institutional framework demanding such closure, laboring on something that cannot know that closure. This tension is nestled in the bodies of the two characters. The one, Fox Mulder, seeks explanations beyond science, and the other, Dana Scully, trained first as a medical doctor, looks for an answer in science in order to administer law. On closer examination, however, Scully is deeply religious, and Mulder's search beyond science is not necessarily antiscientific but rather an example of the scientific process of seeking a science to match a desire. All of this means that their work is never done. In this they both resemble the other series and surpass them. A show like *Law and Order* retains what Félix Guattari and Negri would call a "logocentric and paranoid, authoritarian and potentially destructive" subjugation of work.[21] It functions much more like some readings of Foucault's disciplinary society than Deleuze's social circuitry. Cases are open and shut in each installment. And yet like the *X-Files,* there is an endlessness to the prospects of labor. Crime may go down, but it only goes down and stays down by endlessly working hard to keep it there.

Moreover, the two series share an even more telling imagery of work: its real subsumption under social life. Many of the *X-Files* scenes take place late at night in apartments, offices, or laboratories. The lead characters labor long into the evening in front of computer screens, fall asleep with case folders in their hands, and are awakened by midnight telephone calls from the other worker. Sleep is always in short supply on the program. Green computer lettering on the bottom of the screen indicates the time and place of the next phase of the assignment as if a computer were monitoring the movements of the agents. Of course, it is the viewers who are monitoring their moves, watching them with their coffee cups at all hours of the night and morning. The viewers are the ones learning techniques of participation in labor and the state from Mulder and Scully. And as much as technology enables the endless labor and propels the plot, it also ensures that labor and relies on it. A sudden test result reported by a cell phone pushes forward their work, but the very presence of that cell phone, that other worker, that laboratory, secures that labor too. Not just computers and cell phones but beepers, security cameras, spy satellites, and high-speed travel fill the program. Viewers are in the presence not of semiskilled state soldiers but, in contemporary liberal parlance, knowledge workers in a state service industry. While all of the language of this last sentence must be open to interrogation, these knowledge workers share with the detectives and lawyers of the other series a level of development that places them not secondary to private workers but primary. With the task never finished and technology available to keep work going all the time, labor becomes the normal condition of social life, or in other words, labor becomes naturalized in social life, as once it became naturalized in capitalism.

Whatever other social relations exist encompassing family, sex, or creative interest, relations that traditionally existed outside work even if they often served the reproduction of that labor, are now at play inside labor. Thus, the traditional love interest between the characters is perpetually deferred by work, the only scene where it could occur. Reproduction now becomes a social fact of work, still invisible, covered not as it once was by the wage work in the welfare state but by social production itself.[22] Under this condition, although the woman appears to be fully present in social life, she continues to be subjugated precisely because this social life is the subjugation of labor both productive and reproductive despite its surface of sociality.

But all of this provides only imageries that point to one part of the subjectivity of these state workers. It helps illuminate how they work— they work endlessly, serving a public intellectually, technologically, and legally. The spectacle of social life overwhelms the quality of labor until it is impossible to think of them as anything other than FBI agents in love. It recalls the scene in the film *Sea of Love* where Al Pacino looks at two youth planning to rob a shoe store. They look back at him and see a cop— the camera hanging on him like a life sentence of labor. Direct labor has disappeared and become an act of social being. But why? This is how they work and what they have become, but what holds them in this intensified subsumption of labor? To say with Mulder and Scully it is their search for truth or justice is to answer tautologically, not to mention illogically given the structural barriers to truth and justice in their work. To say with them that it is mere duty like sheriffs and soldiers of the past still fails to account for the pull of duty (and perhaps forgets the subplots of those earlier narratives in which the sheriff—as in *High Noon*—or the soldier— as in the bathos-nostalgic *Private Ryan*—struggles to be free of this labor, returning to a communal-familial life before it).

If one cannot look to Mulder or Scully to express this attachment, perhaps one can turn to the population imageries themselves. Most *X-Files* episodes could be divided into two kinds of cases. In one set, there is a kind of return to an earlier level of sociality, and in the second, a kind of anticipation of a higher level of sociality. Both may read as fantasies of escape from the logocentric rationality of capitalism many still face in the daily law and order of their lives. But only one threatens to reveal and reverse the subsumption of labor under the society of control. Many episodes feature what one might call the threat of primordial social life. In these episodes, the agents encounter phenomena that seem rooted in old myth, ancient story, ethnographic custom, and nineteenth-century horror narratives (these last themselves mostly disruptions of industrial capitalist logic by earlier forms of belief), or else in the seeming devolution of humans into animal, spirit, or devil. The other cluster of episodes, by contrast, focus on the technological hive and governmental conspiracy at the center of an advanced and invading alien people, who significantly may or may not really be us. Furthermore, some of the episodes contain speculation about the biogenetic manufacture of a subject that might either take one beyond the possibility of resistance or establish the cyborg on terms most hostile to this resistance.[23] This second cluster makes for fruitful speculation about what it cannot say about the population imageries of state work in the United States.[24]

The characters labor to reveal this conspiratorial hive—a hive that may or may not be literal. It is as if gradually through their labor they make more and more of the vast interconnectedness of the state, economy, and civil society (to indulge in the current usages of those terms) visible. Of course, one useful way to think of this gradual enlightenment of the conspiracy is as Fredric Jameson has read such action, as evidence of the population's sense of a totality beyond the enforced fragmentation of wage labor under capital.[25] Conspiracy becomes habitable for so many people, according to this view, because it is based on suspicion, an overwhelming emotion of capitalist life derived from alienation, competition, and compulsion. This suspicion is provoked not only by these conditions but by the sense that the conditions have been ordered. But why then would people take such pleasure in conspiracy? Why would it not be a painful experience? To suggest that people are drawn to the satisfaction of a conspiracy exposed may have some validity, but it also leaves people in front of the screen, with only a cognitive capacity for conspiracy. Instead, it might be useful to see the way state workers, like these FBI agents, are fully capable of creating, not just exposing such conspiracies. To the extent that people imagine their own labor through such imageries, it could then be said that pleasure comes also from what can be made, not just what can be undone from the outside. In other words, state labor here appears to implicate other labor, to instigate technique, to form publics with specific responsibilities and abilities. This is a way, as I will argue later, to read what reinvention does particularly—not just reproduce or condition but implicate other labor.

One can move from a perception of totalization by others to one constructed by oneself. In this light, one can in turn understand one cluster of episodes, the primordial ones, as a kind of fear of this construction, more appropriate to an earlier phase of population imagery in which the worker, even the state worker, did not want to be fully bound up in labor and imagined another world of family or community. On the other hand, one can understand the other cluster of episodes, the techno-conspiratorial ones, as a kind of impulse not to retreat from the interconnectedness of capitalist relations but to instead, as the Italian workerists called it, exodus from the state or what one might label instead the state object.[26] One might interpret the strategy of exodus as taking interconnectedness as the property of labor not capital, and taking it with labor out of capital relations. In a sense, it is the opposite move of capital's attempt to leave behind labor and class relations, so prominently displayed in financial markets today. Because it is based on the same organizational underlife, exodus could well be understood as the political strategy appropriate to a society of control, but it could also well be misunderstood as the society of control. Labor disappears into subjectivity, the hardest work of all and the most wealth making. Yet the X-Files cannot really explain this subsumption. It can only fantasize at the point of its muteness.

But it is precisely the burden of the state that makes this property of labor visible; the true basis of its association leaves its trace with each undulation of Deleuze's snake. Unlike capital, the state cannot pretend to lose its labor, and as much as one encounters population imageries of the subsumption of that labor under a new circuitry of social production, guns must still be drawn and duty called. The state must be materially and ideologically produced by state workers and increasingly by other labor against the tension of social life's new claims to naturalness. Reinventing government is just such a claim, and just such a struggle for material and ideological reproduction. State work is visibly work because of this tension, which derives from material labor being ideological in state work and ideological labor being material. More crucially, it is visibly work because of its flirtation with the subjectivity of labor and not just citizenship—a flirtation increasingly necessary to consummate state work.

IN STATE

Then again, public administration can be viewed in part as an effort to contain this politics, although that effort is simultaneously a marker of its very bounty. Population imageries are unstable, but the conditions they organize may be more enduring, and may help to explain the state enough so that one does not fear its forms, do not give into its ghostly effects. My reading of population imageries of state workers yielded three interlocking questions: how do state workers work, why might individuals see their labor in them, and why do they work at all? These questions may lead to a fourth, if people really can see themselves as publics implicated by their labor in the state, and that is why people work at all. All of these questions are raised in the reinventing government discourse, but especially the problem of how individuals are implicated in state labor. Reinventing government, like all public administration, may be a strategy for securing state labor, yet people are asked to do this increasingly in new ways. The strategy for securing state labor derives from more elaborate attempts to secure and contain both state labor and labor beyond the state. These are the strategies of public management in general. Public management takes as its task the problem of arranging state workers in time and space—that is, of how state workers work. Public management is itself a concentration on this problem by public administrationist discourse generally. This discourse must also contend with the problem of why these state workers work at all. But in the reinvention discourse, this implication of labor is taking a new form, and perhaps signaling a new state form and with it a new citizenship.

I should begin this investigation with some of the most prominent statements of reinvention and the coming of public management to U.S. government. These are the writings of Gore.[27] What has been written by or for Gore comes out of an intellectual discipline that takes the state object as bounded and given, the discipline of public administration. He is likely a conduit for this discipline, but he represents a confluence of power and ideology firing a new state project in the United States. Gore's project proposes an autonomy for the state that is not relational, and one that is proposed at exactly that moment when the relationality is intensifying and perhaps even forming a new citizenship in this intensification. This is a citizenship responsible for the state, not to it. Gore's project may also, as Derrida says, phantomalize a transformative project, the way that it pretends "to certify death there where the death certificate is still the performative of an act of war or the impotent gesticulation, the restless dream, of an execution."[28] I will have to overcome this death act.

STATOLATRY ON THE NET

Let me return to an older language for a moment to consider Gore's certification. When Gramsci wrote of the transformation of politics (or what he considered after both Hegel and Marx, civil society), he was addressing the same question that Poulantzas was pursuing in the *New Left Review*. Gramsci was interested in the development of what he called an autonomous state life, one in which the transformation of politics transformed the state. Yet it was also one in which a transformed state transformed politics. This is the heart of Gramsci's argument around the way of position and war of movement. Often, this assertion has been interpreted as offering alternate strategies. This interpretation suggests that if a direct assault on the state is not possible or desirable, a strategy of transformation in civil society, in that separate place of politics, is available. Thus, the organic intellectual wary of political parties or wishing to quarantine the state could operate in this realm of civil society. But it is hard to find that offer in Gramsci's own writings. For Gramsci, transforming a state needed always the ongoing work of transforming society, and transforming society could not be done without transforming, not quarantining, the state. This is Gramsci's innovation in the Leninist problem of the seizure of state power.[29] Gramsci saw the state not only as an object to be seized but also as a form in process within the dialectic of state and civil society—a process that could not suddenly be halted with the formal seizure of state power. Rather, this form was one that would require the continued work of organic intellectuals in civil society and after the seizure of the state, in its trenches too. Nor could this organic intellectual, in Gramsci's view, develop outside a mass organization for that matter.

This does not mean that Gramsci saw the seizing of state power as an unimportant moment in the process of transformation. Indeed, he coined a term, statolatry. This term seems to indicate a recognition that it will be necessary to fetishize the state as object in order to think the transformation of politics, of civil society. Or in a more contemporary language, it may be a recognition that the state "is a resonance chamber" for all other points of power, as Deleuze and Guattari have it.[30] But Gramsci was aware of the danger that this fetishism could become entrenched, warning, "Statolatry must not be abandoned to itself, must not, especially, become theoretical fanaticism or be conceived of as perpetual."[31] Today, however, a kind of statolatry has in fact been abandoned to itself, Gore, and the theoretical fanaticism of public administration theorists. It is the kind of statolatry that manifests all the contradictions of this abandonment and whose normal condition is crisis, especially in the contradictions between its sense of itself as object and its "zones of impotency." Yet it is also a statolatry that has benefited from a sustained war of position by bourgeois theorists who appear set to consolidate a new hegemony with this state project, with this war of movement, with Gore's statolatry.

If there has been a tendency on the Left to want to quarantine this object, such theorists and activists would find no quarrel from Gore as well as the capitalist class fractions and tentative hegemony that intermittently make his work possible. He is only too happy to abandon the state to itself, and certainly the hegemonic project around him requires exactly such a conceit. The chant of "a government that works better and costs less" covers the reality of a state that works more ubiquitously and costs more. In practice, a reinvented government is not a limited, quarantined one but an infectious one. Axioms such as "reducing the size of government" or "bringing it closer to the people" are false not only in practice but within what Laclau identified as Poulantzas's challenge to Ralph Miliband to find the contradictions between practice and theory within the theory of bourgeois political science itself.[32]

Instead, this reading of reinvention discourse may indicate more directly that reinvention marks a new and specific relation to the agency of capital characterized by a new subjectification effort to mark "the end of the dialectic between labor and capital in the constitution of the social state," in the words of Hardt and Negri.[33] This is not to suggest that public administration is the only vessel for this change, but it is part of that resonating chamber dedicated to recording and implementing a new statolatry. The growing presence of administration and management in social life, much of it emanating from the state, implies that this particu-

lar phase of statolatry, a reinvented statolatry, may contribute significantly therefore to what Hardt has speculated is the withering away of
civil society in North America, and not of some putative state object.[34]

This reinvented statolatry is neither a completely new phase nor is it
contained even as public administration within the federal government's
reinvention program. Nevertheless, one can begin to read the outlines of
this statolatry, conceived of as perpetual and carried out not by the class
of producers Poulantzas and Althusser envisioned but by Gore, public
administration professors, and management consultants on behalf of a
buoyant bourgeoisie who have attempted to sever their relationship to
labor as the source of wealth. The spread of the state can be seen on the
Web, a virtual statolatry, as an appearance of the contradiction between
what the public administration discourse is saying and what it seems to
be doing, and of course at the same time as the way the discourse is
trying to bridge that contradiction.[35] In the federal government's National Performance Review (NPR) Web sites, the unfolding of the reinventing government project can be traced over the last six years. The
market success of the book *Reinventing Government: How the Entrepreneurial Spirit Is Transforming the Public Sector, from the Schoolhouse to the
Statehouse, City Hall to the Pentagon,* led the NPR to adopt it as a guiding
text of their work.[36] The book itself is part of a larger movement in public
administration toward public management—a movement that provides
the wider context for the federal government's project.[37] If the sprawling
title of this book does not bring to the surface some irony in a work
designed to fight "bureaucratic malaise" then perhaps the spiraling links
and multiplications of the NPR Web sites seem at least to form an odd
metaphor in this language of restraint and directness. There may be
more than just irony in using a medium that encourages the filling of
space to talk about the way the space of government should be constrained. With the onset of the Clinton-Gore administration's implementation of the "end of welfare as we know it" campaign rhetoric, the Left
has responded with ever-more-vehement attacks on "corporate welfare."
The Web sites of the reinvention project are, in this argument, a classic
example of the mystification of public and private, of the state and private
industry. One did not have to wait long at the annual Socialist Scholars
Conference in New York, for instance, to hear about the subsidies, tariffs,
tax breaks, and state research and development funding that keep private
capital afloat, especially big capital. The development of the Internet by

the U.S. armed services and its subsequent transfer to a few hands in big capital functions as a chief illustration of this corporate welfare for this leftist discourse. The damage caused to the concept of income support itself, not to mention the concept of industrial policy, in the course of this populist counterattack may be less important in the present context here than the assumption that the state could simply transfer its affections. And this is to say nothing of what such a leftist contention does to reinstate the state effect after promising to explain it.

Just look at the most recent overarching policy statement of the NPR, the January 1997 *Blair House Papers*. Whereas the yearly paperbacks published by Gore are public relations documents, the *Blair House Papers* is the principle policy document of the reinvention movement in the federal government. Every federal manager has to know the document, and every senior manager now has the principles built into his or her performance evaluation.

THE BLAIR HOUSE PAPERS: NPR IN AXIOMS

The Blair House Papers features a series of axiomatic statements under three broad strategies, followed by lists of examples where government workers or citizens made suggestions based on these statements. Then there are claims of how the government put the suggestions into highly successful practice. So, for instance, under the heading "Find out How Things are Going by Getting out of Washington," under the strategy "Deliver Great Services," one is told that "people who face the customers every day already know how to improve services." I will come back to these customers. "Hugh Doran," the example continues, "whose first-floor Veterans Affairs [VA] administrative office in Kansas City was right below the second floor VA patient clinic, realized that swapping floors would provide better service for sick vets." One learns that "his good idea has led to floor swaps and better VA service in seventeen cities around the country." The document also lists improvements in service agency by agency, boasting of the use of alternative dispute resolutions to improve management-labor cooperation, providing advice on how to get the best out of state workers, noting partnerships with businesses and local governments, and recording reductions in top-heavy bureaucracies. But like many current popular as well as academic books and articles on management, it is the anecdote, aphorism, and axiom that string together the narrative. Indeed, the most influential article of the 1990s in a business journal may be Michael Hammer's reengineering piece, a series of anecdotes and exclamation marks.[38]

It would be a mistake, though, to miss the underlying systematic thinking of this state project amid the feel-good stories and trite sayings. This proliferation of the axiomatic freely through both managerialist and public administrationist literature suggests that some kind of realization, based on something larger, is possible in both places. Where this axiomatic expression meets technique one finds reinvention.[39] This document echoes the Nixon administration effort, but the forced flowering of those axiomatics point to the problem of viewing capital's agency through the state as willful.[40] With reinvention, however, even public administration theorists who could not acknowledge the basic contradictions of the project recognize the significance of this effort despite the partisan politics and tug of capitalist class fractions that shape it. The NPR has the ambition of recovering the bounded, measurable, and limitable state object in the view of these theorists, something attraction to public administrationists, even if that boundedness comes at the price of further state dispersion and insinuation. Prominent public administration theorists like Donald Kettl of the Brookings Institute and B. Guy Peters thus concur in the importance of the project.[41]

VOICES IN THE HEAD: NPR IN CONTEXT

Yet to read the recent work of Kettl or Peters on reinvention is to be hailed in what well may be considered schizophrenic ways. To the reader of public administration literature, however, these are also familiar ways, reminiscent of founding texts like those of Woodrow Wilson in the 1880s, Leonard D. White's first textbook in the 1920s, contemporary classics such as Aaron Wildavksy's study of implementation in Oakland in the 1970s, or Michael Barzelay and Babak Armajani's *Breaking through Bureaucracy* in the 1990s.[42] There is the strong sense that these works want forcefully to create interpellated subjects, but at the same time become confused about those subjects. Thus, as all these theorists discuss how to administer publics, they appear to address different readers, sometimes even within a sentence. At one moment they appear to be addressing a stratum of state managers, at another all state workers, and at still another some kind of public that must take responsibility for how the state runs. If anything, these voices have grown louder and more competitive in the public management project. Public management concentrates its address, as one would expect, on managers and managerialism, yet it is also engaged in convincing state workers, policymakers, students, and various publics of the correctness of its approach. At any moment, it might address its claims in any of these directions. These multiple hailings are symptomatic of the efforts to hold together an idea of the state as object that at every moment threatens to come apart or join other forms, and yet at the same time is powerfully organized by its relation to capital. Both state workers and different publics must be convinced to labor on the state, and even public management theorists find themselves, perhaps unwittingly, beseeching these managed subjects to help them.

Public administration in general beseeches in ways that recall my earlier reading of the *X-Files*. Reading its classics, it is apparent that they want to make citizens of everyone, as they want to make workers of those who labor in the state. Reinvention is an instance of public administration insofar as it wants to make citizens of everyone and is subject to the constraints of the "administration and politics debate." And even when it has been acknowledged that the two are related, the discourse of governance has always intervened to place limits on the question of what state workers should do—that is, how much and in what ways they may call the public out.[43] Another way of phrasing this last task is to say that public administration has always had to decide on the techniques for forming publics, and has had to account for the reasons and limits of these techniques within representational capitalist democracy. But here the distinction needs to be made between public administration as ideology, where this limit has to be respected, and public administration as symptom of the relation to capital's agency, where this limit is constantly transgressed. In this latter sense, public administration is not an ideology but what Deleuze and Guattari label an "assemblage of signification." Reading Althusser, they add that "subjectification as a regime of signs or a form of expression is tied to an assemblage, in other words, an organization of power that is already fully functioning in the economy, rather than superposing itself upon contents or relations between contents determined real in the last instance."[44]

As an assemblage of signification tied to the agency of capital, public administration's task in forming publics moved, historically, from one of discipline to one of reproduction, and with reinvention is moving from reproduction to instated labor. This claim remains to be explored. But if subjectification under early capitalism produced a disciplinary citizenship for Foucault, and if subjectification in the postwar period has produced a welfare citizenship with the possibilities of de-commodified agency for Claus Offe, then perhaps one could speculate about an emerging subjectification administered by the contemporary state in fully capitalized and commodified societies.[45]

REGULATORY CITIZENSHIP?

If roughly the first kind of administered citizenship made wageworkers and the second consumers, and both remade race, gender, and sexuality in their own image, what might reinvention represent? This new implication of labor in state labor, the way people are asked not to vote, not to realize the value of their work through state provisions, but to finish work that has exhausted the state, such a condition can at least lead to an assertion: that reinvention is trying to subjectify regulators. Reinvention can be seen as symptomatic of a new citizenship, as inadequate as its earlier version, yet looking more insidious for its newness. Regulatory citizenship assists in the administration of both discipline and reproduction directly in the labor of the citizen. What, then, would it mean if Negri is right and subjectification is now directly a force of production? In other words, what would it mean to derive wealth from regulation itself? It would explain, for instance, why the new citizenship itself should be so spectacular, full of refugee crises and racial profiling (and U.S. scholarship), while the exercise of traditional citizenship rights should have become outmoded. Does the society of control work not by getting laborers to vote into existence the state but by having people produce and realize citizenship itself as a commodity?[46]

If the modern state is partly an explanation effect, public administration has been an important part of that explanation. In the past, public administration has explained the state as various kinds of citizenship, but it has also had to explain the state as labor. Where these two explanations meet affords the opportunity to see the limits of the explanation and the new relation to the agency of capital. It is also the point where socialism resurfaces. Explaining the labor of state work has always been public administration's acknowledged object, and especially explaining it to state managers, politicians, state workers, and the consequent publics. So, for example, Mary Parker Follet's 1926 work, "The Giving of Orders," talks about building "mental attitudes" in workers so that "they will see the desirability" of working hard because they hear not an order from an individual boss but "the law of the situation."[47] Parker Follet would later be claimed by so-called human relations theorists as a predecessor, and the human relations school offers the most consistent history of attempting to convince state workers (and managers) to work hard.[48] But these mental attitudes also articulate with the public and state manager coming to accept a law of the situation behind an order. Louis Bronlow, Charles E. Merriam, and Luther Gulick warned President Roosevelt in 1937 in their "Report of the President's Committee on Administrative Management" that "there is much bitter wrong to set right in the neglected ways of human life," and to do this, efficiency "must be built into the structure of the government."[49] The Bronlow Commission, as it became known, was interested in combining the motivational state project of the emerging New Deal with a system of managerial authority that could be relied on to measure workers working, whether or not those workers were inspired by the New Deal. On the other hand, in his 1959 "The Science of Muddling Through," Charles Lindblom acknowledged the limits of a "rational-comprehensive root model" and opted for a "successive limited comparisons branch model" because the first model implied a completion of state work in the state that practicing state managers knew intuitively to be false.[50]

Lindblom's work gave birth to the anecdotal narrative of much management literature, and the antirationalist leadership literature of recent years, all attempting to account for work beyond the state through such mystifying notions as instinct, guts, or foresight. As critical management theorists have also been quick to note, this revolt against the "hyperrationalism" of the scientific management was further confirmation that indeed there was conflict to manage in the workplace, and if Taylor's productivism or Ford's bribery did not work, maybe psychology could tackle this conflict, or at least mask it. But it might also be shown to simply be a step in the modernist project of colonizing the internal space of the worker, as Taylorism worked primarily by subduing the worker. In fact, it is not too much to say that scientific and human resource phases of management, though dialectical and coexisting in much of the twentieth century, roughly conform to Hardt and Negri's recent conception of imperialism versus empire—where the first conquers territories and obliterates difference, making what was outside the imperialist power now inside, and the second infects and manipulates those territories, such that there is no longer an inside and outside at all. It is no surprise that an empire of management has come to dominate contemporary life and that scientific forms of management, such as reengineering and core competencies, to name just two, appear as counterdominant approaches.[51]

These management techniques in the age of what Hardt and Negri call empire can be read as symptomatic of that trench work the bourgeois state engages in beyond its borders—work completed by labor beyond the state; work that takes different forms as representative democracy, as welfare state living, as regulatory state extension; work that belies the autonomy that both public administration and management theorists want to give to state and private industry managers. If one is to read public administration as a way to think about the state and therefore state work, one will be tracing the limits of its own knowledge of itself, precisely because it has always been constrained from problematizing ideas like the state and state work.

REINVENTING STATOLATRY: NPR IN ACTION

These classics, part of every masters of public administration course, are only emblematic of the discipline's concentration on these contradictions—a concentration retained by public management and a source of its multiple hailings. A return to the NPR document illustrates the way the reinvention movement tries to hold together a state object in order to administer a new citizenship. As Gore notes in his introduction to this document, the NPR has settled into three broad strategies under the headings "Deliver Great Services," "Foster Partnership and Community Solutions," and "Reinvent to Get the Job Done with Less."[52] These three strategies can each be read as a construction designed to overcome a contradiction. The first strategy, "Deliver Great Service," can be interpreted as a renewed effort to get at the problem of measuring productivity and efficiency (how should state workers work). In "Foster Partnership and Community Solutions," there is an attempt to address the problem of the way state work is necessarily continued beyond the bounded state (on what should state workers work). Finally, in "Reinvent to Get the Job Done with Less," the problem of why state workers should work is encountered—a question that indicates the interlinked character of these problems. If these three questions can be answered, the state effect can be produced. But if they must find their answers directly in the forge of productive relations, which in turn is embodied in productive subjectivities, the state effect risks being lost to a new politics of real abstraction. Let me work backward beginning with the question of getting state workers to work.

Postwar public administration has had the traditional disadvantage of not being able to appeal specifically to individualized wage incentives to get workers to work harder. It has, however, had recourse to the general Fordist strategy of offering high wages relative to the economy and specific labor pools. Yet while a "good government job" might convince someone to work hard initially, it is no guarantee that such hard work will continue throughout a career. Still, state administrators have often had an ideological weapon at their disposal, and that weapon was the appeal to nation—an extraeconomic appeal to the worker to work hard for some larger good. The nation, or sometimes a community at another level such as the city, took on different versions in this appeal over time, the Progressive spirit, the New Deal, and the Great Society offering the most obvious examples of this extraeconomic appeal. Hindy Lauer Schachter recounts in detail, for instance, the Progressive era motivations of those who worked in New York's Bureau of Municipal Research at the turn of the twentieth century.[53]

This ideological appeal was always imperfect and patchy, often, but not always meaning more to managers than frontline workers. But reading, for one, Jerre Mangione's *The Dream and the Deal,* it is easy to see the way a vision of nation could inspire hard state work. With the challenges to the welfare state, both material and ideological, however, this strategy fell into (another) crisis in the 1970s with the Nixonian dismantling of anti-poverty programs in particular where labor could not be, in Michael Burawoy's language, obscured, and I might add in the military with the Vietnam War where labor could not be secured.[54] The standard narrative of the growing partnership of labor unions in this welfare state arrangement, on the one hand, and the growth of new social movement articulations with the state, on the other, surfaced real contradictions in the appeal of nation as something that could produce citizenship. According to writers like James O'Connor, the statolatry of welfare state capitalism in the United States, and subsequently in the rest of the English-speaking developed world, foundered on tensions caused by the shifts in power and therefore spending realized through the state. For Negri, in contrast, O'Connor's position implies that state spending has either not been understood as productive, and as social surplus value, or it has been, but the politics that follow of merely advising wage laborers to fight for some of this social surplus value is distasteful to him.[55] At any rate in the United States, neither the forces of U.S. capital nor U.S. white workers were willing to sustain this particular fetish of nation. Nor is it clear that it was materially possible without further shifts, whatever the social democratic strategy to extend the metaphor. But the tactic behind "Reinvent to Get the Job Done with Less" marks a new strategy for securing that social surplus value—one that redirects it for appropriation back through labor.

Like new managerialist discourse in private industry, reinvention phrases like "getting the job done with less" in part simply mask retrenchment, coercion, and sweating. The work of the Labor Notes Collective on the introduction into private workplaces of total-quality management and the team concept is an exemplary effort at unmasking the intent of much of this discourse.[56] Reinvention in *The Blair House Papers* is, in many instances, the (re)emergence of such brutal management tactics in state workplaces precisely because a cohered ideological appeal is not fully available. But amid these tactics is a pattern of redirecting state, public, and citizen back through labor, securing its value twice so to speak and obscuring it still further.

THE ETHICS OF EFFICIENCY: NPR ON
WHY WORK

The first subheading in the "Get the Job Done with Less" section is titled "Get the Best from People," and this subsection begins by stating that "federal employees have been trapped in an industrial age management system. They've been burdened by the metaphors of that age. The idea of the machine convinced us to organize our efforts as if the individuals who work together are parts in a mechanism."[57] Thus one learns that the work conditions of the federal employee have been created by the age of Fordism, twenty years after Murray first identified this homology in

Marxism Today.[58] "The assumption was that people can most usefully be employed doing the same thing over and over and over again. Decisions to change were made high up in the organizational pyramid, and instructions were conveyed down through the layers of the organization to bring about a change," this subsection continues. One also discovers that things have changed, that "money is becoming increasingly scarce," and that individuals have to "unlock unused human potential" if they are to get government working. One finds out that "you personally need to see the fixes through." And perhaps most interesting, one learns that the "NUMMI" auto plant in Fremont, California started making spectacular profits after it began treating its workers "as more than cogs in a machine."[59] Most of the other sections in the reinvention strategy can be reduced to the kinds of mean tactics that have come to be associated with U.S. business culture in the 1980s and 1990s.[60] So, for instance, it is easy to recognize the boast that "agriculture is closing 1,200 field offices while maintaining or increasing service to customers by multi-tasking the remaining offices" for what it likely is—an increase in workload for the remaining workers through job redefinitions and the scrapping of old job descriptions designed to protect against such speedups of the line.[61] But this first section hints at something else, something that holds together these cruder strategies of getting state workers to work hard.

In creating the homology of public and private worker in the past and in their common fate, this narrative privatizes the public worker without removing that worker from the state. This is not a matter of applying the standards or practices of private management to the public sector, something that would hardly be new. The state project is instead being cast as one dedicated to the cause of competitiveness, productivity, and efficiency, just as in private industry. It is no longer a matter of using private means for public ends. Rather, the state workforce is urged to use private means for private means. If this sounds contradictory, an example may help. In a linked report from the Federal Benchmarking Consortium called *Serving the American Public: Best Practices in Customer-Driven Strategic Planning*, the "best-in-class performers" are portrayed as being driven and directed by "visions, values, and credos." In exploring what these values are, and why the federal government would want to take them on, the following are listed: service to customers comes first and to employees second; senior leaders involved in planning process; a clear planning process everyone understands; good internal communication;

a sense of urgency to serve; and performance measurements tied to incentives.[62] This study's partners include Chevron, the city of Phoenix, GTE, the commonwealth of Virginia, Dupont, and Xerox, to name a few. Hence the visions, values, and credos that people are asked to take on as a nation, that state workers are asked to embody, do indeed "transcend time, market conditions, executive personalities, and planning assumptions," do indeed "form a core ideology," as the report proudly adds.[63] Again, it would be unwise to dismiss this core ideology in private industry as mere cover for smooth capital accumulation. Management and organizational theory asks that such narratives be taken seriously. For instance, planning is a way to get workers involved in the mental revolution of the corporation all over again. Notions of leadership are a way to blunt the realities of being a boss. The stable accumulation of profit remains available to some extent to permit these values to be judged. But most important, in management theory, the business press, and now in the NPR, these values are presented as values in themselves, as a core ideology that does not require the stable referent of accumulation. It is in its state of putative autonomy that this core ideology has been adopted by the NPR as an extraeconomic approach to getting state workers to work hard. The term efficiency, therefore, should not be viewed in such documents as a description of labor but as a value behind labor. State workers labor to be efficient. They are not efficient in order to labor. Yet if the object of labor is efficiency, how would the increase in productivity of efficiency be measured, and is it possible to know when workers have become efficient? This first question is where the new ideological appeal links to the rest on the reinvention techniques. The second question connects the strategy on getting workers to work to the other two strategies in the NPR project.

With efficiency as the goal, but the accumulation of profit gone as even an unsteady referent, the productivity of today's labor can only be measured against yesterday's, or against another day. A state worker is being more productive when a judgment can be made that more tasks were accomplished today than yesterday or than the worker at the next cubicle or kiosk. These tasks are in turn most easily quantifiable, at first look, when they are services to the public, to customers, that can be measured—number of phones answered, number of permits granted, numbers of patients treated. But without knowing when efficiency has been reached, this system of measuring productivity requires every yesterday to be inefficient compared to every today, with every future looking like harder and harder work toward the elusive goal of efficiency.[64]

THE CUSTOMIZED STATE: NPR ON HOW
TO WORK

It is not clear that state managers, especially senior ones like cabinet secretaries, would be unhappy with this perpetual drive to efficiency, devaluing every past effort of the state worker in the daily calculation of productivity. Nevertheless, the question of measurement eventually will get raised by rebellious state workers or dissatisfied publics, or rebellious state workers who are also dissatisfied publics. And when it does get raised, the focus on customers and information technology is designed by the NPR to answer the question of when a public is efficiently administered. The selection of customers ("identify your customers and win them over") along with the disembodiment of both customer and worker in Internet access represent efforts to reconstruct the autonomous state object against a core ideology that does not permit an autonomous state project even as it insists on the reality of the object. I will sacrifice a full discussion of the implications of high technology for the state form, but it is worth noting that the related arm of the NPR program in this area, called "Virtual Government," is a tempting example of an effort to cut the cost of the state while simultaneously expanding its reach and the demands of customers for more of that reach. That is, the reinvention project once again would seem to be complicit in an expansion and integration of the state into new space.

Looking at the use of the word customer, however, it is useful to recall the way the contradiction in this state project hides in plain sight. I have been focusing critically on the flow of private industry discourse into the state, suggesting it is not merely a set of imported techniques but an integration of the way public and private worker subjectivities are getting produced. It is equally obvious that as the state flows out into private industry, it not only takes on the forms of private industry and begins to speak its language but it also transforms those forms and a new language emerges. The ideas of corporate leadership, business ethics, teams, and total-quality management are all either taken directly from the state or are produced only as a result of changes in the state form. Leadership and ethics, in particular, are taken from public administration as well as orthodox political science and international relations, and teams and total-quality management are responses to the reconstitution of the state by organized labor as well as consumer and environmental groups. "Fostering partnership and community solutions" is an equally obvious and unnoticed flow of the state, not only into private industry but also into a civil society already deep in the process of subsumption under a state that offers this partnership.

The use of the word customer has been much noticed. Traditional public administration scholars, suspicious of the direction of the new public management, note the usage with alarm.[65] They want to rehabilitate the appeal of nation and require the citizen, not the customer for this purpose.[66] They may well underestimate, however, the deterioration of that older citizenship as well as the degree to which the customer is coming to form the mortar of a new citizenship. But the NPR has reasons of its own to speak of customers, and not only because of the flows of the state into private industry and private industry into the state. By reducing the citizenry to specific customers, agencies limit demands and improve the possibility of finite measurement of efficiency and "reaching best-in-business goals." The "key principles in a customer-driven organization," according to *The Blair House Papers,* are first to "identify your customers—start with the reason your organization was set up in the first place," then "continuously to ask your customers what they want—skip this step and you'll get it wrong." The last two principles are to "set standards so people know what to expect," and "measure and publicize results."[67] So instead of citizens determining what services they need, either through the once-fashionable approaches of "street-level bureaucracy" or legislators, customers are chosen who already meet the agency's reason for being set up in the first place.[68]

A customer is a citizen who has already made a claim on the service, where the customer, the claim, and the service are already fixed by the state manager. This orientation has the dual advantage of precluding new services, customers, or claims that might alter the variables needed to "measure and publicize," and appearing to limit the resources needed to reach the best-in-business goal. In fact, it does not limit resources, only citizen participation and access, redirecting that labor involved. So, for instance, in the examples given of "successes" in customer service, one learns that the U.S. Commerce Department "opened Export Assistance Centers with Ex-Im Bank, SBA, USAID, and state agencies providing one-stop help for expanding businesses," the Department of Justice will "provide instant access to electronic fingerprint records for frontline law enforcement officers," and Veteran Affairs now has "service . . . so fast that the NY benefits office turned its waiting room into a museum of six wars."[69] Each agency defines its services by the customers it already has and its customers by those services. The Commerce Department supports mostly large private businesses exporting finished commodities and advertising, and therefore improving services to these customers becomes its goal; the Department of Justice and Veteran Affairs see their customers as law enforcement officers and veterans of wars, respectively. The possibilities that citizens either through agencies or legislators will redefine what Commerce, Justice, or Veteran Affairs should be about is constrained by the exclusion of citizens from access to the agency using the "reason it was set up"—to serve the presently identified customers. In practice, of course, this means that these agencies are closed off to anyone not already served in them, whether Gulf War veterans, lawyers defending political prisoners, or community credit unions looking to link with credit unions in Central America.

But in the process of trying to solve the problem of measurement in public administration, this state project, predictably at this point in my argument, fails to limit state resources and requires customers to labor in the gap. Within the confines of a customer-driven organization, agencies administer to the state's admixture with business in the Commerce Department through one-stop shopping or with what is left of citizenry in the Department of Justice through the ubiquity of fingerprinting or snitching practices. Only in entitlement programs does the opportunity exist for negative growth, and only if citizens do not find ways to become customers, as the Gulf War veterans again make clear. Whether in trade or law enforcement, though, customer-driven strategies give only the illusion of providing finite sets for measurement. Yet the values, visions, and goals of efficiency and productivity, now shared by both public and private workplaces, would not appear to promote limiting resources. Rising incarceration and increasing international business competition may provide comfort in their familiarity, but efficiency dictates that more resources will have to be provided to retain even the same level of services. Hence, while the terms of measurement might remain steady, those who are given license as customers can push forward state presence often to the detriment of those citizens who are nonetheless incorporated in the process.

Even though this last might appear to be a political point and not a problem with public administration, it should be clear that the uneven development of subsumption caused by the divisions of customers and noncustomers can only require still more administering and the presence of state workers precisely at those points in the subsumption most strained by this unevenness. Thus reemerges the question of how to get state workers to work along with the issue of how to measure that work. When the Latino Officers Association in New York City, for instance, placed at such a straining point, questions the performance-by-objectives and "Courtesy, Professionalism, and Respect" public relations campaign of the New York Police Department, it simultaneously calls into question both the ideology of efficiency and that of its measurement. Similarly, when students, faculty, and staff at the City University of New York reject ending remedial programs, they simultaneously reject the customization of state service and ideology of measurement obtaining to it. Now both of these examples are from another level of government and not pure moments of opposition, but rather ruptures in the larger state project exemplified by the NPR. At the federal level, however, the revitalized union democracy movements in public unions, right-wing backlash against the FBI, and Left-populist resentment of corporate welfare could be noted as examples of ruptures in the state project of customization and measurement. In each case, noncustomers or state workers question both their exclusion and unwilling incorporation, and the validity of measuring efficiency and productivity under these conditions. These ruptures are far from unproblematic, and like an episode of the *X-Files*, citizens and workers often have only the sense that some sinister hand is at work in a project of state-society integration not in their interest or under their terms. Yet they have a sense, too, that this hand may be theirs, possessed by a state life electrified into being by the agency of capital. They are asked to complete this project by agreeing that there is no project, only "a smaller government that works better." They must agree to be customers or noncustomers and be measured or excluded from measurement as the project requires.

LIFE DURING GORE TIME: NPR ON WHAT TO WORK ON

And yet this is more than just a request for consent, more than just an invitation to believe in "businesslike government," to use the title of

Gore's 1997 book on the progress of the NPR. The NPR codifies state labor in customer labor. While on the one hand, the state worker is subject to the measurement of the customer, on the other hand, the customer is subject to the measurement of the state. In other words, the customer's labor is implicated in the state, not abstractly but directly in the labor of being a customer and being a customer for a particular state worker. Because the work of the state continues beyond the labor of state workers themselves, measuring that work requires not only that customers complete that work but that noncustomers accept this labor by customers. To put it another way, state services are not realized in the delivery alone but in the way they are taken up and completed by customers. A business that fails to export or a local police force that fails to arrest devalues the federal services provided to them as customers. The strategy to "Foster Partnerships and Community Services" addresses the way customers must realize the value of federal services. It is no accident, then, that the customer becomes the worker in this phase of measuring the value of state services. In fact, in all three subsections, "Focus Regulators on Compliance," "Remove Barriers So Communities Can Produce Results," and "Use Labor-Management Partnerships and ADR [Alternative Dispute Resolution]," it is the customer as worker who must realize the value of federal services, who must in fact complete the work of the NPR.

This third problem for public administration, the problem of how publics are completed, in the case of the NPR, might be better understood as how services are completed by the labor of customers, so that these services can be measured. Some examples of how the NPR tries to explain this problem may be helpful here. In focusing on "compliance not enforcement," the Occupational Health and Safety Administration (OSHA) "identified the 200 companies with the highest injury levels and made them an offer—form worker safety committees with your employees to self-identify and fix hazards, and we'll stop writing tickets and start offering compliance assistance." OSHA claimed as a result that the worker injury rate dropped 47 percent. The Environmental Protection Agency (EPA) identified the seventeen highest-priority toxic chemicals and challenged industry—"commit to reduce emissions by 33 percent in three years, and 50 percent in five." The EPA then "stood aside," asking companies simply to write letters explaining how they would do this. The agency later reported that the 50 percent goal was reached in four years and 750 million pounds of toxic chemicals were removed from the environment. Finally, the INS (Internal Review Service) began "meeting with business owners to help arrange legal replacement workers—many from the welfare rolls—then deported the illegal immigrants," instead of deporting them during raids and then having new undocumented workers take their place.[70]

These examples also stand out to the skeptical reader for their claims, not just for the way they can be used to address a theoretical problem. One might well question the reliability of the kind of self-policing encouraged by OSHA and the EPA, as one might question the immigration laws, free trade acts, and welfare policy that make the INS strategy possible. But for the purpose of my argument, it is important to note that the services to be measured are not completed by EPA or OSHA inspectors, or INS police, but rather by the workers in the factories and companies who implement the safety committees, reduce chemical use, or transform themselves into workers from welfare recipients. In the place of fines, tickets, or arrests, all of which can be regarded as complete and measurable at least temporarily, the movement to compliance seems if anything like an increase in state activity, but activity increased by the labor of workers outside the state. It is ultimately in this reading not just a matter of measurement but task completion, where every state and private worker alike sees task completion as an end in itself. But what does it mean that the state has returned to labor?

ANTISPECTACLE

In her work on Reagan era, political public culture, Lauren Berlant talks about the need for U.S. citizens to try "inventing new scenes of sociality that take the pressure off the family form to organize history for everything from individuals to national cultures."[71] She maps the way the most intimate parts of life had come to fill the public sphere while many matters of common concern had become private. Berlant notes the deterioration of citizenship in the last twenty years and calls, in effect, for a renewed citizenship based on multiple sites of social interaction. Yet it might be possible here to revise this schema by suggesting that common concerns have not so much become private as labored, and thus have taken on the atomistic appearance that labor plays under capital. On the other hand, these matters of common concern, the social constitution, are no longer private matters. They cannot be reenchanted. They can only be Disneyfied, making them stranger still, if more representational of society's condition, and especially making them sources of direct wealth. This privatization produces what Negri calls the social worker.[72] And by going into labor, public administration could be said to change the relationship between labor and capital. The old dialectic of labor and capital that formed the backdrop to the modern state experiences a shift in constitutive power. Instead of exploring the intricate relationality of state and capital, it may now be important to study the intricate relationality between state and labor. Society has been given the state in the name of trying to reproduce capital. It may work, but it is a dangerous move for capital.

This regulatory citizenship does require new forms. Management guru Tom Peters has his suggestion for this statolatry through a renewed citizenship. He approvingly quotes the authors of *Reinventing Government* when they begin their book by saying, "We believe deeply in government." He writes the forward to the first Gore book on the NPR, *From Red Tape to Results,* and admonishes his fellow citizens that "if we don't do most of this, fast, we'll be stuck with a nineteenth-century government in a twenty-first century world." He adds ominously that "competitiveness will suffer, and our very democracy may teeter if the level of distrust and disgust grows—perhaps even paving the way for a raving demagogue to enter the White House."[73] Peters's demagogue is Patrick Buchanan, Republican presidential challenger. He had been Berlant's too. For Peters, a reinvented government can renew citizenship. Another father of reinvention, Philip K. Howard, author of the best-selling *The Death of Common Sense,* writes the forward for Gore's paperback, *Common Sense Government,* and looks ahead to a government based not on what is "legal or illegal" but what is "reasonable." He announces that with common sense, "we can accomplish things we had almost given up on."[74] Poulantzas believed that a quarantine state would turn against its own civil society. The NPR's statolatry seems instead to be turning into society. As work is subsumed under social life, so the state appears now to be constituted in that life. How the state effect will survive the production of difference and its politics that social life implies is an open question.

How should the *X-Files* be read against this question? There appears to be a gap between the spectacle of the social constitution in such imageries and the dull labor of regulatory citizenship as it is administered in countless sites of doing more with less. But the gap exists within the subjectivities that are producing social life. If that social life is constructed on the real subsumption of labor under capital, the price for capital has been its utter socialization. Maintaining the ability to appropriate from a socialized position requires a control of subjectivity. As much as the spectacle is what Foucault referred to as a positive power for this purpose, it only increases the antagonism with that dull regulatory citizenship life. If people watch the *X-Files*, *Oprah Winfrey*, or *The Practice* as positive powers, they may be opting for representation that is free of the instrumental hands of the state, hoping to produce a politics whose abstraction is truly in their service. It will be necessary however, both to say that people are right to seek this politics and that these hands must be confronted as one's own. This is why the aliens are simultaneously fascinating and threatening. When one looks down at one's hands they see the cyborg implant, just as Seven of Nine on *Star Trek*, and just as Seven of Nine is an occasion for an exploration of antihumanist escape from dualities and into difference and partiality, so too does spectacle involve of one in machining one's own subjectivity.[75] State work remains dedicated to making a horror of one's hands. Reinvention wants to make regulation a response to this chaotic embodiment of the machine. If reinvention can make a place for itself in this subjectivity, it can reassert its abstracted duality against this difference and, of course, its oneness, its ghostlike state effect. The danger is that this subjectification will recognize its own power in the meantime.

4. GENERALIZING SOCIAL TERROR:
PUBLIC MANAGEMENT AND PERFORMANCE
BY OBJECTIVES

The brain of capitalism has turned itself precisely into the state.
—Antonio Negri, "Is There a Marxist Doctrine of the State?"

In the last chapter, I tried to give a sense of how citizens and civil servants are mutually implicated in state work, their labor, and even their imaginations. Another way to say this is that public administration has intensified, especially with reinvention, the laboring of publics. And seeing public administration as the laboring of publics returns a politics to those repeatable practices and techniques that Foucault said can give the impression of a state structure as something solid, even natural.[1] This is different than seeing labor in the state—not that the discipline of public administration has shown much interest in this perspective either. The laboring of publics, in the sense that Michael Denning uses the word in talking about the laboring of U.S. culture during the era of the Popular Front, brings something more into play. Denning means to give U.S. culture the benefit of multiple use created by the term laboring, including making visible the labor of making culture and making that culture the culture of all those who labor. The laboring of publics can similarly make state work partisan by opening it up to scrutiny.[2]

In a way, I am getting a lot of help in the laboring of public administration these days. As capital looks for more and new ways to accumulate surplus, pressure on government has been intense to deregulate and scale back social protection. Part of this pressure has also insisted that "government pay its way," that it prove its value to society by measuring its value. With a few exceptions, this does not mean that government should actually make money but rather that it can prove it contributes to private accumulation. Some of this proof comes through evidence of sound investment, through military procurements and technology funding. This is relatively easy to measure, or rather to convert for measurement. The companies receiving the investment make money in the market and government investment is validated. Of course, this is delicate politically because other kinds of investment, for instance in alternative fuel companies, might also be easy to convert, but fractious as policy. Jingoism mostly eliminates this discord while keeping investments flowing.

For these familiar reasons of imperialist hegemony, it is not the capital flowing through state work but the labor that also flows through it that is coming under the spotlight. How can it be cut, or prevented from being cut, by measuring its productivity, or to use the current terminology, by measuring its performance? The state technique that performs is called public management. Conveniently for me, it is forced to look at labor. But unfortunately for public management, this labor proves not so easy to measure.

While it is not so easy to measure, it is revealing nonetheless. In the last chapter, I looked at the way this labor implicated publics, and by measuring this implication, one makes this situation even more self-conscious. One makes more and more labor self-aware as the work of comparison, unitization, and exchange, as state work generalized now, as mass intellectuality. The laboring of publics may therefore be able to open up labor to itself, and perhaps along the way, explain why the state is at the heart of the laboring of culture today, as it was not in the time of the Popular Front. It may be that performance has come full circle.

To see public management as the reemergence of labor, whatever its politics, is to try to overcome once again the repeated reappearance of the state as a collective abstraction that marks work that only goes as far as talking about the state as discourse, just as public management does. Thus, even sophisticated work like the historical sociology of Philip Corrigan and Derek Sayer remains at the level of, as they say, the state stating. By looking at who embodies that stating in labored practices and how, perhaps the state can be kept from congealing and clogging too fast.[3] One way to do this is to look at the increasingly unsatisfactory labor of making publics, both for publics and the workers who daily make this thinning abstraction. The work of Negri, Virno, and Hardt can then be used to see public management in light of the post-Fordist changes in how wealth is produced in many developed countries today first identified by Michel Aglietta and Allen Lipietz.[4] Public management is part of this historical moment and an attempt to reproduce state effects under antagonistic conditions. It is also an example, as Tony Tinker has pointed out about accounting, of the real subsumption of labor under capital. A new unity of labored effects under capital might even be detected—a unity brought together in this instance in the subjectivity of the civil servant.[5] On the other hand, it is also a moment of intensified disaffection for the civil servant and citizen—disaffection not with the conditions to which public management attends but with the impoverished effects for which public management can have no answer.

PUBLIC MANAGEMENT INTRODUCES ITSELF

The reinventing government project of the NPR ended with the new presidency of George W. Bush. There is good reason to believe that public management as a series of linked techniques and practices will survive. Reinvention is easily understood as an ideological project in a larger sense. It reproduces the state effect in aggregate and links it to the much more secure effect called the economy, perhaps even more closely than past representations. It is more closely connected because with reinvention, the state effect is linked internally to the economy in the body of the state worker, not just in the state statistics and aggregate actions characteristic of Keynesian economics. By this I mean that it draws its legitimacy directly from the way state workers labor and how that labor is narrated using private sector terminology. State workers have always had a specific identity of citizenship system maintenance urged on them.[6] One may conclude from this intimate link with the economy through the techniques of workers themselves that reinvention has made the state seem more real than ever, and one might expect this to be the case materially.[7] Yet when one looks at how this ideology works as practice, how it becomes practice and practice takes its name, one senses trouble. There was always trouble, of course, but this kind of trouble is new. In practice, state worker identity has not become more specific but more general. Although a special ethical code is still interpellated, state work is structured and understood like any other work. And any other work is increasingly, as Negri puts it, social work. Public management is both a response to the threat of this immaterial labor and its victim. It asks for a measurement as a way to recover the organization of immaterial labor, searching for a material way to prove the state's naturalness through a kind of quantitative effect. If this quantitative effect is part of the relentless search for new areas of profitability incited by capitalism, it is also a mark of the pathos of state practices that must struggle to assert authority in the face of immaterial labor.[8]

The New Public Management holds that *"how* government manages affects *what results* it can produce."[9] But the rise of what I will call simply public management has met with some skepticism. It is often portrayed either as the triumph of instrumentalism over values or the cover for the retreat from the welfare state and the abandonment of a collective commitment to social justice.[10] Sometimes, these arguments are combined to say that focusing only on how to make government work abandons the effort to seek consensus among citizenry about what it should do. Just as often, though, these criticisms remain separate, with a moderate critique emanating from within public administration scholarship that emphasizes the need to recover the idea of citizenship, civic values, and the ownership of government by the people from a technocratically constrained language, and a social democratic critique usually emanating, especially in the United States, from beyond the field and seeing something more sinister in the stress on private sector technique, the managed decline in commitment to social programs, and scarcity.[11] The conceptual inadequacy of both will become apparent.

Public management as a field is perhaps only ten years old. It is quite self-aware of both its rapid growth and sudden influence. It is aware too of its critics. To the extent that one can talk about the field as a singular subject, it would be fair to say that it sees its role in just the opposite light as its critics. Through good management, public managerialists hope to renew what they regard as the fraying contract between citizen and state, and both through this renewal and its own efficiencies, carry out successful social programming and regulating. In two discipline-building conferences in the United States, in 1991 and then 1995, public management scholars reflected on their influence and tried to define their strengths and weaknesses. Both conferences subsequently led to codifying volumes of essays, first *Public Management: The State of the Art* and then a consolidating volume titled *The State of Public Management*.[12]

Donald Kettl's introduction to the latter volume attempts an explanation for why public management has taken to the field with such confidence. Public management is here because, as Kettl concludes, management matters. It matters because citizens rightly demand high performance for the tax dollars they pay; because disappointing performance signals problems in the administrative system; because the administrative system increasingly stretches past individual government agencies into vast interconnected networks inextricably connected to society's basic institutions; and because in the end the quality of government's performance and public faith in these institutions are inextricable.[13]

Public management, then, is the best way to fix government, and a government that works is one that has the trust and confidence of its people. A working government is thus the basis for renewed citizenship. Kettl also writes an introduction to a volume from the Brookings Institute titled *Inside the Reinvention Machine* reviewing the NPR. Here, he suggests that better management can alleviate the crisis in U.S. government—a crisis in which people no longer believe government can work.[14] From here it is a small step to the question of why the state should rule if it does not work, and at this point arises the kind of crisis of legitimacy about which Jürgen Habermas and other social democrats worried in Europe in the 1970s. Habermas, like some critics of public management in the United States today, advocated keeping the decision making in government away from managers and in the hands of citizens in political dialogue.[15] The distinction that Habermas seemed to make between public and private management, and between technocrat and citizen, are not ones that Kettl and the New Public Management emphasize (nor ones that I will respect). Instead, Kettl's "vast interconnected networks" attached to "society's basic institutions" hint at the citizen as manager of these pathways and mobility of management technique throughout society. Whether the state worker is a spider or fly in this web is an open question.

Kettl asserts that the emergence of public management can be located in the aftermath of the "trauma" that implementation studies caused in the field of public administration.[16] Implementation studies themselves emerged as a way to study state programs resulting from Great Society legislation. They claimed to focus on whether the intended results of legislation were actually produced locally. The most often-cited work here was Jeffrey Pressman and Aaron Wildavsky's *Implementation: How Great Expectations in Washington Are Dashed in Oakland or, Why It's Amazing That Federal Programs Work at All, This Being a Saga of the Economic*

Development Administration.[17] It would be unfair to allege that its influence owes to the fact that people did not have to read it to learn its argument, but perhaps fair to say that its radical pragmatism shoved aside other kinds of analyses. These other analyses were for the first and last time to date threatening to break open the field with the critiques of antiracism, social movement histories, and the apparent growing difficulties of private accumulation in the United States, thereby asking a field that had always tried to quarantine these struggles as environmental pressures on the public organization or specialized questions of governance to account for its own ability to exist.[18] In the end, implementation won the day, and though most of its theorists would reject the connection, their unwillingness to expand their critiques made the appropriation of these critiques by the Right much easier.[19]

Kettl notes that "the implementation movement brought questions of performance to the center of the debate for the first time," but "for all its appeal," it "played a constant note of despair" in recording instances of programs not working at the local level. Public management emerges as a "far more positive view of government and its programs." At the same time, public administration began examining itself in light of the implementation crisis, and other disciplines already engaged in issues of performance and questions of networks joined the debates about public programs. The conclusion, Kettl maintains, was a "remarkable convergence."[20]

Laurence E. Lynn Jr. and B. Guy Peters, two other leading scholars of public management, also speak of public management as an optimistic pursuit, borrowing "what works" from the private sector and deepening the comprehension of why what works does work by borrowing from the "social sciences."[21] Nor has the United States been the only habitat for public management. In the English-speaking developed world, it has taken root in the post-Thatcherite atmosphere of England, as well as in Canada, Australia, and New Zealand to varying degrees. In England, Tony Cutler and Barbara Waine point out in their incisive study of the British public sector in the 1980s and 1990s that "managerialism offered a positive message: goals could be attained with the use of fewer resources if only the appropriate management approach were adopted."[22] Here, too, the focus on results based on proper management offered a way out of implementation narratives of failure, even if that failure was not resulting in the kind of state reorganization, the kind of privatization, witnessed in the United States. More recently, Germany, Switzerland, and many other countries of the European Union have joined in extolling public managerialist approaches.[23]

Public management has also assumed a central place in international development administration. Development administration theorists, the counterparts to beleaguered public administrationists in developed countries, warn that "in the United States and many OECD countries, the intellectual agenda has been seized by the New Public Management. Through offers of aid funding and threats of aid conditionality, the movement is being energetically promoted across developing countries by the World Bank, USAID, and the U.K.'s Overseas Development Administration and other bilateral donors."[24]

The most defining case for public management, of course, has been made by the best-selling book *Reinventing Government*.[25] Its subsequent adoption as the script for the Clinton-Gore efforts at governmental reorganization, the NPR, has only confirmed its influence. Ironically, this book was written by two people who were not in the circles of the public management project in the United States. Equally ironic, the book concentrates on practices and case studies. The emphasis on practice, always key to public administration, is one of the characteristics of public administration against which public management styles itself the new science. Public management in fact regards its emphasis on theory as one of the pillars of its existence.

Barry Bozeman, organizer of the first national public management conference, announced that the new discipline was at its best "when it concerns itself with theoretically informed experience prescriptions." Bozeman is here quoted by H. Brinton Milward, who rejects mere "best practices" accounts about public sector managers and advocates for getting "public management researchers to take social theory seriously."[26] Milward echoes Kettl's remarks on the significance of other disciplines for public management. But the example of the authors of *Reinventing Government* are a reminder that practice and theory are never autonomous. If, on the one hand, *Reinventing Government* evinces the public administration theory that practice is theory, it also contains the public management theory that management is practice. Crucially, it sounds a triumphant note for the techniques of the private sector, competition, entrepreneurship, strategic management, and the attention to "performance and results."

What emerges, then, is a portrait of public management that arrives to reinspire governments by emphasizing the importance of managing them correctly. To focus on management, the new public management draws on other disciplines, especially economics, business, and parts of the social sciences that are already concerned with a bundle of management concepts like performance, outcomes, networks, efficiency, choice, and resource maximization, and rather less concerned with organizational form, process, empirical case studies, resource allocation, and control. In more popular terms, public management has become the common sense that says the management techniques of the private sector can be used to make government work better and thus make it more popular. These techniques can be applied, with some modifications, to public purposes. Yet as I will argue, public management is not the adaptation of private sector techniques to public purposes but rather the attempted reorganization of the state to new private purposes—a reorganization that is both inherently statelike and crisis ridden.

In fact, it can be asserted that the idea of public management as private innovations put to public use may stand what is really happening on its head. It may not be entrepreneurship that will save the government but governmentalization that will save the entrepreneur, by making productive those social solidarities often intent on resisting further incorporation under the terms of accumulation and appropriation. In other words, public management emerges as the organized resistance to the solidarities that previous state-capital arrangements have created. Public management, from this perspective, is not advice from the private sector—and other social science disciplines that study it—to the state but the latest strategy for reproducing society under the conditions of crisis Habermas thought he had isolated in a moment. This reproduction strategy involves more and more of the population and their lives, and more and more of their subjectivity, in accumulation, yet it risks more and more solidarities produced by the logics of management. It remains to be seen how public management tries to resist these solidarities through the mechanism of performance, and how the need to deploy this resistance through the state precisely provides new openings for alternative solidarities, even as it reproduces the state effect.

CRITIQUES OF PUBLIC MANAGEMENT

It might be useful to start by observing how the social democratic critiques of public management from outside the field of public administration have failed to grasp the kernel of this inversion. That public management runs the risk of exposing the politics of performance rather than aiding the performance of politics is a potential point of rupture unlikely to be revealed by these critiques. This is because these readings tend to view the private economy separately from the state, and that economy as basically viable and real (rather than as a material effect), much as the Right does. This stance leads to a kind of politics of redistribution that runs as follows.[27] The wealth-creating economy, currently aided underhandedly by state subsidies to corporations, should be made to fund all the social programming necessary. More local decision making and self-management will help determine how this full funding should be distributed, and will provide people with more meaningful connections to their communities and work. Under such circumstances, consumers and workers will choose environmentally sound programs and products.[28] Into this politics steps public management. It appears to these critics like the antithesis of their politics. It seems to put more power in the hands of managers as opposed to workers or communities, to accept the cost of subsidizing business with minimum redistribution and maximum subsidies, and to commodify the services it does manage. On top of all that, public management proposes itself cheekily as the way to save government.

Social democratic critics have, in response, made some important points about public management's presentation of self. They first note the virtual absence of any history but disciplinary history in public management's account of itself. The new public management has an acute sense of its newness, yet it remains oddly naive about its own currency. Indeed, public management has about it an air of radical chic reminiscent of Theodor W. Adorno's cutting remark about Karl Mannheim's sociology of knowledge: "It calls everything into question and criticizes nothing."[29] Despite the well-intentioned effort to be "more positive" about government, the history around this history shows that the implementation literature was a significant part of the assault in the 1970s, by every administration from Nixon's onward, on Great Society programs and an ideological weapon in the attempt to call the social welfare state, such that it was, into question on supposedly nonideological grounds. To the extent that public management accepted that the state was not performing, it bears the mark of this ideological birth. Consequently, the emergence of public management can be viewed as a kind of complicit acceptance of the smaller government "common sense," meaning less state redistribution downward and more upward, that becomes hegemonic in the 1980s and 1990s, coincidental with the rise of public management. Thus, returning to Kettl's assertion that "management matters," it is easy to recognize the parsimonious language of today's shrinking social welfare programming, such as the movement to health maintenance organizations that manage—that is, limit—health services to the poor and elderly. The demand of citizens for high performance for their dollar has allowed the emergence of the notion of the state as a service in the market, where everyone is entitled to equal exchange, and everyone's money buys a visible and equal amount of a commodity, a government service. From this notion comes not only the idea that it is unfair when rich people are taxed to support programs for poor people but also that each tax dollar should be visible, producing a discount on a subway card or tax holiday on clothing as a way to demonstrate the one-to-one correlation between a dollar taxed and a dollar of service performed by government—an almost pre-Smithian logic.[30]

This social democratic critique thus sees public management either as a dupe of rightist ideologies and policies or as coconspirator in their ascent. Either way, public management becomes the instrument for dismantling the social welfare state in the United States and much of the Organization for Economic Cooperation and Development.[31] To make matters worse, public management appears to introduce private management-labor relations and measurements of efficiency as well as accountability inimical to the de-commodified services of the state. It does so, finally, by centralizing power in the hands of management. On all counts—the lack of redistribution of private profit, commodification of services, and authoritarian treatment of workers—public management represents the wrong direction for U.S. social democrats. It would follow that they dismiss its claims to aiding any kind of legitimacy but that of a "workfare state."

Now this critique based on the politics of redistribution is not without insight. Still, on the fundamental question of why public management has arisen and spread as it has, it seems to me to be of little use. Why has public management been embraced in the state and the discipline of public administration? Why would schools of public administration, so linked to the state in funding and student placement, embrace what has here been described as an antistatist logic? Why, despite the presence of the above critique, has it been able to grow with such rapidity in influence? It seems unsatisfactory to say, as the redistributionist critique must, that public managerialists are being untruthful or deceiving themselves in contending that public management is the best hope for retaining both government programs and public faith in these programs. The only other recourse for redistributionists is to make the technocratic argument that there is a more efficient way through the taxing of corporate or personal profits to fund programs building human capital, as Robert Reich has, or that self-management and decentralization are actually more efficient than so-called command management, as radical democrats have maintained.[32] But it is hard to imagine that explanations of either false consciousness or technical mistakes about how the state might best function would in other circumstances be accepted by the same redistributionist critics.

The flaw in the redistributionist critique may be that it accepts the economy as an autonomous, and known, sphere that the state aids, when it should instead be aiding the poor, workers, or the environment (and by implication, the state too is both autonomous and known). That this state aid might be constitutive of the economy or that the state might be constitutive of these communities cannot be reached from this perspective. It therefore becomes hard to see public management as an attempt to reproduce an unstable relationship where the state must reorganize, but with every reorganization, every privatization, also reconstitutes social solidarities it must resist. For social democratic politics, this relationship suggests that not only do such politics owe their existence to that which they may be asked to deny in power but that a program of putting the state to other uses attacks the wealth-making mechanism on which such a program would be based. It would be difficult to develop an understanding of public management as other than an unfair approach resulting from electoral compromise and the influence of the wealthy in politics, unless public management can be viewed as not a choice but a logic given to undermining itself.

INTERNAL CRITIQUES

A number of other critiques from within the field of public administration share this basic perspective, if in less ideological terms. It might be said of all of them that the laboring subject returns as the citizen to try to extricate him or herself from the very state conditions that produced his or her citizenship. That is, they all assume a plasticity of state agency that could never have created public management in the first place. The *Public Administration Review* recently featured a symposium on "Leadership, Democracy, and the New Public Management." As Harvard University's Linda Kaboolian explains in the introduction, the symposium provides "an opportunity for the adherents of public administration and of public management to engage each other," and "to elucidate their positions on issues that divide the school of public management from that of public administration."[33] Thus, a salient critique in the symposium and beyond blames public management for its lack of attention to ethics, and to a higher constitutional compact between citizen and state, and worries about its accountability and inattention to "politics." Out of this lack of attention comes a calculating rational actor who is unwilling to sacrifice for the state or other citizens, and hence one is left with a state unable to build collective projects.[34] A more pragmatic version of this critique suggests that the importation from the private sector of the focus on service to the customer should be replaced by the no-less-market-derived idea of the citizen-owners who are willing to accept the no-less-market-derived idea of the choices of others as well as themselves.[35] Yet this symposium cannot explain public management's growth any more than can social democrats, without resort to saying public managerialists have been mystified by the language of business or have simply not thought through the consequences of their techniques.

In response, public management theorists have claimed that it is they who are interested in these larger questions. Laurence E. Lynn Jr. stakes out this claim in his article, "Public Management Research: The Triumph of Art over Science."[36] But public management's own expressed preference for social theory has even been trumped by other public administrationist theorists using, for instance, Jacques Lacan. Lacanians have attributed the decline in the welfare state, in which public management seemed too willing to participate, to the problem of creating a polity that can imagine Alterity.[37] This Lacanian approach comes out of a group of self-labeled critical and postmodern public administrationists who nonetheless naturalize the state despite their professed antiessentialism.[38] This Alterity, moreover, quickly degenerates into pressure-group politics. How can one account for the specific public managerialist flavor that the end of the social welfare state has taken, without resorting to pluralist models for an explanation? Perspectives that do not call into question the state effect, no matter how adventurous otherwise, cannot say. But if one suspects that these various public administrationist approaches misunderstand public management's inversion, if one senses that their acceptance of the state object does not permit a reversal in the terms of debate, where can one turn to instigate these terms?

It follows that if the false consciousness argument of the redistributionist and public administrationist critiques alike has been rejected, the claims of public management must be taken seriously. Central to these claims is the notion of performance: how to get better performance, and how to measure it.[39] What can be observed is that public management employs performance to solve a problem, but at the same time reconstitutes that problem. Rather than viewing public managerialists as thinkers who do not understand or have the wrong approach to the state, they can come to be seen as thinkers whose understanding and approach successfully reproduces the conditions they seek, but that these conditions press the contradiction that called public management into being. Let me spend a minute, then, on this question of performance to see what it might reveal about public management.

PERFORMANCE

Performance is indeed a term borrowed directly from the managerialist literature coming from and concerned with the private sector.[40] Looking at the managerialist literature, however, one immediately encounters two senses of performance: a narrow one connected to a worker's output, and a broader one connected to a firm's or, in government, an agency's outcomes. From the former, there is an individualist emphasis on pay incentives and promotions, and from the latter, a collectivist stress on the organizational results of performance. For instance, public managerialist B. Guy Peters questions performance measurements in government, claiming they are more easily measured in program than policy areas.[41] What he is questioning is a truncated idea of performance based only on the first sense of worker output. But in the private sector literature, this kind of performance measurement is matched by a broader measurement of the firm. Prominent strategic management theorists seek to build "a better theory of firm performance, as well as informing managerial practice." For them, this kind of performance measurement is a way to understand "how firms achieve and sustain competitive advantage."[42] In terms that oversimplify, the first sense of performance involves getting workers—including managers—to work hard, and the second involves organizing that hard work in a way that makes the firm a winner in the marketplace.[43] These two senses of performance rely on each other in the literature on firms; in fact, they form the theory of the firm.[44] In some way, how workers work in the firm must be connected, by the act of organization, to competitiveness. Competitiveness—that is, success in the market—ultimately measures how workers work and how they are organized. Yet the temporal and spatial question, which is the question of the firm, is all-important. The market cannot measure how workers work directly but must wait to measure it through the way the firm organizes this work. Management's object becomes this time and space in which workers are re-created and reorganized. Of course, that time and space is not only apparent to management; it is also a source of politics for workers.[45]

Attention to performance in the managerialist literature involves not just the management of workers, nor the planning of firms, but the anticipation of market organization and reorganization in that time and space between managing workers and managing capital. This is the task of what has become the most influential subdiscipline in business schools, strategic management. Now what does it mean for public management to speak of performance?

Despite B. Guy Peters's reading of performance as only a worker-management issue, public managerialists have been aware that they must deploy both meanings of performance if they hope to make sense of either meaning. But Peters has correctly identified the problem public managerialists face. It is at first much easier to implement performance as a strategy for getting workers to work hard than as a strategy for organizing and directing their productivity. Even this ease soon breaks down, however, in the absence of this organizational moment—that is, without the dialectic of the market. How can organization be anticipated and subject to reorganization without direct reference to the market? The answer to this question is, on the one hand, the key to the spread of public management, and on the other, the contradiction of its reproduction. In the process, it becomes apparent how wrong redistributionist critics are to suggest that public management is not clear about its object or not technically competent to engage it.

To help think about how the state complicates the use of performance, how public managerialists eventually invent a kind of performance more complex than that in the managerialist literature, and how this new kind of performance finds a way to anticipate and be organized by the market, one might turn to a discipline immersed in these questions differently.

PERFORMANCE IN PUBLIC

A sociological understanding of performance can place public management back within the general contradiction of wage labor and at the same time, when placed together with the field of performance studies, explain something particular about public management's dissembling. Irving Goffman notes that in contemporary life, people presume they will be measured against others and therefore perform their identities in public. But such judgment on the basis of social codes is so omnipresent that it produces constant pressure and constant tactics on the part of the performer to avoid unacceptable representations of self, often by directing unacceptability toward others. Michael E. Brown places Goffman's observations within the context of historical materialism as a way to account for the "terror" of social life under capitalism. He sees in these pressures, among other things, the need "for the managerial detachment in the representation of the self that must be embodied in such interactions and that marks them as analogous to the class relation of property to labor power."[46] This management has as its goal the ability to withstand constant comparison and comparability under the sign of exchange value, and simultaneously to participate in this comparison. With the growth of immaterial labor, it has become more difficult to compare and measure, and thus various strategies for intensifying this management have emerged. For public management, the chosen strategy has been named performance. Performance, then, is a technique of intensification of comparison where comparison is necessary as the basis for practices that assume universality and naturalism (citizenship, voting, rights, laws), and permit the continuing state effect. An intensification of performance risks drawing attention to the historical dynamic that makes such comparison possible—that is, the "process of realizing the contradictory and therefore unrealizable commodity form of the individual," as Brown puts it.[47] And this risk grows all the more with immaterial labor. As it becomes harder to separate labor from labor power, it becomes hard to separate the citizen and laborer, and harder to organize both—a practice essential to generating state effects.

Performance as the intensification of management, of people in the process of incessant comparison without regard to value other than what can be rendered the same for exchange purposes, courts a heightened consciousness among workers who sense the frenzy of arrangements and artificiality that make this measurement possible. In public management, this frenzy leads to an even more apparent organizational moment. A glimpse of how this intensification runs such risks in state work can be seen in the field of performance studies, where one conception of performance posits the possibility of the commodity form of the individual, while another uses the heightened occasion of the performance to recognize the social cooperation that makes it possible. The latter reveals a dialectic of abstraction of exchange value and measurement of labor's sameness that informs performance—a dialectic that as it grows more intense, can potentially expose the specific kind of appropriation that leads to this specific kind of alienation.

PERFORMANCE STUDIES

Another group of scholars also works on what it terms performance. In the discipline of performance studies, theorists have developed a body of work designed to address those live aspects of artistic performance that are neglected by the traditional textual, and Western cultural, focus of theater, dance, and film and music studies. Presenting what she calls "one potent version of the history of performance studies," Peggy Phelan suggests it may have been born by bringing theater and anthropology together to consider the "extraordinarily deep questions these perspectives on cultural expression raised." Phelan asks,

> If the diversity of human culture continually showed a persistent theatricality, could performance be a universal expression of human signification, akin to language? If performance communities continually made themselves into mini-cultural ensembles, how did their rules and responses reflect larger cultural imperatives?[48]

In the attempt to find this language of performance, and with it the discipline of performance studies, theorists take a number of approaches. One way of understanding the theoretical orientation of performance studies scholars is to divide them between those who see primarily what might be called the antiorganizational moment in the performance and those who place more emphasis on the organizational one. On the one hand, scholars like Phelan favor an "elegiac" approach that stresses the performance's reliance on an unrepeatable performativity and therefore its quality of loss.[49] Victor Turner and Richard Schechner prefer the notion of studying performance as something that happens "in-between" social space.[50] Rhetorician Judith Butler, from outside the field, expands the performative to the social spaces Turner and Schechner would transgress.[51] Without flattening the richness of any of these approaches, it is possible to point out that they share an interest in the politics of the antiorganizational moment—that moment when social order is performed in a way that reveals its lack and contradiction. While for Phelan this is a special moment reserved for art, albeit not necessarily Western art, for Butler these moments are a constant challenge to the reproduction of order, when they are not the stuff of that reproduction.

For other theorists of performance like Randy Martin and Fred Moten, such moments are noteworthy for the attention they draw to organizational possibilities. For Martin, such possibilities become abundant through the conditions of crisis that are both the conditions of the suspension of social life for performance and the conditions for organization in social life generally. From this comes the realization that organization always occurs within crises in modern capitalism and so a politics of organization will do likewise.[52] In his introduction to a special issue of the journal *Women and Performance,* Moten notes that the exclusion of sound from the discipline of performance studies is based on an overly simple understanding of sound's temporality—one that guarantees a kind of presence that performance theorists are trying to call into question. He suggests, following Martin, that the reduction in the sensual ensemble may be tied to a reduction in the social ensemble in dominant conceptions of performance studies. From here, he speculates that since sound necessarily represents the body, it may lead to "a non-pathologizing, non-moralizing understanding of fetishization" useful for thinking a new politics that would allow one to be "interested in the future that sound produces and reproduces."[53]

The complexity of performance studies thinking goes beyond the uses required here, but that thinking does yield a way of understanding the connection between performance as a measured act of intended productivity in management, and performance as a bounded act intended to represent the production and reproduction of the social. Martin and Moten see in the persistent "trouble" or "crisis" such representation yields the opportunity for a politics through and beyond such performance. In this sense, they look into an organizational moment and the way it constitutes the moment of performance and is open to performance's reimagining. By contrast, Phelan and Schechner investigate an antiorganizational moment, a "rupturing disappearing," of social life, a commodity form of subjectivity. It might be said that private sector performance theory is focused on a similar antiorganization moment, hiding the organizational moment in the market. That is, performance is made up of the antiorganizational act of getting workers to work harder by breaking down old systems and solidarities, and on the antiorganizational act of breaking down old systems of capital as a part of this gamble. What actually organizes both worker and capital is not that management decision but the market's confirmation, just as the market prompted the initial gamble. Conversely, in the public sector performance act it could be expected that whatever the organization broken down in decisions of how workers work or funding is applied, the organizational moment that actually decides cannot be had directly from the market. The organizational moment in the performance act cannot be ignored by trusting in the market to re-create the conditions of its possibility. That organizational moment must be included to complete the performance. It becomes necessary to be conscious of the act of organizing publics for market confirmation or rejection. Or more precisely, it becomes necessary to see that worker or agency performance has no meaning without the market, and that its meaning is therefore reduced to the management of self under conditions of incessant comparison and replaceability. In other words, the social basis of performance hidden in the antiorganizational moment surfaces in the organizational act of performance in the state, revealing the nature of that organizational form.

Let me return now to public management's original contention—that it can make government work better, perform better. It employs the popular managerialist concept of performance to do this. But now it must measure its results, or in the language of argument, it must be reorganized based on what works best. The market is not directly apprehendable for this purpose, however. Thus, public management has to find a way to measure itself. It has to extend the performance act into its organizational moment. What this means in practice is that the state must reach beyond itself to organize publics in such a way that this organization can be measured by the market. Or at the level of worker performance, it means that the worker must actively create the basis for comparison even as she or he compares, thereby opening up social life to labor again.

It must be quickly highlighted that it is not the act of reaching out beyond the state to organize publics that distinguishes public management from public administration. It is rather the need to organize publics under the logic of performance. As should be clear by now, this is a logic of the labor process, and more especially of the process of extracting surplus value. Public management's uniqueness stems from its imperative to organize publics to extract surplus value in order to bring market measurement into government. This is, moreover, precisely the point— the key point of this argument—that is missed by a redistributionist or public administrationist ethical critique of public management. Public management operates under a logic of the labor process. It is not an attempt to bring the market, or private sector techniques, into the state. Nor is it against an ethical—that is, antiorganizational—impulse of individualism. Just the opposite, since it realizes it cannot bring the market into the state to organize it, it cannot directly ground itself in the terms of exchange that gave rise to an ethical position based on the individual-citizen, itself based on the commodity form.

Public management instead becomes extraordinarily statelike, intensifying the state effect.[54] This is central to its growth and influence. It practices through necessity an organizational moment, a state moment, in order to make the state work. This insistence is its strength and honesty. It reveals how public managerialists could be advocates of both the market and state, without having to resort to suggesting they are not being honest or clearheaded. It also clarifies the way public management spurs experiment in practices that produce intensified state effects. These are effects that can be understood neither as the simple abandonment of the state through budget cutting or privatization nor, alternatively, as the mere tool of capitalist interests. Rather, public management pursues a larger logic of the market, itself a search for survival, for reproduction. This pursuit is, of course, also what exposes public management to the trouble, the crisis, of alternative solidarities, alternative forms and directions of organization.

PERFORMANCE BY OBJECTIVES AT THE
NEW YORK POLICE DEPARTMENT

The New York Police Department's attempt to become a performance-based organization illustrates the way this new view of public management alters an understanding of the criminal justice system in three fundamental ways.[55] First, it points toward the problem of managing state labor.[56] Second, it shifts the focus on a justice system of control to one of constant reorganization. And third, it underscores the resistance that the state must maintain in the face of other social solidarities proposing the organization of labor. Policing makes a good case study here precisely because, on the one hand, it is a place where the state effect is produced so readily. Despite the growth of private security, public security has also grown to address populations that do not appear immediately profitable to those funding private security. On the other hand, policing has taken on a central role in forming the organizational moment in public management, permitting the measurement of performance far beyond its own agency boundaries. In fact, it has a kind of metamanagerial role—a role still resolutely dedicated to state effects and distinctly linked to the new forms of production as any since Friedrich Engels identified the "special bodies of armed men." Like those bodies, however, state effects are not reducible to this role.

ONE HUNDRED BLACKS IN LAW
ENFORCEMENT

But it might be appropriate to start with some of the ways public management troubles the police and reproduces its ongoing crises. There are two reasons to "maximize productive and allocative efficiencies that are hampered by 'bureau-pathologies'" in the police force.[57] The first is to lower crime statistics, and the second is to root out corruption among the workers themselves. Leaving aside for the moment the method of lowering statistics, how is corruption decreased as a bureau-pathology? It is done by the concentration of power in management, and in the case of police, in their union as well.[58] This concentration is a familiar move for public management, which advocates an entrepreneurial manager with the flexibility and freedom to manage for performance.[59] What it means in practice is a retreat from community policing, a style of managing workers and publics that leaves too much control in the hands of frontline workers and the communities with which they come in contact.[60] Unfortunately for the district commanders, such a pullback produces higher crime statistics as police are both less visible and less knowledgeable once they are returned to centrally dispatched squad cars. Public management would thus seem to face a contradiction. To get the workers to perform, they must be on the street, but on the street they are out of reach of the entrepreneurial manager with his or her targets, incentives, and objectives. Yet that is not the end of it. Such a pullback also produces both more brutality and more divisions within the force. Police accountability to management goes up, but accountability to communities decreases.[61] The anonymous officer leaps from the patrol car with nightstick or gun in hand believing he or she can reconcile his or her distance from the community with the need to produce lower statistics by unloading blows or bullets. Brutality becomes the only labor-saving device capable of reconciling managerial control with the hunt for numbers. With the rise of such brutality, the workforce fractures. The Latino Officers Association forms and breaks with the Hispanic Officers Association over questions of brutality in the Latino community. One Hundred Blacks in Law Enforcement forms out of the Guardians to conduct exactly that kind of community policing that management now forbids, visiting African American youth outside the officers' work hours to advise them on how to act when confronted by their coworkers.

If the story ended there, performance by objectives in the New York Police Department might have failed long ago. By failure, I mean that it would have been supplanted, in the pendulum swing of police organization, by a reorganization into a community policing model. This swing has historically followed a series of high-profile conflicts with communities. Yet such a swing has not taken place.[62] The department has preferred to live with brutality as a way to reconcile central control with the need to lower statistics. But it might be wrong to attribute this obstinate approach either to the personal outlook of Mayor Rudolph Guiliani or the lack of organized pressure from communities, though both may contribute to the department's confidence. Such contributing factors, for instance, cannot account for the way the department has ignored the foundational rule of management: do not let alternative social solidarities develop to provide proof of other labor arrangements. Nevertheless, the continuing strength of One Hundred Blacks in Law Enforcement, the Latino Officers Association, and the growing voice of gay and lesbian officers appears to be outpacing any managerial response or co-optation.

The dismal failure of the New York Needs Courtesy, Professionalism, and Respect initiative as well as the recent controversies around the Labor Day Parade and the Patrol Benevolent Association awards dinner indicate how these alternative solidarities are only growing stronger.[63] These solidarities are no longer easily detached from protest communities following the Amadou Diallo and Abner Louima incidents, and even recent trade union rallies include police officers for the first time in recent memory.

Instead, it could be suggested that public management has forced a basic change in how policing must be understood—one that has committed policing to a kind of reproduction of itself fraught with contradictions. Paul Chevigny, for example, reads police behavior as a search to restore a dominant social order.[64] He notes the way their sense of order is inscribed with race and class. Their reaction to social life conducted outside this order is more severe the more that life appears to transgress the order. But what if the police are not involved any longer in preserving a social order but in the reorganization of that order, a sometimes radical reorganization? What if policing is now understood as part of the reorganization instigated by the logic of public management, the very state-like moment when the administration of publics must be shaped forcefully to yield to market measurements? It is the moment of welfare to work, corporate charter schools and Channel One, health maintenance organizations, harvesting from public lands, speedups and cutbacks in every public service designed not to punish in a moral universe but produce in a capitalist one. It is a moment, in fact, now known in virtually every agency when public managerialists gain the upper hand in the reform process.

This process originates in the language of scarcity, competition, and efficiency brought on by the crisis in accumulation in the 1970s, but in the hands of public managerialists, it must be transformed into a reorganized state capable of articulating with both the demands of new accumulation strategies and those of its ideology—in short, with its political economy. Just as these new practices are crucial to the success of public management, so too are they likely key to the perseverance of the performance by objective model of the New York Police Department. In this universe, antimarket solidarities do not necessarily start as threats but certainly become them. A public managerialist police agency is no different from any government agency in this sense. It is asked to re-create itself to make its public measurable by the market. This imperative effects its core public, suspected criminals. We will see below the ways this reorganization works. On the other hand, beyond the core public, social solidarities that do not yield (enough) private profit—whether public housing residents, community gardeners, trade unions, or street vendors—do not necessarily want to be reorganized for private profit accumulation strategies. The police play a metamanagerial or co-optive role in these cases by taking over parts of these publics and enforcing such reorganizations. To refer to this as the criminalization of these populations is not inaccurate, only insufficient.

BAD BOYS, BAD BOYS?

Angela Davis and others struggled against one part of the reorganization of the core public in policing: the prison-industrial complex.[65] It stands, or rather grows, as an odious emblem of the logic of public management. The prison-industrial complex is that configuration of private and state capital invested in the building of prisons, supplying of prisons, and industries inside prisons, in articulation with the reorganization of policing and the courts. The term stands also for the configuration of ideology that accompanies this new strategy of accumulation. Like all growing industries, and especially an industry full of capital from the state, the prison-industrial complex has an appetite for cheap and plentiful labor.[66] And like other state-funded industries, it worries little that such labor will undermine its strategy since the invocation of national interests, of the interests of the citizenry, provide exceptional protection of private property, as it did for the railroads and military at various points in U.S. history. The broken-window strategy and hard-fought battle to introduce New York City police into the schools, both discussed below, can be seen as points of articulation with this new accumulation strategy as well as an impulse to retain a public managerialist approach to policing in New York.[67] It is not a functional argument that is being made here, although too often this is how the prison-industrial complex is understood. Rather, it indicates the logic of a technique and its consequences. This technique starts as a limited strategy for intensifying comparison and ultimately contributes to producing the state effect called the prison-industrial complex—a complex no less real for these origins.

The broken-window strategy relies on building the case for incarceration based on public infraction, especially among the young and working class. In New York City, that profile means African American and Latino male youths whose presence in public, particularly in any organized form, is already regarded by many citizens as an infraction.[68] By lying in wait for these youths when they jump subway turnstiles, drink beer and malt liquor in public, or jaywalk, police not only record the infraction but gain the right of search and seizure, sometimes finding concealed weapons, carried mostly for protection, or small amounts of cannabis or cocaine, carried mostly for personal use. A youth first caught jumping a turnstile at the age of fourteen may, by the time he or she is caught shoplifting some pants at the age of eighteen, have a police record of half a dozen petty counts. Such a record allows the state to make the claim that there is a pattern of habitual criminality requiring real prison time. Such a youth then enters the state penitentiary system for a period of one to five years, and in so doing also enters into an accumulation strategy that must house, feed, and put this youth to work. Together with petty drug dealers, these youth now make up the vast majority of the prison population.[69] They join prisoners convicted of serious crimes whose sentences have grown more severe and are more often the product of automatic penalties like the "three strikes you're out" laws. These latter form the workforce for the growing number of industries in prison as a supply of long-term, often docile because defeated, labor supply with no cost of reproduction. Both populations contribute to the overall strategy. If there is something to Negri's contention that public spending should be understood as a second kind of expropriation, then this strategy is one of expanding extraction that gets more from the laborer through state taxation, but by charging the laborer to house their own competition.

The most recent extension of supplying labor and a kind of human raw material to the prison-industrial complex is occurring in the New York City public schools, where even the compliant Chancellor at the time, Rudy Crew, resisted the presence of police officers for several years. The process of building records among youth has now moved out of the public space into the latest contagion of citizens' fear of such youth, the public schools—this despite the fact that more students have been injured or killed by dilapidated buildings and buses than by each other in the schools in 1997–1998.

Thus, the core public administered by the police, suspected criminals, who in New York are youth from communities of color, is reorganized not simply to be controlled but to be "eliminated tout court from the world," as Gramsci phrased it.[70] Such youth are far less evident as youth in New York City today. They exist as workers, prisoners/prison workers, or students en route to one of those destinies. They exist much less as youth, youth culture, or solidarities in public in opposition or diffident to these destinies. This is what people with property in New York mean when they say that the city is not only safer but it feels safer. It is no mere coincidence that one of the leading proponents of public management at the Brookings Institute, John Dilulio Jr., is also the author of the infamous "superpredators" article about youth of color in the United States that characterizes them as defying measurement as potential workers (or productive members of society), thereby placing them outside the category of human beings under this episteme.[71]

The prison-industrial complex has always been around, and even if it is increasingly important, representing for instance the part of the construction industry with the highest rates of profit, it cannot explain the choice of investing in this strategy as opposed to another, such as a training and apprenticeship approach to the disciplining of youth. That is, although I have identified the technique of performance as a way of understanding in part how a state effect like the prison-industrial complex is produced, I have yet to explain the choice of technique. For this understanding, the youth in question can help. The youth of color caught up in the new logic of policing are no more automatically wageworkers than they are criminals. In fact, youth of color in New York are involved in a broad array of potentially self-directed labor that is increasingly regarded as antisocial and antiproductive, as criminal. Those who practice such self-directed labor need to be reorganized as publics subject to corporate accumulation strategies. Youth of color are prominent among those who practice exactly this noncorporate, self-directed labor.

COMMUNITY COURTS, CREDIT UNIONS, AND STREET VENDORS

If one looks in New York at community-based credit unions, street vendors and small craftspeople, community court projects, advocacy groups like ACORN (Association of Community Reform Now), or even insurgent political campaigns, one finds an intriguing pattern of involvement among youth of color. What is common is short, intense periods of participation. In most cases, direct state actions like closing down vendors or cutting funding play a significant role in ending these relationships. What seems clear is that youth of color are attracted to the possibilities of escaping corporate accumulation strategies, as they are surely not attracted to prison-industrial accumulation strategies. But all such alternative solidarities, as well as more individual strategies of self-directed labor, are the primary targets of public management's reorganization of publics.

Such alternative solidarities, having been created out of the social relations of capital including state welfare programs, now stand in opposition to the logic of public management, and that means youth of color do too.[72] Policing must intervene here, with these solidarities and youth, in instances of reorganization in which other state agencies cannot by themselves resist the power of these solidarities. This is the other source of support for a public managerialist approach to policing: the active use of policing in other public managerialist reorganizations. Whenever an agency is involved in reorganizing, it is always far from clear that the logic of that reorganization is superior to the solidarity in place and often the case that this solidarity has precisely provoked the reorganization, exposing the weakness of its claim to objective measurements of efficiency and productivity. This would be a strong thesis version of an argument common in critical accounting about efficiency—an argument whose weakness, in both senses, is a lack of dialectic that flattens power (and the work of Foucault on which it is based). Thus, these theorists believe they are seeing an increasingly social construction of efficiency because of changes in technology and management techniques designed to be more efficient. This tautological approach is all that is left as an explanation for power's dispersion without some sense of the ongoing dialectic of capitalist relations as encouraging and then impoverishing sociality.[73] It might be better to recall the example of unionized hospital workers in the New York Hospital Corporation who fought the coming of McDonald's to public hospital cafeterias as an attack on their union strength and solidarity, unconvinced by the public managerialist argument of contracting out. Teachers continue to challenge the voucher systems and charter schools where unionized workers are the first to go. Housing advocates continue to resist attempts to close or sell off public housing. Social service and welfare rights advocates contest workfare programs. The contention here is not that these solidarities represent noncommodified social space, as Karl Polyani might once have viewed these blocs. Yet even if one accepts Claus Offe's claim that ideological state apparatus are in fact noncommodified spaces needed to reproduce labor and the market, one would have to explain how it was possible to convert these spaces so easily to spaces of profitability in aid of that market rather than at its peril.[74] The reorganization led by the logic of performance in public management demands this direct profitability from these spaces. Such reorganization often goes by the name of privatization.

OVERCOMING A PERFORMANCE
PROBLEM: PRIVATIZATION

One of the ways to increase performance, privatization, can now be seen in a new light. Privatization is only the most direct kind of state reorganization, and as the public managerialists themselves like to say, not appropriate for every service. But the fact that it can be carried out in any service as part of the reproduction of state-capital relations forces one to ask how this shift is possible. After all, leaving aside the different qualities of the welfare states in Europe and the United States, should not the privatization of schools, along with the further privatization of health care, security, public health, and transportation, lead to some great difficulty in producing the workers needed in the United States? Just such an assertion has been made by both social democratic and public administrationist critics. Yet the U.S. political economy has grown tremendously and is by most accounts no more crisis ridden than usual. Why has privatization not threatened this stability more, as critics of public managerialists predicted? Older social solidarities have instead been destabilized and dispersed by this reorganization, and have failed to mount the predicted counterassault.

In fact, privatization now can be read as that statelike movement of reorganization that seems to privatize management of reproduction without losing the state effect of that reproduction. If this is governmentality, it must be one that can explain the instated self. It would appear that a statelike concern for social-capital arrangements enters via management technique in these privatizations. As Pasquale Pasquino remarks,

If one rids oneself of the idea of the state as an apparatus or instance separate from the social body, the focus of all political struggle, which must be either democratized or destroyed once its veritable nature has been revealed, or which must be appropriated in order to take power; if one frees oneself of this old idea, canvassed in the political theatre since Kant at least, one can perhaps recover another meaning of this word state. . . . [T]his would mean resituating the analysis of relations of power wholly within the interior of this social body. . . . [T]he state would then signify not the site or source of power, the one great adversary to be smashed, but rather one instrument among others, and one modality of government.[75]

But if the state is one mere modality of government, how is it that this care of reproduction so necessarily statelike in one moment can be entrusted to individuals in direct contact with markets the next? Has the state entered the management in a way that permits the individual to produce her or himself in a sufficiently instated way? Is it an afterglow of the state effect that suggests it travels with management, not with conventional governance? This is to say, as citizen-workers read health magazines, go back to college, take responsibility for their families, and support zero tolerance for drugs, sex, and violence, how does technique maintain the corporate directedness of at least most of this self-management and the reproduction that the techniques producing state effects saw as their task? For the most part, these questions will have to remain unanswered in this book.

Yet perhaps this dynamic reveals the incompleteness of considering community courts, credit unions, or the activities of One Hundred Blacks in Law Enforcement as instances of a general governmentality where authority has become unmoored from these techniques. Instead, governmentality may mean a discipline directed explicitly at labor forms in which the reproduction remains alive in the care of the self. This is a view of governmentality that acknowledges the troubles, the crises, under which the care of the self develops, and the limits of its autonomy from practices driven to reproduce these conditions. If discipline alone were the goal of these practices, how to explain the intervention to prevent self-directed labor? By the same token, though, more can be expected from moments of organization under such conditions. Because does not the movement of these techniques into the subjectivity of labor in general threaten to undermine any distinct separate effects that could be taken to stand for a real and bounded structure called the state? Let me complete the more speculative side of this look at public management by considering one such moment of organization.

The Stolen Lives project is a collective of parents whose children have been the victims of alleged police brutality. They have organized national days of protest against police violence and been a significant voice in the fight against police brutality in the wake of the Abner Louima brutalization, Amnesty International report on New York City policing, and Human Rights Watch report that singled out the New York Police Department for severe criticism. How can such a movement as Stolen Lives now be thought of not as a resistance to state violence but as that movement of people toward self-directed labor and social solidarity against which the state must deploy violence as resistance, against which ultimately it would wish to deploy this kind of governmentality?

What Stolen Lives is proposing is the assertion of youth of color public life. This is an assertion of a certain kind of solidarity against which public management is deployed generally and performance-based policing specifically. Rather than seeing Stolen Lives as a resistance to state violence, it might be more appropriate in light of this discussion to see performance-based policing as a resistance to the assertion of youth of color public life so forcefully envisioned by the Stolen Lives movement. Not that this public life is innocent of technique or practice; just the opposite. It has been exposed to the effects of exchangeability and rejected them in favor of a rich conception of social life. The danger for these practices then becomes doubled. First, more technique may lead to more ways of seeing the solidarities it attempts to resist, and as these solidarities become bound up with immaterial labor, they become a source of wealth that must be confronted anew with still more techniques of organization that must be developed based on this source.

With the intensified moment of performance in public management, the impossibility of founding subjectivity on the image of the commodity is confronted, and it is confronted at a particular, post-Fordist historical moment. Law, citizenship, and at one time welfare enforced such an exchangeable subjectivity in the abstract, deflecting attention from the abstractions that laborers produced through the workplace or household, or appropriating them. But without the mock social surplus of welfare, and with changes in production toward reliance on the general intellect along with the unity of culture and production exemplified by immaterial labor, state work enters a crisis. Or rather, it enters less a crisis than a mix of pathos and danger. This pathos is the dominant new state effect, just as cynicism, as Virno notes, is the dominant effect of labor experiencing this state effect.[76] The pathos derives from a practice in which the state, in the labor of the state workers, must beg its status from the citizens from whom it seeks a priori acceptance. Public management attempts to manage such a crisis through more technique and more state effects. But it finds that technique increasingly within directly productive subjectivities—subjectivities that cannot easily be split between state and society. State effects have become personal. The cops thus become *COPS*, and the very cycle of differentiations, organization under exchange, and then new differentiations becomes a source of wealth directly through the cultural industries. There is the sense that this organization under the sign of exchange may be subsumed now in this new kind of social production, where culture and production are fused, and the state effect is a moment in this labor, not something apart.

5. THE ADMINISTRATION OF MOTIVATION:
ANY COOK CAN NETWORK

The destruction of the State can be envisaged only through a concept of the reappropriation of administration—in other words, a reappropriation of the social essence of production, the instruments of comprehension of social and productive cooperation.—Antonio Negri, "Constituent Republic"

Public administration reaches into subjectivities to realize and regard itself. These practices I have called reinvention and public management, and they are simultaneously techniques for arranging state labor and the laboring of publics. They produce state effects, but because they rely increasingly on subjectivities that are part of a new social production, these techniques expose their effects to other kinds of abstractions amid these subjectivities. Yet there is a third practice that produces state effects about which I have not yet spoken. This is the administration of motivation. As with state work's realization and self-regarding, motivation is a necessary part of organizing labor, and it requires the labor of publics to succeed. If the techniques of policing, welfare, citizenship, and law have been manipulated to ensure the reproduction of state effects under new conditions of wealth making, so too have the techniques of motivation. What was once the material practice of patriotism, nationalism, and family, or the American dream, today must find a new technique in this new form of social production. If the problem of labor I have named performance is that of arranging workers and capital in space and time for measurement, behind this difficulty lies the fundamental, but also historical problem of all management: how to get workers to work hard throughout that space and time. If public management focuses on the first problem, public administration has always grappled with the way to solve the more basic problem of labor, as a specific formation called state work. The question of public administration is that of how to get state workers to work while at the same time creating publics through that work that also labor. They are the same concern, requiring and constituting each other. But they hide an even deeper question of why wage laborers labor in the first place.

Although this was not an issue Marx and Engels addressed much, perhaps because in their day coercion looked like a sufficient explanation, it has subsequently become an important question for theorists, especially those associated with the labor process theory in the 1970s that suggested that "in the long run capital has succeeded in imposing its techniques of control [rationalization and mechanization] over the work process."[1] By asking why workers work to produce state effects, some insights not previously pursued may emerge. One starting point is to look at the limits of labor process theory and then use the work of Maurizio Lazzarato to hasten not only the implosion of the firm but the labor process critique that reinstates it. Looking at why state workers work can help in first moving beyond the reference of the firm, and then under certain post-Fordist conditions, recasting the notions of networks and webs not as descriptions of the way state workers work but as attempts to enforce such work out of labor after the fact of its social cooperation.

At the risk of stating the obvious, I must begin by saying that to work for the government is to work for someone else. It is to be a wage laborer. Like all wage labor, state work (that process of working in government to produce state effects) presents an enduring problem for the power that would extract surplus from it: how to get the wage laborer to labor well, and how to get that wage laborer to labor more. It is first necessary to confront the relation between this question and that of why wage laborers labor at all. The first question is at least implied and occasionally even stated by public administration, but the second is beyond the epistemic pale of the discipline. Public administration may not have as its aim harder and better work in the state, yet it certainly recognizes this harder and better work as a means. On the other hand, it cannot even recognize the question beneath this means: Why do these workers work at all? Public administration is not alone, of course, in sidestepping this deeper concern. When it has been confronted, the question of why wage laborers labor was traditionally answered with recourse to ideology, relying ultimately on a false consciousness argument on the Left, and one about expectations and calculations on the Right.

The labor process literature represented an advance over these positions by locating some kind of rational agency within what it regarded as the limited options produced by the subsumption of labor under capital, and in some sense combined the explanation of the Right with a capitalist critique, especially in Michael Burawoy's work discussed below. In this synthetic view, capital secured the consent of workers through elaborate games and maneuvers in and around the workplace between workers and managers, while simultaneously obscuring its own true workings.[2] The advantage of this approach is that it took the explanation out of the minds of workers and into their material relations in production, and thus made it possible to study the creation of this consent in a new way. Another way of looking at this labor process literature, then, is as an attempt to bring the question of why workers work together with a study of the technique of how those in control get workers to work hard. Producing consent recognized that the efforts of management went beyond the mere arrangement of workers in time and space to this fundamental arrangement of the politics of consent. But the politics of consent was itself then limited to management-labor relations. The gain of bringing together the questions by materializing them in relations at work also brought the diminishing of the world beyond these relations and within them. British labor process theory, to the extent that one can group theoretical trends nationally, has acknowledged that world beyond on occasion, although it is still dominated by the workplace as the unit of study. Despite some fine attempts to gender subjectivity and acknowledge resistance, however, it does not see any other labor out there in the world (except household labor, which it treats as a sociological problem).[3]

LABOR PROCESS IN THE STATE

A study of public administration confronts a theory of labor process in government in the first instance because public administration wrenches apart these two concerns.[4] Public administration focuses on how to get workers to work harder (or as they would say, smarter or more efficiently) to the utter exclusion of the question of why they should want to work at all. But perhaps labor process theory also is confronted by public administration and challenged to try to bring the world back in, not as an ideological effect or the starting point of consciousness before the labor process but as materially involved with the production process and the way government workers produce themselves. Seeking out the labor process that produces state effects may offer some special vantage points for seeing the insinuation of ideology in labor as well as labor in ideology. It will require working through the twin discourses in public administration of scientific management/public management and human relations/organizational theory, which only seek to explain how to get the state worker to work or how to get that worker to work harder. This search gets formulated as the divide between theory and practice, or between theorist and practitioner. Attempting to understand how the state worker works is theory. Attempting to push that labor harder is practice. No conference, collection of essays, or master's program escapes formulating this duality as a tension either to be resolved or tolerated. This duality makes no room for a theory of why—theory already being attached to how. Such an attachment is reinforced by a perceived reality where only how is available for abstraction from practice. Public administration as a discipline is therefore incapable, even in its radical and critical moments, of theorizing in any way that might make practice impossible. It cannot think about why workers work for fear of the disappearance of its object— an object already difficult to hold steady.[5] In fact, even its critical moments serve to obscure this fear.

But the question of why the state worker works moved away from the instrumentalist imperative in public administration. It is not attached to the issue of how to generate surplus labor, but owes its allegiance to the categories of ethics and governance. Although these categories may be rendered instrumental, and may be attached to the approaches of scientific management and human relations, they are also the only subjects of public administration permitted to drift into idealism and a kind of metaphysics of presence where the state worker acquires his or her putative humanity. In other words, the obscuring mechanism that complements the one in labor process theory takes place through the discourses on ethics and governance. The worker is thereby addressed in multiple ways: as part of the production process in the state in scientific management discourse, as part of the community of workers in the state in human relations discourse, and as the guardian of a citizenship in the discourses of ethics and governance, where citizenship is, as Althusser understood it, the burying of the state in the individual. A multiple interpellation in public administrationist discourse becomes the ghostly effect of carving up the fundamental problems of why and how a state worker works.

It might be said, then, that much as it does not admit it, public admin-istration does point to a theory of its labor process in the act of trying to constitute that process through various addresses. The question of how a state worker works cannot ultimately be separated from that of why a state worker works, any more than the labor process in general could survive such a separation. That such separations are always attempted, placing the working subject into a schizophrenic condition, only belies the instability of the separation, even if an easy opposite must be resisted. In public administration, the constant return of this other question is encountered under the address of ethics and governance. The state worker cannot be put back together again—that is an impossibility—but an attempt can be made to discover the way state work nestles in the body of that worker through this multiple interpellation. If public manage-ment has revealed a citizen instated through labor, a look at labor in the state can reveal the concentration and experimentation of this develop-ment—what might be called the mass intellectuality produced by imma-terial state labor. Taken up critically, this language may help unearth a socialism in the state not to be quarantined but to be worked at.

Some objections, however, might be raised to seeing public admin-istration as a discourse about the state's capacity to labor. Viewing these diverse strategies as aimed at extracting labor power and surplus labor may come at the cost, at least temporarily, of an understanding of the other ways in which the strategies attempt to operate. Ethics in govern-ment, as in business, effect the circulation of commodities and their realization as they do the conditions of their production by labor. Ques-tions of entitlement and responsibility operate to configure services just as they do to configure markets for Gap clothing or Starbucks coffee. But to answer this objection, I should tip my hand in this argument and suggest that the labor of the state is disarticulated with the related uses of these strategies in circulation and realization, that the state labor process is specifically characterized by advancing conditions of circulation and realization within it.

A second objection might question whether the focus on surplus labor, on getting more labor power out of the worker than that worker might want at first to give, and why that worker consents makes sense in the state workplace.[6] It could be suggested that in the Fordist bureaucracies of the past, hard work was less the goal of state managers and politicians than a kind of systems maintenance, whatever the influence of certain theoretical perspectives on how those bureaucracies were viewed. But maintenance is still harder work than skipping off at 10 A.M. for the breakfast special at the local diner. The image of the lazy or uncooperative state worker as a problem predates the new managerialist assaults on the public sector of the last ten years. It is a cliché interrupted by the New Deal and briefly by the war on poverty when bureaucrats are perceived as cooperating with social goals and willingly giving up their autonomy to do so.[7] Yet it might be helpful to answer this objection by making clear that what I am contending is that the unifying problem of public administration is the problem of what Burawoy called the effort bargain, whatever the level of effort.[8] In this sense, if one wanted to pursue the question of why people work, the state presents perhaps the most fruitful challenge as a workplace with less wage incentive and less competitive pressure.

There are, of course, difficulties with considering the state worker as a wageworker. While it is certainly true that this worker has nothing but his or her labor to sell and will starve if he or she does not sell it, it is less clear how one would make available related concepts like the ownership of the means of production in this context, or whether value is being added to a commodity or labor in the work of the state worker. This makes the question of what is being obscured more difficult. Some of these questions connect to conventional political science and notions of sovereignty. Others might lead away to what Jacques Taminiaux calls the problem of adequation and a consideration of the marxian aim of work as self-production versus a Nietzschean aim of work that cleaves to the "unveiled" in the unveiling.[9] I will suggest a way of understanding the obscuring of how the state operates. But I will leave open the question of a transformative fetish.[10] It can be said, however, that the state worker is similar enough to other wageworkers that to give the answer that the state worker works for the money or to avoid being fired is as inadequate for these workers as for other workers. The entire history of management begins from the inadequacy of this answer, and has developed workplace space, culture, and ideology on the basis of that perceived inadequacy. This is to say nothing of sociology's own project to explain effort through consumer culture, leisure, and status.

It might also be supposed that the obscuring of profit making remains operative at some more complex level, and that the foundations for wage levels and control of what is produced must still be constructed. Here is where the discourses on governance and ethics are deployed, although never without management and human relations theory. It is fine to claim that what the state does and how much money it has to do it are decisions coming from the sovereign people through their representatives, and that state workers work within those limits. But how that work gets done and why workers actually make any effort requires the full force of management, human relations, and the ideologies of state and nation—in short, the full and also tenuous force of a labor process. If this moves beyond the obscuring of profit, it may also serve as a reminder that if the obscuring of profit is understood in the narrow sense of keeping people from seeing who controls the wealth rather than how they do not control the generation and definition of wealth, and thus seeing a way to generate the end of control, of management including self-management, there is not much to work with from labor process theory in the way of a politics anyway.

SCIENTIFIC MANAGEMENT

Management, including self-management, has been as much at the core of public administration as it has been of business. Public administration shares with private management an early history based on the concept of scientific management and an interest in the mental revolution proposed by Frederick Winslow Taylor. Taylor's presentation to the Special Committee of the House of Representatives to Investigate Taylor and Other Systems of Shop Management is often credited with having a profound impact on the emergent field of public administration in the United States.[11] Others followed, like Frank Goodnow with his separation of politics and administration in search of an administrative science, Leonard White with the first textbook, and Luther Gulick and Leon Urwick promoting scientific approaches from Taylor and Henri Fayol.[12] All of them were inspired by what Alfred Chandler records as the managerial revolution that occurred in private managerialist action and reflection in the first half of the twentieth century in the United States. This managerial revolution made an appeal to both worker and management—an appeal of the machine. It promised both worker and manager that a machinelike association would yield material benefit. It did. But in the process, it produced both the degrading of managers and workers into parts of that machine along with the effects of association on the subjectivities of workers. This led to both trade union consciousness—and under some circumstances, revolutionary consciousness—and conversely, human relations as a way to recapture managerial consciousness.

The effect of the appeal to the social machine was countered by Elton Mayo, A. H. Maslow, Robert K. Merton, Herbert Simon and others who began calling this approach into question by introducing behaviorist concerns. Underneath this appeal, in part, was the recouping of middle-management power against upper management and ownership as well as the blunting of trade union power. It was C. Wright Mills who condemned this emergent human relations school as trying to create "pseudo-gemeinschaft islands" in a gesellschaft swamp.[13] And it was an appeal to community where an older, gentler class order would restore harmony in the image of the small town. This is exemplified in Dwight Waldo's famous comment that "administration is everyone's concern." Indeed, the Fordist care of the self as consumer, family man, and patriot already implied this even for those who were objects of administration.[14] Not surprisingly, then, the impact of this human relations revolution was as pronounced in public administration as it was in private managerialism. Yet in a sense this work was only the other side of Taylorism, as with Fordism, returning to question itself. In his history of Taylorism's legacy, Stephen P. Waring asserts that Taylor himself in his plea for a "mental revolution" appealed to a language of "corporatism" as much as to the bureaucratic division of decision and task that was to be his more commonly acknowledged legacy. Waring notes that notions of harmony and rationality that sit together in Taylor found differentiation in his disciples, and thus in managerialist history in the twentieth century. The search, Waring writes, "for rationality and harmony quickly led to a schism, and partisans were divided into two philosophical schools, post-Taylorite bureaucrats and post-Mayoist corporatists."[15]

Despite their common origin and common object of securing effort from the worker and obscuring the process beyond production, both private managerialist and public administrationist discourses have presumed them to be separate approaches. In public administration, with its special relationship to ethics and governance, this presumption has resulted in a legacy of theorists attempting to put back together what were really just variations on the same approach. This attempt begins with

Dwight Waldo after World War II, and with the revalorization of Woodrow Wilson and Mary Parker Follet as progenitors of the task of making whole what are still considered the warring sides of the science and art of public administration.[16] Minnowbrook's New Public Administration in the early 1970s, as much as the implementation studies and New Public Management discussed in the last chapter, tilted the balance back and forth between science and art. Part of this struggle has always been the insistence on the art inside science and science inside art. Similar patterns can be observed in the private managerialist literature over the past century.

The split itself may have been a result of thinking functionally about the labor process rather than having an interest in its contradictions. But the legacy of the split has most certainly boosted a functionalist approach. Thus, if a workplace appeared dysfunctional, the first recourse was to change the formula, injecting more human relations or more hard-nosed management, depending on the diagnosis. The split and the attempts to fix it also gave the appearance theoretically of a totality. The terms of the debate were circumscribed by this duality. This kind of thinking has been powerful enough to seduce critical theorists from outside the fields of management, including cultural studies, as we will see below.

COMMUNIST CONSENT

So, for instance, one of the weaknesses in labor process theory has been to accept the idea that consent is what human relations theorists say it is. For human relations and organizational theorists, consent is tied to showing workers their "true" interest in creating a certain kind of workplace and engaging in a certain level of cooperation. Labor process theorists describe astutely the way this interest is constructed through a perverse republic of work. But what if this is not what consent is? Then the construction of it would also be vulnerable to reinterpretation. What if consent were the term for trying to explain how both cooperation and autonomy had been taken to a higher level? Then the process of management constructing such a notion of consent takes the form of a story, an explanation for a social development that cannot know its name.[17] In other words, consent can become, in its manipulation, not the securing of effort but the undoing of those who would tell tales about it. The inability of labor process theory to offer a politics out of its insights stems perhaps from accepting a notion of consent derived more from the liberal idea of the trade-off between cooperation and autonomy in human relations theory than the marxist one of consent as a principle of social development as in Gramsci. This notion of what might be called communist consent uses cooperation's growth to make an autonomy of the multitude into something that knows itself not as the limiting movement of choice but the ever expanding movement of possibility.

Communist consent helps clarify the unease critics feel with British labor process theory. The combination of identity work derived from power relations is critiqued from within this field by Chris Smith and Paul Thompson. They refer to the work of colleagues David Knights and Hugh Willmott as "discourse analysis" that "is antithetical to historical analysis, and leads to grant theory without a context." Furthermore, they complain that "the voice of labor is not accessed, but constituted within managerial discourses."[18] Management is allowed a collective presence, but workers have only individual subjectivities.

Consent is viewed by these theorists as something constructed on the terrain of the individual and then added up to create a version of hegemony. So, for instance, conclusions like this are commonly made: "Whether explicitly gendered in form or not, individuals' exercise and defence of control through skill and consenting practices can be accounted for by their interest in securing identity within capitalist production relations."[19] But if consent is understood instead as the seeking of cooperation for the purposes of autonomy, this view breaks down. Rather than seeing consent as a game of pluses and minuses for the individual, communist consent is always positive, seeking involvement, cooperation, and collectivity as the path to autonomy, and then crucially, finding the politics in this search. Even if the new level of cooperation fails to yield new levels of autonomy, a newly enriched politics is possible nonetheless, based on this higher level of cooperation. By contrast, the consent of human relations, and of Knights and Willmott, is always a zero-sum game.

A good example of this ahistorical approach, based on the liberal notion of "freedom from," can be found in Knights and Theo Vurdubakis's article "Foucault, Power, Resistance, and All That," in the book *Resistance and Power in Organizations*.[20] It is an admirable and judicious defense of Foucault. Still, it reads discipline and resistance without any curiosity about the history of these terms. It simply presumes that resistance comes after discipline. If discipline is understood as social cooperation, however, then resistance becomes the politics of that cooperation, and therefore constitutes it, comes before it. This is a point made by Hardt, Negri, and Deleuze. It is also made by Gramsci. Moreover, resistance seeks a not-yet-constituted discipline for the possibilities that this discipline as social cooperation might hold for autonomy, and then creates a new discipline when this disappoints. Resistance, in other words, seeks cooperation, and workers, quite evidently in state work, seek something more than the construction of individual or even collective identity. They seek in consent the ladder of cooperation and autonomy that leads to something more fulfilling than choice, more abundant than identity. They seek communism through the fetish of a spiraling cooperation that management needs and narrates, but cannot contain or respect. If communist consent is directed toward collectivity, a politics is possible in the struggle over the nature and direction of cooperation.

LIBERAL CULTURAL STUDIES?

But it is not in labor process theory alone that one encounters the baleful influence of this human relations/scientific management split or the limits of accepting a definition of consent derived from liberalism, Western psychology, and human relations theory. In cultural studies, Avery Gordon and Christopher Newfield have explored the corporation to good effect in an issue of the journal Social Text.[21] Gordon discusses the way management consultants have developed a discourse on diversity. His warnings about the adaptability and flexibility of the corporation have an underlying organic image of the corporation in them that suggest that race, gender, or sexual differences really could be engulfed by the corporation, managed into submission by it. The specter of this functionalist model leads Gordon to call for an antimanagerialism that advocates self-management. Thus, the antidote of self-management can provide the autonomy threatened by the corporate model of cooperation. Gordon accepts that human relations takes as its task the manipulation of consent, neglecting the relation between the manipulation of consent and effects of cooperation that would open up a politics that did not rely on a liberal notion of autonomy and cooperation as opposites.

To its credit, Newfield's work does imply a politics of consent where the growth of cooperation and autonomy could be narrated. The visceral optimism of Newfield's piece in contrast to the pessimism of Gordon's is the first clue to this politics. Newfield begins unpromisingly. Discussing the writings of the management theorist Tom Peters, Newfield criticizes him for what he leaves out of his accounts, but he also finds something seductive in Peters's use of pleasure to offer a kind of liberation in the corporate world. Newfield describes this as "positive alternative systems for a multiracial corporate populace . . . addressing its need not just for culture in the sense of arts and media but for work culture, for a positive, alternative, post-corporate business culture, [one that] will arise from ideas of liberation that are more carefully targeted to separate liberation from management for the large numbers of people who now mostly find liberation through management.[22] He wants to harness what attracts people to Peters and use it to promote a noncorporate culture. With this last move he disappoints. Like Gordon, he cannot entertain the idea that cooperation and autonomy might need each other. This idea is a ruse employed by weak liberals like Robert Reich who have been swept aside by the robust corporatism of Peters. Newfield is probably right about Reich's motivation, but he is not correct to presume that the only choice is between individualism and corporatism. In search of what he labels "radical individualism," Newfield abandons the field on which he gained his insight from Peters.[23] Rather than engage Peters on his own terrain— the immensely interdependent work world where Peters, without serious rival in either Newfield or Reich, tells a story about a higher level of social development he cannot actually understand but like some religious prophet, repeats with absolute belief—Newfield imagines a noncorporate world where autonomy can stand against cooperation. Here, autonomy extends into cooperation through a kind of liberal choice making at the level of the local. There is no sustaining relation between the two. Still, like Peters, Newfield does sense an excitement about the possibility of struggling over the politics of consent, even if his liberalism displaces it to the local, just as Peters's shamanism displaces it to the spiritual.

PUBLIC ADMINISTRATION

Public administration's part in making rather than receiving all this management history might at first seem minimal. It is often portrayed by public administrationists as such. But it is helpful to employ this history briefly in order to see where public administration enters on the stage. Although the divided discourses often obscure their identical object, the

science of management and art of human relations have arisen historically as the answer in modern capitalism to a problem at the point of
production: how to get workers to work, and work hard. Workers are
either managed and supervised into productivity or else they are coaxed
and massaged. Both seek to overcome the wage laborer's intrinsic resistance to making good on her or his sale of labor power. I have hinted
that the resulting consent produced by the combination of these pressures and techniques may reveal a complex politics not fully appreciated
by some inside or outside the field of business history. Yet again at the
risk of being mundane, let me add that state managers have a third
approach to the effort bargain and search for consent, one historically
regarded as less available to the private firm—until, it might be argued,
the state makes it available.

To work for the state is to work for someone else, but to be told you
work for yourself. The state has always had the appeal of nation, of the
people—an ethical appeal at its service in disciplining and enabling state
workers. This appeal takes many forms, from discourses on ethics, to
governance, to the difference between public and private goals, to technologies of accountability, transparency, and efficiency. Most commonly,
an ethics discourse is also linked to a concept of governance understood
in public administration as a kind of pragmatic manipulation of sovereignty. Ethics becomes the guide for determining the action of governance, yet governance also can act to set boundaries on ethical applications. I will call this dynamic the ethical state. The ethical state discourse
is used to appropriate the state from the workers who make it and to
show to them an image of their relations. In other words, the ethical state
in practice becomes an alien ethical state.[24] Noting the ideological nature
of the state in capitalist societies is hardly news, but looking at this
capitalist state in the context of the administration of the state worker
might yield another dimension of the critique. Ralph Miliband's classic
work stops short of considering labor as more than decision making in
the state.[25] A fuller construction of state labor is the purpose here. I am
less interested in the inability of the state to stand for society than its
inability to stand for its own labor.

ETHICS AND GOVERNANCE

What is the importance of the ethical appeal in public administrationist
discourse according to public administration? The answer has been that

the centrality of ethics, of ethical conduct, and the ethical goals of public administration are said to distinguish administration and management in government from managerialism in the private sector. As mentioned earlier, this position is most famously announced from within the public administrationist discourse by Wallace Sayre over seventy years ago when he stated that public and private management and administration are "fundamentally alike in all unimportant respects." This pronouncement has survived even public management. Graham T. Allison, in a call in 1979 for a field of public management that would soon be answered, saw the creation of the Senior Executive Service in the Civil Service Reform Act of 1978 as the opening for a consideration of the specifically statelike character of public management.[26] The growth of business ethics and corporate governance as concerns in the private sector in the last two decades would seem to undermine this defense of public administration and the special place of ethics within it. But business ethics does take many of its themes from public ethics, as does the discourse of corporate governance. In fact, this reversal in the logic of the common sense that innovation occurs in the private sector and can be harnessed in the public sector—a common sense boosted by public management discourse—should give pause to analysts who would model a mechanical interaction between the state and economy. Toby Miller makes this point with regard to cultural policy, noting the way oppositional theory has been tied to cultural consultancy and state funding in Umberto Eco, Chomsky, and Lyotard. The genesis of their work would seem to call into question where the state is and warrant some investigation into what it is, perhaps even from the thinkers named. These encounters should have led to more, not less engagement for the purposes of Left politics, and to an engagement with "the rich literature in business and professional ethics that has arisen over the past dozen years."[27] Miller contends that this has not happened, however, and no one has yet explored the implications of a state said to be giving ideas of ethics and government to a corporation.

Public administrationists may not be wrong to insist that this question of the ethical state appears to distinguish state labor from labor in general. But in looking more closely at the question, it is less its presence than its form and use that distinguish state labor. In public administration discourse generally, both ethics and governance are deployed within certain limits, within what is regarded as the proper field of study and action for public administration. Rather than being used to explore limits, both ethics and governance in this discourse imply other powers that set those limits. In the case of ethics, those powers are the courts; in the case of governance, they are the legislative and executive branches of government in the United States, and parliaments in other nation-states. Sometimes these authorities are transposed, and this is due in part to the mutual insinuation of ethics and governance in terms like public trust, public interest, and public good. To put it another way, ethics and governance are not terms that open up public administration. Despite a recent flourish of scholarship on ethics, for instance, public administration continues to understand ethics as obedience to law and sovereign wish. Despite evidence from across the globe on the dangers of understanding governance as a constitutional construction, public administration in the United States—and in its imperializing form—continues to regard governance as a matter of negotiation between branches of government.

This self-limiting discourse has rarely, if ever been characterized as stemming from the problem of how to convince state workers to work hard. If one tries to understand the ethical state as the basis for the statelike solution attempted again and again to solve the problem of convincing state workers to work, one may expose the limits of this discourse, including its explanatory limits. One might then see the labor process in the state more fully and develop an explanation of the discipline public administrationists exhibit in the face of these concepts. It would also help source the multiple interpellation, the fractured subjectivity, of those who try to form the state object. The ethical state discourse wants to recompose this subject, rid it of uncertainty, humanize it. But the desire is set against itself. Using ethics and governance to make the state worker work does not dehumanize that worker so much as it challenges the humanizing project of the ethical state, thereby potentially providing an opportunity for state workers.

Edward Pendleton Herring made an early formulation of the connection between ethics and governance in a 1936 book.[28] He maintained that because of the growing complexity of government and vagueness of the sovereign will, the task of the state worker was to use ethics in creating the rules and regulations that would flow from legislation. This account offers an early example of the way public administrationist discourse gives the humanizing project of ethics with one hand and takes it away with the other. For Herring, ethics becomes a tool in the hands of the state worker for making policy and programs. The state worker may use either what he or she has in the way of an ethical view or the ethical view derived from the elsewhere of governance. But the state worker may not make the ethical state. In fact, Herring's use of "public interest" as a criterion to guide the state worker turns out to be a purely relative term based on the weight of all the pressures bearing on that state worker, from his or her superiors, to the courts, to the legislature, to interest groups. Ethics are brought to labor and at the same time they are used, but not possessed by that state worker. Public administrationist critiques questioning the interest group pluralism that emerges from this work, including directly in Herring's work, have accepted the terms of this alien ethical state. They want to locate a more principled approach either in the worker or community, avoiding the making of ethics in state labor. This is exactly how Theodore Lowi criticized this ethics in his famous *End of Liberalism* in the late 1960s, when he demanded a performed ethics in the state worker unsullied by state labor. And it is the position of H. George Frederickson writing about the New Public Administration at the end of the 1960s and Frederick C. Mosher writing about a post-Watergate public service in the 1970s, both of whom seek to locate the alien ethical state in a new and more democratically sensitive governance that nonetheless comes to the state worker as the already-formed ethics of community. Today, even the position of critical public administration-ists associated with the Phoenix project in public administration hardly escapes this trap, substituting hermeneutic questions about ethics for a discussion on the politics of a labored ethics.

All these critiques may miss the central point about the ethical state as the pluralists described it from Herring onward. The pluralist approach does not lack principle. It lacks a politics of labor. The pluralist con-struction of the alien ethical state is an essentially ideological effort to account for a process of state formation without investing state workers with the power to produce the state—an ideological effort that continues to this day in such recent critical studies as James L. Nolan's *The Thera-peutic State.*[29] Locating moral or ethical values outside the state worker in interest groups, legislation, court decisions, or democratic culture gener-ally, or inside the state worker through professionalism, education and training, and workplace culture, pluralism depicts the labor process of state formation as a matter of choice, measurement, and balance of external elements with reference to an ethical state. In this sense, both Lowi's call for a democratic centralism as well as the localism and advocacy of Frederickson and Mosher seek to locate these ethics either more firmly in the state worker or more firmly in communities and publics. Mosher actually tries to do both at once, appealing finally to public administration schools to teach more ethics. Instead of pursuing the limits of the dominant pluralist explanation for the role of ethics and governance in public administration, both seek to rationalize them in a single subject, whether worker or public.

But from the vantage point of the labor process, if the ethical state is understood as both an effect of labor on capitalist conditions and a condition of labor under capitalist conditions, it might be possible to move beyond the ethical inside and outside. If a state worker, as Herring says, uses ethics to make state programs and policies, and at the same time, if a state worker, as Dennis Thompson claims fifty years later, uses "crit-icism of one's past and current performance" as the "last refuge of moral responsibility," ethics would appear to be both produced and reproduced in and through state work. As well, if public administrationist discourse insists on locating ethics instead in either the worker or public, then it is precisely because this humanist impulse is used to alienate the state from the worker that it produces the conditions of its own instability and enforces, in the public administrationist who must explain it, an extraor-dinary ideological discipline. Though the state worker is producing and manipulating the state itself, in other words, ethics constitutes another state that expropriates the labor of the state worker. By having the state worker use ethical tools and suggesting that there is a humanizing proj-ect in that worker's labor, and at the same time locating these ethics outside that labor, as something to be used but not produced and pos-sessed, public administration produces its own predicament. The ideal is located outside labor for ideological purposes, yet inside the laborer for exploitative purposes. Public administration presents ethics as the means of production of the state even though these means are not pos-sessed by the producers. The producer is asked to pursue her or his humanity with an ethics placed in or beyond them, but not developed through them. The project of humanization, of uniting the subjectivity of the state worker around the ethical state, is undermined by the need to alienate that ethical state so that any emerging social principles of labor do not produce and transform that ethical state.

But how does this happen? Where is the agency of alienation? This operation is neither the creation of a perverse republic of work within labor-management relations, as Burawoy has identified it, nor the standard return of citizenship rights in place of alienated rights in the workplace. It is instead the engine of both, the living skeleton of the actual rationalizing project at the heart of citizenship and individualism. It is the incompleteness that drives the worker in this operation, the way things fall short. Citizenship, individualism, subjectivity, and constitutionalism, which are the work of the state worker, cannot simultaneously be the reward without coming to belong to that labor. Therefore, incompleteness—the humanizing project that is also the driving project to make state workers work, to live up to that humanity, that now alien ethical state.

How, then, does this ethical state come to stand against the state worker as something alien, timeless, as the measure of the worker not one's social product? I can suggest two avenues of agency. The first one is the way the worker is called into being by public administrationist discourse, by the schools that Mosher appeals to, by the professional development seminars and retreats, by the codes and mission statements as well as culture of the workplace, by the restrictive appeals of nation, citizenship, and law that bound this subjectivity (and in turn have their own schools, workplace codes, and cultures, including the political science department in the industrialized and proletarianized university). The second one lies in the claims the worker makes on the ethical state as a representation of the collective efforts of state workers. This agency may or may not serve alienation of this kind. Yet in the search for a representation of itself, it often does. This search, though conjunctural, derives from the passion of social labor, from the sense of pleasure that comes from working with others to represent that passion. Here I cannot follow Judith Butler, who wants to explain the love of law as "the passionate pursuit of the reprimanding recognition of the state."[30] For the state worker, the relation remains material even as it remains alienated, and it derives from the social even as it falls short of that social imaginary. The limits of interpellation of the state worker point not inward to a deeper self but outward to the limits of interpellation of the public. The police officer knows something about the limits of address. What public administrationists do to that officer, they do to others. They may not locate ethics where the address would have them located. They want credit for their work.

Let me begin by restricting myself to some examples of how the alien ethical state emerges in state workers' work. Worker-subjects are addressed directly and indirectly by public administrationist discourse, producing a multiple interpellation as workers emerge in their labor. Workers also use the social product of this labor to revise their subjectivity, trying to claim the growing autonomy produced in the imperative of further cooperation. It should be clear by now that this subjectivity presents itself as individuality, but is made possible by social relations that hold a far richer possibility of autonomy and cooperation than the mere "identity" that is displayed to others in face-to-face work in government. I will look at three examples: Philip Selznick's *From the TVA and the Grass Roots*, a classic 1949 account of a major New Deal program; Charles Lindblom's seminal *The Science of Muddling Through*, published in the *Public Administration Review* in 1959; and Jeffrey Pressman and Aaron Wildavzky's *Implementation*, published in 1973.

ALIEN LIBERAL DEMOCRACY

In Selznick's account of the Tennessee Valley Authority and its use of citizen's committees, he identifies a problem: co-optation. Based on a democratic ideal of participation, these committees quickly become victims of the "needs of administration" that "become dominant," resulting in "the tendency of democratic participation to be reduced to mere involvement."[31] What state workers and publics are able to make out of this democratic experiment, then, becomes subject to two contradictory invocations of an alien ethical state.

On the one hand, this alien ethical state is invoked in the discourse to suggest that whatever the state workers and publics have made is not the state but rather some degraded copy of it that stands in contrast to the ideal. Thus the labor of the state is hidden in the ideal. But the labor must also be spurred, and so the alien ethical state is presented as something that must still be attained, even though the principles of this alien ethical state—that is, the principles of liberal democracy—cannot be developed by state workers and publics because they are contradictory. At the same time, the more satisfactory principles that might emerge in the labor of the state are always subject to the degrading action of the alien ethical state. Only the principles found in the experience of the labor of state workers and publics could form the basis of an ethical state, one that would stand for the labor they were presently engaged in developing. This does not have to be an ideological assertion. Creating an ethical state would require seeking out and addressing obstacles to that project, but the alien ethical state explicitly limits the state worker to accepting its production elsewhere. The ethical state placed against this labor and derived from elsewhere, from principles of liberal democracy, cannot but tyrannize both state worker and citizen in this project. Fortunately, the alien ethical state is itself forced to return to the state worker and citizen with each exhortation to copy it. It returns not as untapped subjectivity but as untapped relationality.

PIECES OF CITIZENSHIP

In a different discursive mode, one devoid of the overt liberal democratic politics of Selznick, this alien ethical state can still be seen at work in the writings of Lindblom. Here, the alien ethical state both degrades and exhorts state workers too. Lindblom begins by criticizing the suggestion in decision-making and policy-formation literature that one can take a full inventory of values and then make the right choice. He labels this approach the rational-comprehensive or root model and sets it aside because he says it is impossible to use to solve complex problems. Instead, he advocates what he refers to as muddling through, a pragmatic approach based on experience, comparison, and compromise.

By foreclosing this rational-comprehensive model, Lindblom degrades the work of state workers, and by advocating muddling through, or what he also calls successive limited comparisons, he nevertheless exhorts state workers to continue despite the limits of their efforts. Once again the ethical state is alienated. Ethics in the state are not the product of state work but something that stands against state work, beyond its reach. They can be used, though not possessed by the state worker. They are part of another order, available only in pieces to the state worker as he or she continues his or her efforts at the degraded state. But at the same time, the state worker is responsible for these ethical tools while in his or her possession, and must work to reproduce them without ever believing he or she has created or possesses the means of their production. To muddle through is to be addressed as a state worker whose citizenship is something that returns to one in pieces through one's labor on the state.

THE HUMANITY OF POLICY

Finally, in considering the famous book that began what became the implementation movement, one can see the way Pressman and Wildavsky employ the alien ethical state as a device for convincing workers to work, while denying them the political implications of that work. They take an exactly opposite view to Lindblom, and by extension Herbert Simon and others, by insisting on an empirical analysis of how programs are actually delivered and a positivist approach to the action that would follow. Yet despite their faith in a rational methodology, they too close off access to the ethical state. They alienate it in favor of the delimitations of implementation—something that occurs after policy formation and up to the point of delivery. Told to implement, the state worker is both degraded in scope and exhorted to realize the humanity of completed policy. This occurs through the degradation of implementation itself as a collective action. In the view of Pressman and Wildavsky, collective action is the decay of the humanity in the state worker, public, and ethical state. It has to be contained. Pressman and Wildavsky do entertain the possibility that collective action will highlight problems in this humanity, but not that collective action, that this labor, could come to produce an alternative to the humanity of policy. The humanity of policy remains subject to a severe separation from execution, and thus, from the experiences of labor that might transform it.

Policy as something that emanates from the mystery of the ethical state might best be understood as Althusser understood humanism, and especially as he criticized the notion of reification. Policy is not a thing but what Althusser called "a money-thing."[32] It represents the power state workers actually confront as they labor within the image of their relations to the state. But here it is a power weakened by its inability ever to free itself of the labor that produces it in the state. Unlike money, the trace of its labor resurfaces in each implementation, each muddling through, each co-optation.

As much as public administration has provided this reading, it cannot move further. Like the question of performance, that of why a state worker should work edges to the limits of conventional analysis. Public administration might be said to "tell the truth about the object that it loves," as Hardt and Negri put it. Public administration "raises the veil from that reality that critical reason wants to understand in order to subvert."[33] I have tried to isolate in public administrationist discourse a worker who is called out in various ways, yet also one who struggles not only in the rules of the game but with the rules of the game, and who has productive access to both. I have not sought in public administrationist discourse a de-commodified world, in Claus Offe's sense of this region, but a laboring one.[34] Let me leave public administration's own account now to pursue this state labor process.

ABSTRACTING THE STATE WORKER

Conceiving of all three of these approaches as ways of getting the state worker to work aids in bringing together their common object: the state worker and that worker's labor process. In so doing, the state labor process can be abstracted. The worker is asked to think about him or herself through these three kinds of addresses: an address of the machine, the community, and the ethical state. If all three are in part ways to get that worker to work, then the labor process they produce and especially the consequences of the way this occurs through the work of the worker should be investigated. Some thought should also be given, however, as to the limits of the way this labor process is understood by public administrationists as well as the way the state labor process tends to exceed the limits placed on it by its theorists. An understanding of the way this excess develops should be attempted through a reconception of consent in the state workplace. Finally, it is important to get a sense of the way consent in the labor process is worked out on the field of the state. Let me begin by returning to U.S. labor process theory.

RECONCEIVING RELATIONS IN
PRODUCTION

The key to worker consciousness in Burawoy's view can be found in the relations in production—that delimited, though complex field in which workers and managers act out power games around the question of the effort bargain. In this process, capital secures surplus labor while obscuring surplus value. The consent of the workers is obtained by hiding from the workers the true value of their efforts while bargaining and skirmishing with them about how hard they work. Burawoy insists that "variations in the character and consciousness that workers bring with them to the workplace explain little about the variations in activities that take place on the shop floor."[35] This was also the position of other theorists within the capital-logic school, criticized by Stanley Aronowitz for emphasizing the power of capital to subsume workers under its logic at the expense of analyzing the power of workers to transform their world.[36] Aronowitz contends that Harry Braverman and others pay insufficient attention to the contradictions that develop in culture, ideology, and the uneven development and internationalization of capital. Burawoy does not dismiss these others but holds to his view that the consciousness of the worker is produced primarily in his or her relations at work. Aronowitz disagrees, yet he tacitly accepts the split between two spheres of consciousness, inside and outside the workplace, thereby excluding the powerful material he brings in as evidence about the production of consciousness of that worker from the sphere of work itself.

The first thing to notice when the different ways to convince workers to work in the state are brought together is that a consciousness alleged to be outside the workplace is being applied as part of the subsumption labor in the state workplace. But it is now also apparent that the public administrationist discourse on the ethical state is produced in a way that permits one to question the politics in subsumption, perhaps bridging in state work the arguments of Burawoy and Aronowitz. As suggested earlier, public administrationist discourse reaches its limit because it must both discipline that state worker and try to contain the resulting cooperation that deepens against the image of the ethical state. This contradiction is present for managerialist and human relations discourses too, but in questions of ethics and governance, the need to place state labor always in its own past conflicts with the need to secure its present.

Now it might be argued by Burawoy or others who study the labor process that such an ideological technique as the appeal to the ethical state is strictly secondary to more direct applications of management and human relations as well as an internal constitutional subject. It might be asserted that conceptions like an alien ethical state can be relevant at most when political struggles have broken out on the shop floor, not when the more common economic struggles are in motion. Nonetheless, it is clear that even if the language of games Burawoy employs were to be used, a case could be built for the dangerous instability of rules designed to contain the police officer's understanding of her or his call to the citizen. In fact, in discussing so-called real-life police dramas below, one can see representations of this instability. I have already suggested that brutality can be understood as a reaction to the evident moving on of the game. Rule breaking has no meaning when the game changes.

RELATIONS IN PRODUCTION AND
RELATIONS OF PRODUCTION

But there is a reason beyond this gamesmanship to take account of ideology in the state workplace. Burawoy's advance comes from his application of structural Marxism to the labor process, in part as a corrective to Braverman's classic work.[37] Burawoy makes especially fruitful use of Althusser's conception of interpellation as an institutional address to the subject, constituting that subject as, for instance, "free" or "a citizen." Through that constitution, though, the subject obtains consent to live that freedom or citizenship specifically as it has been interpellated by these ideological state apparatuses. Burawoy shows how this happens in contract negotiations between labor and management within a capitalist institutional framework such that workers come to consent. Yet it is worth recalling Althusser's famous illustration of this interpellation— the police officer who calls out to the citizen. The resulting instatement of that subject as citizen has too often been taken in the direction of surveillance and control, partly under the influence of the earlier writings of Foucault.

In the third chapter, I began the process of understanding this instatement as an enabling one of labor, as the later writings of Foucault explore the enabling "technologies of the self."[38] In the last chapter, I began to blur the place of labor in this interpellation. Now I must admit that my focus is ultimately on the labor of interpellation itself. That police officer is a state worker laboring to interpellate the citizen, who in turn is addressed ultimately as a coworker in an announced enlargement of the state-capital arrangements needed to secure private accumulation on an ever greater scale. From this contention, it should be noted that workers in general are not only arguably produced by this interaction with ideology "outside" the workplace but they also produce it. And state workers in particular not only are made by but make ideology. If the claim is to be taken seriously that the subjectivity of the worker for capital-logic theorists is produced through work, as it is in fact for Marx, it must be concluded that state workers are intricately constituted by the very cultural and ideological conditions that for both Burawoy and Aronowitz come from outside the workplace. By extension, if that interpellation of the original police officer of Althusser's example is an interpellation as much about the labor process as about "outside" culture, nation, identity, or postcoloniality, then a consideration of the state labor process may require also a reconsideration of the labor process in general and its historical agencies. In other words, what should be made of the labor of a worker who calls out to another worker about work on behalf of the state? Is this not the founding of the labor process in general through labor?

IDEOLOGY RECONSIDERED

As much as this vantage point of the state worker helps to trace the limits of the labor process debate, it is also useful in reconsidering ideology. Theorists like Michele Barrett and Terry Eagleton reject a false consciousness model of ideology in favor of a broadly defined notion of mystification in the case of the former and a struggle for imaginary unity amid material disunity for the latter. But despite Barrett's use of Foucault and Eagleton's recourse to discourse, both end up posing "the people" somehow in successful or unsuccessful opposition to ideology. It is interesting to see instead how considering state work leads to Michael E. Brown's discussion of how people's "obligation to dissemble" under capitalist relations might be evident in the "infraprocess" of state labor.[39] The police officer, caseworker, environmental protection investigator, prison guard, and civil rights lawyer—to live they must ideologize. Their labor is both the imperative to dissemble and impossibility of labor ever equaling the commodity, ever reaching its universality. Within this labor, the ethical state stands against the worker like Marx's famed commodity, and as mentioned earlier, policy may then be thought of as its money form. The obligation to dissemble returns as policy. To think of policy this way is to dispense once and for all with policy science as the occupation of measurement and adjustment. It is also to move past the dominant ideology debate of the 1980s in which a hegemony was said to be necessary or unnecessary to the workings of capitalism. No certain subject position can obtain in the worker who works by producing subject positions and equivalencies.[40]

CONSENT

In turn, it may be necessary to rethink the notion of consent itself, so much at the implicit heart of managerialist and human relations literature as well as the explicit heart of the labor process advance. In both literatures, the meaning of consent is taken for granted, and only its construction and stability are in question. Yet this may now seem odd if, in fact, state labor is not consent to but consent through ideology. Gramsci explored the new role of consent, of answering the question of why workers should work, with the advent of Americanism and Fordism, an early instance of the nation nestled in the body of the (private) worker among other things. The opportunity for those who sought and constructed this consent was also implied in his early work. Not only were they constructed themselves by their efforts, creatures of the Fordism and nationalism they built; so, too, was there constructed a new level of recognition of the social basis of their private wealth. This consent was a complex construction. It enunciated the advantages of further cooperation among workers in exchange for the renunciation of control over the nature of that cooperation—what was here referred to earlier as the really real meaning of Taylorism.[41] Despite contemporaneous attempts to separate these two elements into scientific management and human relations, and then to make great efforts to reunite them (a move Marx understood well when he studied politics and economics), Gramsci knew they could not be separated. Further cooperation was ensured by a mental revolution in the worker that saw him or her willingly give up one level of autonomy for a greater piece of the greater wealth. From a reverse angle of the same scene, giving up that autonomy willingly, as in human relations, leads inevitably to further cooperation. Public administration, like management sciences generally, has often denied this connection, even by suggesting it needed to be made.

Both labor process and traditional public administrationist literature share in this fallacy. For U.S. labor process literature, this fallacy stemmed from playing a zero-sum game with cooperation and autonomy. Advancing cooperation was seen largely as a negative condition for worker autonomy, causing de-skilling. The question then became, Why do workers work under these advancing negative conditions? They find little politics because they look for that politics in autonomy, in the actions of individual actors, rather than in the potential desire of the cooperative life that may also explain making-out. Thus comes the answer that workers work because they are cheated out of their autonomy on the shop floor through accepting citizenship in an unequal and distorted republic of work. Never can the answer be that workers work because they sense they produced this republic and desire something about what it represents, even as that representation falls consistently short. A rule-bound understanding of the two as separate antagonisms neglects the transformative relation inherent in such consent, one that becomes clearer when the particular republic of work must include the work of the republic—that is, when state work makes explicit the desire.

Public administrationist literature also sees a zero-sum game in cooperation and autonomy. But because it secures the politics of autonomy with the alien ethical state, like the labor process theory—despite their seemingly opposite politics—it worries about the lack of autonomy. For them, however, this is a worry because they see in autonomy the ideologies of ethics, accountability, nationalism, and professionalism necessary to ask for more cooperation. Hence, one of the major criticisms leveled against public management has been the erosion that its new forms of cooperation have caused in the state worker tradition of ethics, professionalism, and selflessness. This has been particularly pronounced in England. Further cooperation is held to risk exposing to a de-skilling and de-trusting market exactly those so-called de-commodified socialities that from another political view Offe wanted to locate in the state.[42] Yet neither public administrationists nor labor process theorists could explain the growth of de-commodified space using a model of consent in which more cooperation always entailed less autonomy. Indeed, Offe himself might have difficulty accounting for the history and growth of his phenomenon of de-commodification to the extent that he characterizes it as an autonomy from the market rather than a new principle of cooperation born of the market.

This notion of consent not as the opposite of coercion but as a complex construction of cooperation and autonomy, which can be differently configured in different prepolitical moments, helps recast public administration's official history and perhaps even the history of the labor process. It might be said that in these politics, a certain ethics of practice is worked out in the labor process. This ethics of practice can be generalized precisely because it exists not only as capitalist constraint, not only as a capital logic or mode of production, but as the production of that logic where the underlife of revolution sees something in social relations and tries to capture it in an ethics of practice. Thus, Alan McKinlay and Ken Starkey in the final chapter of their collection *Foucault, Management, and Organizational Theory,* grasp half of this dynamic when they call for a reapplication of Foucault in management and organizational studies. They maintain that the focus on managerial panopticons has degraded attention to "technologies of the self, forms of self-discipline that are willingly embraced." This new research agenda would "examine both the limits of organization but also organization's potentially liberating qualities." This is so because "organizations bring individual selves into contact with others and allow, if we are willing, new definitions of the self and, therefore, of organization itself."[43]

McKinlay and Starkey labor under the sign of organizational theory in which form always presents itself first. This should be reversed, however. What organizations are able to become has strictly to do with what is already in motion and what captures a form that can then be presented as an organization.[44] The state worker captures a form that becomes the state labor process, but because of the agencies of capital with which the form is invested, that labor process develops a general character. To rephrase it, the state labor process might be understood as the place where the underlife of revolution chooses a form of self-discipline to express itself as a relation, an organization.[45] But if the form of organization is to hold, and is to contain this underlife even temporarily, it must generalize itself. It must produce the homogeneity of form that capitalism requires. This remains so difficult because the genesis of that form is not in the process of planning but the restlessness of labor to find itself. This means that public administration cannot plan or conceive of this form, it can only try to convince labor to rest—the one thing it cannot do under capitalism.

GOOD FORM

Thus there is what Toby Miller calls a kind of technology of self-improvement, where self-improvement is here interpreted as the exhortation to hold a form.[46] The fact that capitalism undermines stable subjectivity and relies on textual presentations to reconstitute it through, among other things, state cultural policy is for Miller a political opening born of textual analysis and its indeterminacy. Good form, as both C. L. R. James and Miller would attest, is a term that cannot be known only by those who know cricket. Bad form is a problem for both the creeds of individualism and constitutionalism—that is, for the representations of organization in capitalism. It signals a new ethics of practice with more representational power. It threatens to become good form. Public administrationists seek stable form in worker as well as organizational subjectivity. Even the network is that. But the state worker seeks the form of her or his labor, and that cannot rest so long as it is agitated by the underlife of revolution that cannot find itself in exchange and equivalency.

VON STEIN AND WILSON

The technology of self-improvement is thus at work in the public administrationist, too. The state labor process, then, can be understood historically as the attempt to hold steady in subjectivity the worker in general, in the first instance through the state worker. Reading public administration, from Woodrow Wilson to Dwight Waldo to Gary Walmsley, the texts appear one minute to address everyone as members of a nation-state, another minute to address a class of managers in the state, another minute other public administrationists, and yet another minute all workers in the state. Public administrationists produce evidence of their humanizing project, of their search for a steady worker subjectivity, as they try to constitute this state object. But their labor is always fractured by another labor—one they attempt to contain in their discourse but cannot. And if public administrationists are the ultimate example of instated labor as both academic laborers and laborers on the state process, they are also part of what Foucault dubbed one of those "less consolidated disciplines whose constitution was relatively more recent, and in a certain sense closer to their origins and their immediate urgency."[47] The urgency of forming the state object and the immediacy of the effort problem are never far away.

Mark Rutgers, for instance, argues that to start the study of public administration with Woodrow Wilson is misleading, not because Wilson's famous article was only later recognized as originary but because

Wilson himself acknowledged forerunners in German cameralism and polity science. Rutgers's argument is that this history helps in reconsidering the obsession in the public administrationist discourse with establishing itself and developing overarching paradigms for public administration. In other words, he is seeking a disciplinary explanation for something I am trying to explain here by going beyond the discipline to labor process theory. He notes that Ludwig Von Stein in his 1887 *Handbook of Public Administration and the System of Political State Science* had already "stated that there is hardly a science that must consider so many preliminary theoretical and philosophical ideas before its object of study appears."[48] It is for this same reason that public administration has been called the ultimate modernist discipline.[49] Rutgers concludes that multiple discursive strategies make sense in the face of this project. He traces the discourse through its search for its object of study back to the seventeenth century. Yet even in this prehistory can be seen the erasure of state work in the search for the state object. Coming out of the literature of "advice to the prince," cameralism in Germany and polity science in France grapple with an administrative science from the seventeenth to the nineteenth century before losing out to the study of administrative law promoted by both liberal ideas suspicious of the state and capitalism's expanding market domain and legal frameworks. When U.S. public administration begins at the turn of the twentieth century, not much is left of this European discourse on administrative science. Rutgers considers this history only to trace the rise and fall of ideas in the discourse, and to suggest that the fractiousness of the discourse makes sense in such a modernist project as public administration. Left out of this account is the rise of colonial administration, or rather the movement of European discourse on administrative science into an imperial form. Nor does he make use of Foucault's work on the transition from cameralism to a liberal polity—the foundational work on governmentality. The notion of the hollow liberal state requiring only administrative law becomes evidently a false one based on a European state object that did not exist in this period, and on expunging the state worker by not accounting for his or her continuing labor in the state, colonies, and labor process in general through governmentality.

Yet Rutgers's attempt does lead to speculation about the historical relation between a state labor process and the labor process in general. One can point to an archaeology around the labor process. The rise of cameralism and polity science represent the rationalization of state work in the seventeenth and eighteenth centuries in the first phase of capitalism. The absent colonial administration and governmentality in Rutgers's analysis is the extension of that rationalization to colonized nations. U.S. public administration subsequently stands for a new rationalization based on an industrial capitalism, and hence the solidification of both colonial administration and governmentality. All these phases of state labor rationalization are accompanied by a new public address. That is, publics are constituted discursively as they are constituted administratively. But this public address is not for the public alone—much attention has been based on this focus. It is also for the state worker and, anachronistically, public administrationist—as the writer might have once addressed the prince. And yet there is a difference. The writer spoke directly to the prince and later the prince's administrators as extensions of the prince's sovereignty and located subjectivity in this relationship. In these phases of rationalization, the writer speaks to the nation, the constituted publics, the emerging sovereigns, and through them addresses the state worker. The state no longer belongs to that worker as prince or princely representative, and the new worker in the state now works not for him or herself but for someone else.

The effort problem as a problem of subjectivity emerges in these rationalizations, and with it the multiple interpellations of manager, worker, and citizen that represent the attempt to constitute the nation in and conversely through the body of the state worker. The further from managerial control, the more the effort bargain looked perilous, the more the public was imagined as labor, spoken about as work, as the state worker's burden, one that nonetheless had the rewards of nation, of greater glory, behind that work. As such, controlling colonial state workers required extreme appeals to nation, race, and gender, just as the attempt to control the labor of development administrators today requires the extreme appeal of a human rights discourse. Ultimately, however, the aim of the state project is not to have the nation nestle only in the state worker but rather to have it germinate there first, until like some alien creature it is popping out of every worker.

TAYLOR AND THE MENTAL REVOLUTION

Public administration can be read as a way to work out in and through the state the never-ending problems of how to get workers to work by trying to solve this problem of subjectivity—a problem that has attracted notice at certain conjunctures during the past century and can therefore be emplotted. By reversing the order, seeing the state not as the committee constituted by the bourgeoisie first and foremost when crises surface, sense can be returned to Marx and Engels's original phrase. In this logic, the key word in that phrase becomes manage. Any good manager will tell you that you have to anticipate crises. Public administration, of course, does not understand crises as persistent and inevitable, any more than the good manager does, but it does understand the working out of the labor process as its job. One can see the state's, and thus the state worker's, more intimate relation to capital. The state does not in this logic constitute programs to address crises. It constitutes a new state labor process as a model for a new labor process in general to try to overcome the danger in an unstable regime of accumulation. That is, it works out the new way to get workers to work.

The Taylorization that occurs in industrial capital at the turn of the twentieth century is unstable and disruptive at its inception. Taylor himself is called before the Congress to explain his methods because the nation is so concerned about the transformation. The mental revolution he advocates asks workers to give up another level of autonomy for the material gains that further cooperation promises. In the last decades of the nineteenth century, amid stellar corruption of the federal government and the growth of anarcho-syndicalism, public administrationists are proposing a similar separation of control and execution. They are doing it to fight corruption. This underlies both Woodrow Wilson's and Frank Goodnow's work. But another way of saying they are trying to combat corruption and retain faith in the U.S. government, at all levels, is to say they are trying to control state workers and convince them to work hard. What they invent will save Taylorism and secure a new regime of accumulation. It will form a subjectivity of citizenship and worker, textual although relatively stable for a period.

With attention to the effort problem, but also awareness of the various ways to address, the public administration discourse of the time can be looked at as a kind of vanguardism of scientific management in the state. Goodnow as much as announces the production of this new worker as the "authorities which are attending to the scientific, technical, and so to speak, commercial activities of the government."[50] The separation of conception from execution, legislation from administration, is enunciated here three years before Taylor publishes his first work. Goodnow anticipates the separation, but does not understand the effect of workers. His administrative authorities would have to be differentiated within the task of execution, and both manager and worker would have to be Taylorized, brought into the system of production in ways that increased their collective labor power.

The Progressive era in government might be said to produce a working subject for the subsequent regime of Fordism. New Deal state workers anticipate the subjectivity of the postwar bargain. New Society state workers anticipate quality circles, teams, and flexi-time. The subjectivities traced here do not appear as labor subjectivities in the state but only take on this quality when they are generalized in the labor process subsequently. In fact, they might be seen first as publics that need to be administered into work. This happens through a state process, through the labor on ideology that constituting publics as labor requires. In this process, a labor process, new subjectivities become new labor subjectivities. Through the state labor process, forms of subjectivity that labor to produce value for others—in their identities, products, and services—become available as steady forms. That people accept these forms as personal and collective organization has again to do with their sense of the approximation and usefulness of these forms to the association they perceive in their social relations. Understood by public administrationists as graspable, a steady form, a steady state object, this underlying state labor process in fact derives from the instability of what capital relations produce, and what must be transformed into publics and eventually laboring publics.

Progressivism, then, can be read not as a new administration of things but of people, as a new labor process as a model for the future. By 1918, William Willoughby has introduced budgetary reform as a way to ostensibly improve democracy and accountability, but with the effect of introducing a new way to form publics as budget categories, and differentiate and control those concurrently differentiated state workers. By the time Leonard White sits down to write the first textbook on public administration in 1926, he can admit that "public administration is the management of men and materials in the accomplishment of the purposes of the state."[51] The New Deal state worker who emerges as "Bill Bureaucrat," a national hero first to some during the 1930s and then to all during the Second World War, nationalizes worker subjectivity around the grand bargain. The Great Society state worker could be said similarly to reintroduce difference into worker subjectivity—one that capital uses to push forward acknowledgments of class, gender, and sometimes race, in quality circles, teams, flexible time, and the rhetoric of globalized scarcity. But is there not still something taking the state effect for the state in this account I have developed using a critique of the labor process?

THE END OF LABOR PROCESS

Networks are the buzz of public management at the start of the twenty-first century. At their most prophetic, network analysts in the policy sciences speak of a new kind of governance without government, with networks of policymaking, decision making, and implementation that are "a challenge to governability because they become autonomous and resist central guidance."[52] This prophesy has both leftist and rightist appeal. On the Right, it is bound up with capital flows, with the deinstitutionalization of the welfare state, even with memories of an older class privilege.[53] On the Left, it rings true for radical democrats who see it as the antidote to hierarchy and complex organizations.[54] Both positions claim to be making their predictions and taking their advantage from observable changes toward the network form in social relations. Public management has been most enthusiastic about what it regards as these evident social circumstances.[55]

Samuel R. Delany has a different view of networks.[56] He sees them as intraclass and instrumental in an extremely straightforward way, and believes that interclass and less competitive forms of interaction, what he describes as contact, have suffered with their growth, and so has city life. He calls attention to a couple of qualities in networks without demonizing them or romanticizing contact. First, he insists both kinds of interaction occur against a backdrop of class struggle. Networks, then, might be said to encourage the ideology of mobility, and contact an ideology of class consciousness. One networks for success, but hangs out for reasons often at odds with such self-disciplined productivity. This is reminiscent of the question of labor for a state said to be becoming a network. A network society is one that, on the one hand, knows no boundary between work and nonwork time, yet on the other hand, knows more severely, as Manuel Castells has pointed out, about class boundaries and other sharp social differentiation that if put in network contact, threaten the productivity of the network. But all of this begins to unravel the very idea of a labor process, not to mention a state labor process. Consent and cooperation must surely have preceded a form of organization labeled here the network. Technique must certainly have had to draw from this cooperation. Thus labor process cannot contain labor. It can only serve to naturalize an organizational form derived of practices that themselves had first to be invented among the society of producers.

NETWORKS AS ONLY LABOR PROCESS THEORY

Yet it is wrong to give so much to public administration. Its techniques are not the future but the past. Labor process theory is deceptive in this way. It continues to come after the fact, of organization, ideology, sociality, and wealth making. Networks and webs are not a more elaborate way to explain the contemporary world but a more parsimonious one. This parsimony is generated in the name of a new appropriation that must nonetheless operate on the old principle of the price-making market and commodity. But this parsimony is also generated to resist a richness of subjectivities that cooperate in producing identities and hence social wealth as plentiful as difference itself. By contrast, network theory can only hope to use its lines to destroy difference while at the same time reaping its benefits and leaving it to generate again. Or as Maurizio Lazzarato puts it, "For economics there remains only the possibility of managing and regulating the activity of immaterial labor and creating some devices for the control of communication and information technologies and their organizational processes."[57] As a labor process, this is after the fact of the social, not what determines it. Donna Haraway and C. L. R. James, though, can break out of this trap.

THE COMMUNISM EFFECT

When James spoke of good form in cricket or Haraway of the pleasure of being a machine, the consent that West Indian cricketers or cyborgs accept is not in exchange for the chance to cooperate as labor process theory (and public administration) has led one to believe. Instead, consent can be historicized as the last technique embodied in cricketers or cyborgs. But the body as the site of modern subjectivity is a factory of difference, and the social cooperation that produces the West Indian cricketer or cyborg is the transformation of that embodied technique into higher forms of cooperation based on the creativity that only abstractions premised on difference not exchangeability can provide. Public administration, like all techniques of organization ultimately in the service of capital, thus only motivates with its death, just as cricket form or cyborg pleasure motivates people with new forms of social life. I sensed, yet could not realize such forms in my government work. But what of the future in the present, as James would say?

SOCIAL MOVEMENT, CIVIL SOCIETY, STATE WORK

Since the days of the NDP government, the city of Toronto has been largely disenfranchised by gerrymandering conducted unilaterally by the statist, reactionary provincial government that replaced the NDP. The rapaciousness of that new party in power has been checked only by a federalism it has yet to overcome. In New York, the crypto-racist and crypto-fascist tendencies in the Guiliani administration have finally been checked by the mayor's own weaknesses, but not before much loss of life and damage to social capabilities in the city. In Washington, D.C., the specific fate of the NPR hangs in the balance, but one can expect a new mix of post-Fordist state work and anachronistic disciplinary state work aimed with malice at the laboring, prison, and dissenting classes, especially as the country heads into recession. What was the use, then, of this exploration of state work? Is the constituent moment always lost to the constitution of law? Two thousand newly naturalized Haitians organized by their labor union local went to vote in Miami in the 2000 presidential election only to be refused the Creole interpreters who were on hand and turned away en masse based on nefarious technicalities. Neither the corporate press nor Gore or Ralph Nader ever mentioned them. No court will ever hear their case. Instead, a constituted politics babbles away about *the will of the people* in an ersatz public sphere. This *will* becomes the greatest enemy of the multitude. But what can this examination of state work offer them?

Public administration is a primary labor of constitution. At first, it might have seemed an odd focus for communists like me. Moreover, public administration is in many ways stronger than ever. It would hardly seem to hold much hope. The laboring of publics is intensifying in policing and surveillance, laws of credit and debt, enclosure and migration, hyperpatriotic news media and standardized education. It is also deterritorializing, however. This is most apparent in the dominant state effect of the day, globalization. Far from being an effect of the economy, globalization is generated by state work. Finding new ways to exchange, unitize, and compare citizenship and fictitious capital, state work generates globalization. State work was unable to maintain its old comparisons of citizenship and fixed capital because this technique was either refused by workers or co-opted by movements to deepen the technique, and often both. Not without struggle (resistance to free trade) and mistakes (national bailouts), state work took the extraordinary risk of linking citizenship to fictitious capital. Needless to say, this links citizenship to a higher level of capital—a socialized capital. It bases citizenship on precisely that mass intellectuality that supports such capital and on which such capital must always wait. A factory can fail, or it can secure a hierarchy of labor, market, and state arrangements that can reproduce capital. The rights of citizenship could be fought out discretely in this world. But this socialized capital cannot fail, and its network is too vast to be secured except as a general proposition. The rights of citizenship, then, are calculated at the very level of social reproduction as a whole. Public administration had to become the work of comparing, unitizing, and exchanging social reproduction itself. Yet this is impossible, as I have tried to show, even though it leads to many popular biological fantasies. It is perhaps most impossible in the work of those state workers themselves, who generate an increasingly impoverished vision of the world they encounter and know that they must wait on this world to complete even this slight labor. The more they give their consent in this process, the more they see themselves cooperating in outdated forms of discipline or unrealized networks, impoverishing the differences they touch.

Perhaps it is possible to continue state work only at the risk of wanting what it cannot have, revealing what it does not want—a society of labor as the pleasure and fantasy of social reproduction. Public administration can only give over administration to this machine of difference, and that may be finally what I have to offer to two thousand Haitian American trade unionists. I have tried to show that the state as a field of labor would be hard these days to quarantine in favor of generating politics from a new social movement or a nongovernmental organization, and on the other hand, would be hard to smash without damaging ourselves. Poulantzas has perversely gotten his wish. The state is with us, in capitalism or revolution. But perhaps this is not so perverse. Perhaps these popular fantasies, so inarticulate without an analysis of the labor that generates them, are also eloquent about the pleasures at stake. Perhaps in walking away from those polling booths, one is walking away with administration itself, giving one's communist consent.

NOTES

INTRODUCTION

1. That the image is male is most famously analyzed by Catherine McKinnon, *Toward a Feminist Theory of the State* (Cambridge: Harvard University Press, 1991), but in contemporary history, it is also important to note the feminization of much of its labor. See Mimi Abramovitz, *Under Attack, Fighting Back,* 2d ed. (New York: Monthly Review Press, 1999).

2. Toby Miller, *The Avengers* (London: British Film Institute, 1997), 199.

3. Sydney Pollack, *Three Days of the Condor* (Los Angeles, Calif.: Paramount Pictures, 1975).

4. Terry Gilliam, *Brazil* (Los Angeles, Calif.: MCA, 1985).

5. Jean-François Lyotard, *The Postmodern Condition: A Report on Knowledge* (Minneapolis: University of Minnesota Press, 1984); and James C. Scott, *Seeing like a State: How Certain Schemes to Improve the Human Condition Have Failed* (New Haven, Conn.: Yale University Press, 1998).

6. Fredric Jameson, *The Geopolitical Aesthetic: Cinema and Space in the World System* (Bloomington: University of Indiana Press, 1992).

7. Michael E. Brown, *The Production of Society: A Marxian Foundation for Social Theory* (Totowa, N.J.: Rowman and Littlefield, 1986); and Randy Martin, "Fragmentation and Fetishism: The Postmodern in Marx," *Critical Perspectives on Accounting* 9 (1998): 77–93.

8. Other approaches to the everyday, such as anthropology, ethnomethodology, and symbolic interactionism, although less prominent, have been less phobic about the state and labor, but more phobic about the political implications of their work, with some exceptions in reflexive ethnography and the sociology of science.

9. See Cary Nelson and Lawrence Grossberg, eds., *Cultural Studies* (New York: Routledge,

1991); and Cary Nelson and Lawrence Grossberg, eds., *Marxism and the Interpretation of Culture* (Urbana: University of Illinois Press, 1988).

10. Cultural studies explains itself best in the face of this politicization of knowledge in Stuart Hall's work. See, for instance, Stuart Hall, "The Problem of Ideology: Marxism without Guarantees," in *Stuart Hall: Critical Dialogues in Cultural Studies*, ed. David Morley and Kuan-Hsing Chen (London: Routledge, 1996), 25–46.

11. The three most influential, and the ones that inform this study, are Nicos Poulantzas, *Political Power and Social Classes* (London: New Left Books, 1973), *State, Power, and Socialism* (London: New Left Books, 1978), and *Classes in Contemporary Capitalism* (London: Verso, 1979).

12. Harry Braverman, *Labor and Monopoly Capital: The Degradation of Work in the Twentieth Century* (New York: Monthly Review Press, 1974). Michael Burawoy's sophisticated critique and extension of Braverman's work was published five years later as *Manufacturing Consent: Changes in the Labor Process under Monopoly Capitalism* (Chicago: University of Chicago Press, 1979).

13. Tony Tinker, "Braverman's Return: A Reexamination of the British Labour Process Critiques" (9 June 2000, paper).

14. Even when "the need to look behind official claims for up-skilling in the quality of work" is acknowledged as "central to Braverman's work" (Tinker, *Braverman's Return*) the state is still taken as an external actor on the workplace and thus the worker, imparting only a national form. See, for instance, Chris Smith and Paul Thompson's otherwise competent review, "Reevaluating the Labor Process Debate," in *Rethinking the Labor Process*, ed. Mark Wardell, Thomas L. Steiger, and Peter Meiksins (Albany: State University of New York Press, 1999), 205–31, esp. 228–29.

15. Timothy Mitchell, "State, Economy, and the State Effect," in *State/Culture: State-Formation after the Cultural Turn*, ed. George Steinmetz (Ithaca, N.Y.: Cornell University Press, 1999), 76–97. See also Mitchell, "The Limits of the State: Beyond Statist Approaches and Their Critics," *American Political Science Review* 85, no. 1 (1991): 77–96.

16. Mitchell, "State Effects," 77.

17. Quoted in Mitchell, "State Effects," 91.

18. Mitchell, "State Effects," 77–78.

19. Here I am indebted to Randy Martin's original reading of Marx's commodity fetish in which he poses the society of producers as the alternative fetish always shimmering below the surface of the commodity. See Martin, "Fragmentation and Fetishism."

20. I will explore later the one area of state work as here understood—modern science—that cultural studies has productively engaged.

21. Michael Hardt, "The Withering of Civil Society," *Social Text* 45, vol. 14, no. 4 (winter 1995): 27–44.

22. Ibid., 41.

23. See Fred Moten, "The League," paper on *Finally Got the News*, a film made by the

League of Revolutionary Black Workers, presented at the Rethinking Marxism conference, Amherst, Mass., December 1997.

24. In the first instance, we can emplot the work of Herb Simon, Charles Lindblom, and James March, and in the second, the constant protestations against private sector management initiatives like Frederick Taylor's *Scientific Management* and Al Gore's *Reinventing Government.*

1. YES, MINISTER: THE RISE AND FALL OF THE ONTARIO ANTIRACISM SECRETARIAT

1. A note on terms: I will generally use the term "state" in the pursuit of what Michael E. Brown calls its relation to the agencies of capital. I will sometimes use "government" to remind the reader of the ordinariness of the techniques that make up the effects of this state. "Work" and "labor" will operate similarly, with labor being that world-making activity that can come to know itself, as Randy Martin puts it, and work indicating its quotidian appearance. The term "state work" will be reserved for the kind of labor that emerges in this investigation. See the introduction for an elaboration of this term state work. See also Michael E. Brown, *The Production of Society: A Marxian Foundation for Social Theory* (Totowa, N.J.: Rowman and Littlefield, 1986), esp. 94–100; and Randy Martin, "Rereading Marx: A Critique of Recent Criticisms," *Science and Society* 62, no. 4 (winter 1998–1999): 513–36.

2. Sometimes this has taken the form historically as a distinction between administration and politics (and hence, a distinction between public administration and political science), and at other times between public and private management (and hence, the distinction between public administration and management and business studies). Although they recur through the discursive history, these distinctions were first articulated by Woodrow Wilson and Frank Goodnow in the case of the former, and Wallace Sayre and Paul Appleby in the case of the latter. See Jay M. Shafritz and Albert C. Hyde, eds., *Classics of Public Administration,* 4th ed. (Fort Worth, Tex.: Harcourt Brace, 1997), where all these thinkers are excerpted and well introduced by the editors.

3. Two collections published in the 1990s by scholars associated with the Public Administration Theory Network epitomize this struggle: Henry D. Kass and Bayard Catron, eds., *Images and Identities in Public Administration* (Newbury Park, Calif.: Sage, 1990); and Jay D. White and Guy B. Adams, *Research in Public Administration: Reflections on Theory and Practice* (Thousand Oaks, Calif.: Sage, 1994). A more recent Lacanian ambition is pursued in O. C. McSwite, *Legitimacy in Public Administration: A Discourse Analysis* (Thousand Oaks, Calif.: Sage, 1997), also arising out of the Theory Network, but oddly silent on the alterity of labor, instead marrying Jacques Lacan to a kind of liberal public sphere multiculturalism.

4. For an account of this demise and the most sophisticated statement of labor process theories recovery of the workplace, see the opening pages of Michael Burawoy, *Manufacturing Consent: Changes in the Labor Process under Monopoly Capitalism* (Chicago:

University of Chicago Press, 1979). In the last chapter, I will try to show how even this statement is deconstructed by public work.

5. In Canada's decentralized federal system, and as a legacy of British colonial policy toward both the French and indigenous peoples, the provinces have been left to attempt to produce with the national government a constitution. Such a constitution was attempted during the New Democratic Party (N D P) government's tenure. Through the specific intervention of the N D P premier, Bob Rae, a Social Charter was for the first time included. This Social Charter, modeled on early version of the European Union Social Charter, introduced social and economic rights into the constitutional debate, and against all predictions, was included in the final constitutional proposals approved by the provinces and national government. The resulting referendum was rejected by the Canadian people, however, who were suspicious of the special rights granted Quebec to protect its majority French-speaking culture. There is no room here to explore other important dimensions of this constitutional episode, such as the party political efforts of the N D P, led by the highly skilled Jeff Rose, deputy minister of intergovernmental affairs, a trade unionist, and a confidant of the premier, to wrest the constitutional initiative successfully away from Prime Minister Brian Mulroney and his Thatcherite Progressive Conservative Party, effectively ending Mulroney's last best chance to be reelected as a champion of Canadian unity. I worked for the policy manager Bill Forward and his senior policy consultant Frank Longo, who developed the idea of the Social Charter for Jeff Rose and Bob Rae (who took the intergovernmental portfolio as his own), but I played no role in this crucial intervention, except as an observer.

6. For an overview of the Whitehall model, see Kevin Theakston, *The Civil Service since 1945* (Oxford: Basil Blackwell, 1995).

7. Michael E. Brown and Randy Martin, "Left Futures," *Socialism and Democracy* 9, no. 1 (spring 1995): 59.

8. An interesting account of labor-management relations in the state is Peter Fairbrother, *Politics and the State as Employer* (London: Mansell, 1994). For the politics of privatization inside the state, see Harvey B. Feigenbaum and Jeffrey R. Henig, *Shrinking the State: The Political Underpinnings of Privatization* (Cambridge: Cambridge University Press, 1998).

9. Martin, "Rereading Marx," 524.

10. The journals I initially sought out were *Public Administration Review, Administration and Society, Administrative Science Quarterly, Canadian Public Administration,* and *Journal of Public Administration and Research.* I then sought out *Dialogue,* published by the Public Administration Theory Network, and several international journals, including *Indian Journal of Public Administration, Public Administration* (Australia), and *Journal of Organizational Behavior* (U.K.), all of which had more theoretical content.

11. Mark H. Moore, *Creating Public Value: Strategic Management in Government* (Cambridge: Harvard University Press, 1997), 20.

12. Ralph P. Hummel, *The Bureaucratic Experience* (New York: St. Martin's, 1987), 269.

13. Michael Barzelay and Babak J. Armajani, *Breaking through Bureaucracy: A New Vision for Managing Government* (Berkeley: University of California Press, 1992), 9.

14. Robin Murray, *Breaking with Bureaucracy: Ownership, Control, and Nationalisation* (Manchester, England: Centre for Local Economic Strategy, 1987). His initial ideas are elaborated in the British context by a number of authors in Roger Burrows and Brian Loader, eds., *Towards a Post-Fordist Welfare State* (London: Routledge, 1994).

15. This is important. Often, citizenship is seen as the best that can be done under conditions of the exploitation through the wage, and thus, workplace democracy is seen as the only path to socialism. Evidence for this supposedly comes from the infection of capitalist terms of thought when wage laborers turn to wider politics, and vice versa, and local conditions must therefore first be liberated. Not solely. Once the state is seen as labor under capitalism, it produces its own dynamic of exploitation and abstraction in the labor of making publics (a labor not bound by the government). In fact, wage laborers are not limited by a false consciousness when approaching questions of government (or else how would Communist parties have developed) but by the actual practices of state work. Hence, not only do government bureaucracies produce their own abstractions through their own labor processes but also, however full and different workers intend to make their understanding of politics, as soon as they give it over to a category of wage labor discipline called government, they are forced to translate it to abstractions produced by that discipline, like public value. The power of these abstractions to translate workers' dreams come precisely from their being produced, not imported as ideology, and thus appearing to be organic to government, as in some readings of Max Weber. Historically, wage laborers have indeed overcome the public-private split to dream about socialism, principally through parties. But they have not overcome the public-private split created in the very labor of government itself, even when reactionary forces did not end the experiment first. Perhaps the cooperation of state workers, brought together in governmentality, can be refashioned to turn state work on itself by revealing it as a labor already hiding the interdependencies of the society of producers.

In fact, the problem of Eurocommunism and even social democracy is this problem. Much can be dreamed under conditions of wage labor when that dreaming is labor protected by a party from a field of wage labor. But once in power, such parties are also inserted into the field of wage labor, both the government as workplace and administration of publics—in short, state work—and their dreams are reduced by the very labor they then use to realize them. This would argue for the importance of parties, but the need for those parties to confront categories like government and people before they are confronted by them utilizing the experience of state workers. By contrast, workplace democracy presumes that this confrontation of dreams with state work yields no sociability worth building. In Communist countries, the jostlings of party and government, read in the United States as power struggles, might more accurately be understood as an effort to protect dreams from exploitative reduction through the return of categories of governmentality.

16. Nicholas Henry, *Public Administration and Public Affairs*, 7th ed. (Upper Saddle River, N.J.: Prentice Hall, 1999), 471–73.

17. Graham T. Allison, "Public and Private Management: Are They Fundamentally Alike in All Unimportant Respects?" in *Classics of Public Administration*, ed. Jay M. Shafritz and Albert C. Hyde, 4th ed. (Fort Worth, Tex.: Harcourt Brace, 1997), 383.

18. Barbara Koremenos and Laurence E. Lynn Jr., "Leadership of a State Agency," in *The State of Public Management*, ed. Donald F. Kettl and H. Brinton Milward (Baltimore, Md.: Johns Hopkins University Press, 1996), 213–40.

19. See Michael E. Brown and Randy Martin's critique of various updates of systems theory in "Socialism in Transition: Documents and Discussion; An Essay on Rethinking the Crisis in Socialism," *Socialism and Democracy* 7, no. 3 (1991): 9–56, esp. 13–14.

20. Michael Hardt, "Empire: Social Struggles and Globalization" (presented at New York University, December 1999). This talk was based on his book with Antonio Negri, *Empire* (Cambridge: Harvard University Press, 2000).

21. Kathi Weeks, *Constituting Feminist Subjects* (Ithaca, N.Y.: Cornell University Press, 1998), 123.

22. Antonio Negri, *Insurgencies: Constituent Power and the Modern State* (Minneapolis: University of Minnesota Press, 1999).

23. Paolo Virno, "Notes on the General Intellect," in *Marxism beyond Marxism*, ed. Saree Makdisi, Cesare Cesarino, and Rebecca E. Karl (New York: Routledge, 1996), 271.

24. This term is associated with Italian marxist theory of the last twenty-five years, and especially with Paolo Virno and Antonio Negri.

25. Karl Marx, *Grundrisse: Introduction to the Critique of Political Economy* (New York: Vintage, 1973), 93.

26. I take "movement organization" from Michael Brown in his reinterpretation of the historiography of the Communist Party in the United States. I will take it up again in chapter 2. See Michael E. Brown, "The History of the History of U.S. Communism," in *New Studies in the Politics and Culture of U.S. Communism*, edited by Michael E. Brown et al. (New York: Monthly Review Press, 1993), 15–44.

27. Bob Rae, "Why I Am a Socialist," *Toronto Star*, 1 October 1990, 25.

28. For a competent and not unsympathetic account of the Conservative government, see John Ibbitson, *Promised Land: Inside the Mike Harris Revolution* (Toronto: Prentice Hall, 1989).

29. *Stephen Lewis Report on Race Relations* (Toronto: Government of Ontario Printing Office, 1992).

30. For the overwhelming West Indian black community, this play did not evoke a cultural memory of Paul Robeson but was encountered directly from the Edna Ferber book (parts of which were distributed at protests) directly as a set of denigrating images (personal correspondence with Martin Kilson).

31. Pierre Elliott Trudeau's speech has been widely interpreted by historians as part of a strategy to contain Quebec's claims to cultural equality in Canada by introducing so many other cultures. But this interpretation has to account for Trudeau's staunch stand on national bilingualism, Quebec's inwardness, and the internal diversity of the province, which has overwhelmed anything other than a linguistic identity.

32. Robert F. Harney, "So Great a Heritage as Ours: Immigration and the Survival of the Canadian Polity" *Daedalus* 117, no. 4: 51–97.

33. In their book *Mapping Multiculturalism* (Minneapolis: University of Minnesota Press, 1996), editors Avery Gordon and Christopher Newfield offer an account of how multiculturalism had its politics deflated or redirected, but the question of what happened to what multiculturalism named remains open.

34. Etienne Balibar, "Is There a Neo-Racism?" in *Race, Class, Nation*, Etienne Balibar and Immanual Wallerstein (London: Verso, 1991), Paul Gilroy, *Small Acts: Thoughts on the Politics of Black Cultures* (London: Serpent's Tail, 1993).

35. Gordon and Newfield, *Mapping Multiculturalism*.

36. Charles G. Haines and Marshall E. Dimock, eds., *Essays on the Law and Practice of Governmental Administration: A Volume in Honor of Frank Johnson Goodnow* (Baltimore, Md.: Johns Hopkins University Press, 1935), xxi.

37. Matthew Holden, *Continuity and Disruption: Essays in Public Administration* (Pittsburgh, Pa.: University of Pittsburgh Press, 1996), 44–45. The book was the winner of the National Conference of Black Political Scientists Outstanding Book Award. Holden teaches in the Woodrow Wilson Department of Government and Foreign Affairs at the University of Virginia.

38. See Shafritz and Hyde, *Classics of Public Administration*, 8–13.

39. Leonard D. White, "The Meaning of Principles in Public Administration," in *The Frontiers of Public Administration*, ed. John M. Gaus, Leonard D. White, and Marshall E. Dimock (New York: Russell and Russell, 1936), 21.

40. Ibid., 25.

41. Max Horkheimer, "On the Problem of Truth," in *The Essential Frankfurt School Reader*, ed. Andrew Arato and Eike Gebhardt (New York: Continuum, 1994), 426.

42. Ibid., 438.

43. Rosabeth Kanter, "Women and Power in Organizations," excerpted in ed. Frank Fischer and Carmen Sirianni *Critical Studies in Organization and Bureaucracy* (Philadelphia, Pa.: Temple University Press, 1994), 335.

44. See Frank E. Marini, ed., *Toward a New Public Administration: The Minnowbrook Experience* (New York: HarperCollins, 1971).

45. James Q. Wilson, *Bureaucracy: What Government Agencies Do and Why They Do It* (New York: Basic Books, 1989), xii; and Marc Holzer and Kathe Callahan, *Government at Work: Best Practices and Model Programs* (Thousand Oaks, Calif.: Sage, 1998).

46. Martin Albrow, "The Dialectic of Science and Values in the Study of Organizations," in *Control and Ideology in Organizations*, ed. Graeme Salaman and Kenneth Thompson (Cambridge: MIT Press, 1980), 295.

47. Frank Fischer, "Organizational Expertise and Bureaucratic Control: Behavioral Science as Managerial Ideology," in *Critical Studies in Organization and Bureaucracy*, ed. Frank Fischer and Carmen Sirianni (Philadelphia, Pa.: Temple University Press, 1994), 175.

48. Andrew Ross, "Cultural Studies and the Challenge of Science," in *Disciplinarity and Dissent in Cultural Studies*, ed. Cary Nelson and Dilip Parameshwar Gaonkar (New York: Routledge, 1996), 183. Sociology of scientific knowledge scholar Steve Woolgar appears to recognize the problem of the reconstituted object in his retrospective, *Science: The Very Idea* (New York: Routledge, 1993).

49. For a clear summary of organizational sociology's debt to both structural functionalism and systems theory, see John Hassard, *Sociology and Organization Theory: Positivism, Paradigms, and Postmodernity* (Cambridge: Cambridge University Press, 1995), esp. chap. 2.

50. See Alan McKinlay and Ken Starkey, "Afterword: Deconstructing Organization: Discipline and Desire," in *Foucault, Management, and Organization Theory: From Panopticon to Technologies of Self*, ed. Alan McKinlay and Ken Starkey (Thousand Oaks, Calif.: Sage, 1998), 230–41. The struggle over what to make of discipline and desire in Foucault is illustrated by the fact that the editors stand alone in their use of his interest in the possibilities in the subjectification process in organizational theory in this way—the other contributors preferring to concentrate on a negative disciplinarity.

51. Instead, a series of tentative explorations in a special issue of *American Behavioral Scientist* devoted to "Public Administration and Postmodernism" includes an article by R. McGregor Cawley and William Chaloupka titled "American Governmentality: Michel Foucault and Public Administration" (vol. 41, no. 1 [September 1997]: 28–42) in which Foucault is portrayed as providing an antihumanism, read as cautionary and skeptical, antidote to public administration's quest for an objective social science and a functional state object.

52. Although my study takes as its object the ontology of labor and not the epistemology of the state, for a sophisticated discussion of "the state effect," see Timothy Mitchell, "Society, Economy, and State Effect," in *State/Culture: State-Formation after the Cultural Turn*, ed. George Steinmetz (Ithaca, N.Y.: Cornell University Press, 1999), 76–97. Mitchell's central point is that "it is not sufficient simply to criticize the abstract idealist appearance the state assumes in the state-centered literature. . . . The task of a critique of the state is not just to reject metaphysics, but to explain how it has been possible to produce this practical effect . . . the apparent autonomy of the state as a freestanding entity" (84–85). His answer is to consider the abstraction process characteristic of modernity as the source of this effect. Since the focus here is on labor, it is the appropriate quality behind the abstraction process that will be foregrounded.

53. Pierre Bourdieu, *The State Nobility: Elite Schools in the Field of Power* (Oxford: Polity Press, 1998).

54. For a comprehensive review of Canadian policy studies, which subsumes public

administration under its rubric, see Laurent Dobuzinskis, Michael Howlett, and David Laycock, eds., *Policy Studies in Canada: The State of the Art* (Toronto: University of Toronto Press, 1996). As in its U.S. counterpart, a recognition of policy as justification and speech act develops by the 1980s, undermining policy's claim to organize public administration. See, for instance, M. E. Hawkesworth, *Theoretical Issues in Policy Analysis* (Albany: State University of New York Press, 1988).

55. See Marini, *Toward a New Public Administration*.

56. In his memoirs, *From Protest to Power* (Toronto: Viking, 1996), Bob Rae is candid about the problem of the "permanent government" he believed his party faced in the senior civil service and the need to centralize power because of this hostility. See the chapter titled "Hard Choices."

57. *A Guide to Key Anti-Racism Terms and Concepts* and *On Anti-Racism and the Ontario Antiracism Secretariat* are both published by the Ontario Antiracism Secretariat (Toronto: Government of Ontario, 1993), 24 pp.

58. John M. Cammett, *Antonio Gramsci and the Origins of Italian Communism* (Stanford, Calif.: Stanford University Press, 1967).

59. This management group included all those workers outside the bargaining unit of the secretariat. People self-identified in the following ways: three as white, four black, one Chinese, and one Sikh. The dialogues rarely led to a single view, and I am reporting what I took away as the thrust of the arguments, not formal minute decisions.

60. This is the faulty reasoning in Noel Ignatieff, ed., *Race Traitor* (New York: Routledge, 1998), where the opposite of white privilege gets understood as equality, a social conception that only has meaning in a capitalist world of equivalency abstractions that are themselves fundamentally depleted.

61. Holden, *Continuity and Disruption*, 246, 209.

62. Camilla Stivers, "Toward a Feminist Perspective in Public Administration Theory," *Women and Politics* 10, 4 (1991): 120.

63. Dwight Waldo, *The Administrative State: A Study of the Political Theory of American Public Administration*, 2d ed. (New York: Holmes and Meier, 1984). This "system-steering" perspective on the legitimate governing role of the bureaucracy reemerges, after the challenges of democratization and difference in the late 1960s and early 1970s implicit in the Winnowbrook conference, in the "Blacksburg Manifesto." See Gary Walmsley et al., "Public Administration and the Governance Process: Refocusing the Dialogue," in *A Centennial History of the American Administrative State*, ed. Ralph Clark Chandler (New York: Free Press, 1987).

64. Nancy Fraser, "Rethinking the Public Sphere: A Contribution to the Critique of Actually Existing Democracy," in *The Phantom Public Sphere*, ed. Bruce Robbins (Minneapolis: University of Minnesota Press, 1993).

65. See Martin, "Rereading Marx," esp. the concluding passage on 534, which "presents an implicit socialism the specter of which extends far beyond any given historical or organizational manifestation."

66. Bruce Robbins, Introduction to *The Phantom Public Sphere*, ed. Bruce Robbins (Minneapolis: University of Minnesota Press, 1993), xxiv.

67. Another way of saying this while retaining the public sphere is to claim, as Oskar Negt and Alexander Kluge do, that a proletarian public sphere would include the totality of workers' experience and therefore the struggles that failed to produce more than such a sphere—a historical memory that could become a spur to going beyond publicity. See Oskar Negt and Alexander Kluge, *The Public Sphere and Experience: Toward an Analysis of the Bourgeois and Proletarian Public Sphere* (Minneapolis: University of Minnesota Press, 1993).

68. Mitchell, "Society, Economy, and State Effect."

69. C. L. R. James, *Every Cook Can Govern: A Study of Democracy in Ancient Greece* (Detroit, Mich.: Bewick, 1992).

2. REENGINEERING IMMATERIAL G-MEN

1. Michael E. Brown, *The Production of Society: A Marxian Foundation for Social Theory* (Totowa, N.J.: Rowman and Littlefield, 1986), 76.

2. Sheila Slaughter and Larry L. Leslie, *Academic Capitalism: Politics, Policies, and the Entrepreneurial University* (Baltimore, Md.: Johns Hopkins University Press, 1997).

3. Pierre Bourdieu, "Rethinking the State: Genesis and Structure of the Bureaucratic Field," in *State/Culture: State-Formation after the Cultural Turn*, ed. George Steinmetz (Ithaca, N.Y.: Cornell University Press, 1999), 55.

4. A lot of good work has been done in England on labor subjectivity, especially on the creation of the masculine and feminine through labor. The collection, edited by John M. Jermier, David Knights, and Walter R. Nord, *Resistance and Power in Organizations* (London: Routledge, 1994), is exemplary. On gendered subjectivity specifically, see Sheila Walby, *Patriarchy at Work* (Cambridge, England: Polity Press, 1986): and the essays in David Knights and Hugh Willmott, eds., *Gender and the Labour Process* (Aldershot, England: Gower, 1986). But perhaps there is room to expand the gendered labor process to the labor of gender itself, or so this chapter will argue.

5. Thus, George Yudice is forced to guard against this humanist tendency from the Left at the same time that George Soros pushes it as a view of human nature from the Right.

6. Michael Hardt, "The Withering of Civil Society," *Social Text* 45, vol. 14, no. 4 (winter 1995): 27–44. Hardt also makes the point that even if the conditions for civil society were historically present today, such a term underplays the discipline and exploitation that civil society institutions produce.

7. Michael E. Brown, "The History of the History of U.S. Communism," in *New Studies in the Politics and Culture of U.S. Communism*, ed. Michael E. Brown et al. (New York: Monthly Review Press, 1993), 31.

8. See the interesting discussion of the relevant passage in Marx in Peter Hitchcock, "The Value Of," in *Class Issues: Pedagogy, Cultural Studies, and the Public Sphere*, ed. Amitava Kumar (New York: New York University Press, 1997), 117–24.

9. This is precisely how the N D P government was understood even by its leftist critics, most prominently *Toronto Star* journalist Thomas Walkom and York University political scientist Leo Panitch.

10. Jose Esteban Munoz, *Disidentifications* (Minneapolis: University of Minnesota Press, 1999). Munoz's work suggests a way to address the challenge that Jacques Derrida poses anew to the social science conception of agency as always past (and passed on to new operations of difference) at the moment of its recognition.

11. This look will partly be informed by notebooks I kept from 1993 to 1995 summarizing the training sessions and discussions that became a frequent part of our work lives as the Ontario Antiracism Secretariat expanded in those years.

12. Michael Hardt and Antonio Negri, *Labor of Dionysus: A Critique of the State-Form* (Minnesota: University of Minnesota Press, 1994).

13. Brown, "The History of the History of U.S. Communism," 41 n. 16.

14. Deborah Brandt, *Naming the Moment: Political Analysis for Action* (Toronto: Jesuit Centre for Social Faith and Justice, 1989).

15. Antonio Negri, "Constituent Republic," *Radical Thought in Italy: A Potential Politics*, ed. Paolo Virno and Michael Hardt (Minneapolis: University of Minnesota Press, 1996), 213–21.

16. Randy Martin extends George Bataille's use of the social surplus to the performativity of everyday life in his *Critical Moves: Dance Studies in Theory and Politics* (Durham, N.C.: Duke University Press, 1999).

17. This could not in fact be said of capitalist interests where construction firms want more housing or department stores more credit in that these are displacements of scarcity.

18. The body as mere machine rather than machine in the body is reconstructed by Bernard Doray, *From Taylorism to Fordism: A Rational Madness* (London: Free Association Books, 1988).

19. Body and machine in contemporary theory are more often portrayed as vying for attention, or working out a more intricate division of labor, than cohabitating in subjectivity. See, for instance, Donald M. Low, *The Body in Late-Capitalist USA* (Durham, N.C.: Duke University Press, 1995); or for a marxist discussion, Jim Davis et al., eds., *Cutting Edge: Technology, Information, Capitalism, and Social Revolution* (London: Verso, 1997). Of course, the major exception to this is Donna Haraway's work, *Simians, Cyborgs, and Women: The Reinvention of Nature* (New York: Routledge, 1991).

20. Michael Hammer and James Champy, *Reengineering the Corporation: A Manifesto for Business Revolution* (New York: Harper Business, 1993). For a summary, see Michael Hammer, "Reengineering Work: Don't Automate, Obliterate," *Harvard Business Review* (July–August 1990): 104–12.

21. Jon R. Katzenbach and Douglas K. Smith, "The Discipline of Teams," *Harvard Business Review* (March–April 1993): 111–20; and Rosabeth Kantner, "The New Managerial Work," *Harvard Business Review* (November–December 1989): 86–92. Also distributed was Steven Stanton, Michael Hammer, and Bradford Power, "From Re-

sistance to Results: Mastering the Organizational Issues of Reengineering," *Insights Quarterly* (fall 1992): 7–15.

22. These Drucker quotes were pulled without reference, but are restated and summarized in Peter Drucker, "Really Reinventing Government," *Atlantic Monthly* (February 1995): 49–61.

23. James Champy and Donald Arnoudse, "The Leadership Challenge of Reengineering," *Insights Quarterly* (fall 1992): 17.

24. This quotation is from a useful introduction to Negri's thinking in an interview translated by Michael Hardt and posted on a Web site called Amnesty for Toni Negri. The interview, titled "Back to the Future," is a transcription of a videotaped interview with Negri in France shortly before he returned to Italy to begin serving his still-scandalous sentence in Rebibia Prison in Rome. An extended version of the interview has been published as *Exil* (Paris: Editions Mille et Un Nuits, 1998). The Web site address is http://lists.village.virginia.edu/~forks/exile.htm.

25. Robin Murray, "Life After Henry," *Marxism Today* (October 1988): 24–29.

26. See Robert Boyer, "The Eighties: Search for Alternatives to Fordism," in *The Politics of Flexibility*, ed. Bob Jessop et al. (Aldershot, England: Edward Elgar, 1991); Werner Bonefeld and John Holloway, eds., *Post-Fordism and Social Form: A Marxist Debate on the Post-Fordist State* (London: Macmillan, 1991); and Anna Pollert, "The Orthodoxy of Flexibility," in *Farewell to Flexibility?* ed. Anna Pollert (Oxford: Blackwell, 1991).

27. Michel Aglietta, *A Theory of Capitalist Regulation* (London: Verso, 1979). Aglietta has some interesting things to say about the state as a process of the institutionalization of the wage relation under conditions of class struggle, which is his way of trying to prevent the state from appearing as a reflection of this struggle.

28. Pierre Bourdieu, "The Left Hand and the Right Hand of the State," in *Acts of Resistance: Against the Tyrannies of the Market* (New York: New Press, 1998), 1–11.

29. Bob Jessop, "Regulation Theories in Retrospect and Prospect," *Economy and Society* 19, no. 2 (1990): 153–216.

30. See Michael J. Piore and Charles F. Sabel, *The Second Industrial Divide: Possibilities for Prosperity* (New York: Basic Books, 1984); and Helmut Kern and Michael Shumman, "New Concepts of Production in German Plants," in *Industry and Politics in West Germany: Toward the Third Republic,* ed. Peter J. Katzenstein (Ithaca, N.Y.: Cornell University Press, 1989).

31. See Stuart Hall and Martin Jacques, eds., *New Times* (London: Lawrence and Wishart, 1989).

32. A record of these projects is preserved in a publication produced by the unit as it became aware of the impending N D P election loss and guessed correctly that it would be shut down by a new government. Titled "C E D at Work in Metro Toronto: A Report Prepared by the Community Economic Development Secretariat in Partnership with the Social Investment Organization 1995," it is currently available only in the Legislative Library of the Government of Ontario.

33. Matthew Holden, the president of the American Political Science Association and author of the prizewinning book *Continuity and Disruption: Essays in Public Administration* (Pittsburgh, Pa.: University of Pittsburgh, 1996), exemplifies this approach. See especially his tributes to public administration forefathers Leonard D. White and John Merriman Gaus.

34. Michael Hardt and Antonio Negri, *Empire* (Cambridge: Harvard University Press, 2000), 273–274. Near this passage, they cite Stanley Aronowitz on U.S. social movements in the 1960s, in his *The Death and Rebirth of American Radicalism* (London: Routledge, 1996), 57–90.

35. Lawrence Grossberg, "Toward a Genealogy of the State of Cultural Studies: The Discipline of Communication and the Reception of Cultural Studies in the United States" (131–48) and Bruce Robbins, "Double Time: Durkheim, Disciplines, and Progress" (185–200), both in *Disciplinarity and Dissent in Cultural Studies*, ed. Cary Nelson and Dilip Parameshwar Gaonkar (New York: Routledge, 1996).

36. See Tony Bennett, "Useful Culture," in *Relocating Cultural Studies: Developments in Theory and Research*, ed. Valda Blundell et al. (London: Routledge, 1993), 67–85.

37. These observations of our work with the CED program should not be taken for a general law of development, as globalization sees at work everything from this altering real subsumption, to formal subsumption, to primitive accumulation.

38. Louis Althusser and Etienne Balibar, *Reading Capital* (London: Verso, 1986), esp. pages 159–64.

39. Timothy Mitchell, "Society, Economy, and the State Effect," in *State/Culture: State-Formation after the Cultural Turn*, ed. George Steinmetz (Ithaca, N.Y.: Cornell University Press, 1999), 89.

40. Alisa Del Re, "Women and Welfare: Where is Jocasta?" in *Radical Thought in Italy: A Potential Politics*, ed. Paolo Virno and Michael Hardt (Minneapolis: University of Minnesota Press, 1996), 110.

41. Ibid., 100.

42. Ibid., 110.

3. REINVENTING STATOLATRY: FROM NICOS POULANTZAS TO AL GORE

1. See Timothy Mitchell, "Society, Economy, and the State Effect," in *State/Culture: State-Formation after the Cultural Turn*, ed. George Steinmetz (Ithaca, N.Y.: Cornell University Press, 1999), 89.

2. See, for instance, the "Reinventing American Federalism" issue of *Issues of Democracy: Electronic Journal of the U.S. Information Agency* 2, no. 2 (April 1997), which quotes *The Blair House Papers* on reinvention published by Al Gore extensively.

3. Hilary Wainwright, "A New Kind of Knowledge for a New Kind of State," in *A Different Kind of State? Popular Power and Democratic Administration*, ed. Gregory Albo, David Langille, and Leo Panitch (Toronto: Oxford University Press, 1993), 120.

4. Gregory Albo, "Democratic Citizenship and the Future of Public Management," in *A Different Kind of State? Popular Power and Democratic Administration*, ed. Gregory Albo, David Langille, and Leo Panitch (Toronto: Oxford University Press, 1993), 23.

5. Leo Panitch, "A Different Kind of State?" in *A Different Kind of State? Popular Power and Democratic Administration*, ed. Gregory Albo, David Langille, and Leo Panitch (Toronto: Oxford University Press, 1993), 11. Panitch does talk about sensing a fear in civil servants that reminded him of talking to people in Communist Eastern Europe, but this observation implies state workers threatened more by the state than the state object.

6. David Langille, "Putting Democratic Administration on the Political Agenda," in *A Different Kind of State? Popular Power and Democratic Administration*, ed. Gregory Albo, David Langille, and Leo Panitch (Toronto: Oxford University Press, 1993), 229–43; and Robert Reich, ed., *The Power of Public Ideas* (Cambridge, Mass.: Ballinger, 1988).

7. For a good, if partisan review of the marxist debate occurring in Western Europe from the 1960s to the 1980s, see Simon Clarke, "The State Debate," in *The State Debate*, ed. Simon Clarke (New York: St. Martin's, 1991), 40–78.

8. Nicos Poulantzas, "Dual Power and the State" *New Left Review* no. 109 (1978).

9. Ibid., 75–87.

10. This contemporary impulse of quarantine owes a lot to Ernesto Laclau and Chantal Mouffe, *Hegemony and Socialist Strategy* (London: Verso, 1985).

11. Wendy Brown, *States of Injury: Power and Freedom in Late Modernity* (Princeton, N.J.: Princeton University Press, 1995); and Arturo Escobar, "Imagining a Post-Development Era," in *Power of Development*, ed. Jonathan Crush (New York: Routledge, 1995).

12. Louis Althusser, "The Crisis of Marxism," *Power and Opposition in Post-Revolutionary Societies*, ed. Il Manifesto (London: InkLinks, 1979), 225–37; Antonio Gramsci, *Selections from the Prison Notebooks of Antonio Gramsci*, ed. Quentin Hoare and Geoffrey Nowell Smith (New York: International Publishers, 1971); Antonio Negri, "Is There a Marxist Doctrine of the State?" in *Which Socialism?* ed. Norberto Bobbio (Minneapolis: University of Minnesota Press, 1987); and Michael Hardt and Antonio Negri, *Labor of Dionysus: A Critique of the State-Form* (Minneapolis: University of Minnesota Press, 1994).

13. Quoted in Graham Burchell, Colin Gordon, and Peter Miller, eds., *The Foucault Effect: Studies in Governmentality* (Chicago: University of Chicago Press, 1991), 48.

14. See, for instance, Patricia J. Arnold, "From the Union Hall: A Labor Critique of the New Manufacturing and Accounting Regimes," *Critical Perspectives on Accounting*, no. 10 (1999): 399–423.

15. Tony Tinker, "The Accountant as Partisan," *Accounting, Organizations, and Society* 16, no. 3 (1991): 19–39; and Marilyn Neimark, "Regicide Revisited: Marx, Foucault, and Accounting," *Critical Perspectives on Accounting* 5, no. 1 (1994): 87–108. Critical accounting in general is a complex field of struggle, including Foucauldian and Haber-

masian variants, as well as a more old-fashioned professional reformism, but its marxist (to some extent, potential Foucauldian) insights come closest to doing for accounting what this book would like to begin to do for public administration, and they draw on some of the same sources not surprisingly to do so.

16. See, for instance, Chris Smith, David Knights, and Hugh Willmott, eds., introduction to *White Collar Work: The Non-Manual Labour Process* (Basingstoke, England: Macmillan, 1991).

17. See Randy Martin, *Critical Moves: Dance Studies in Theory and Practice* (Durham, N.C.: Duke University Press, 1999), 151–79. See also his "Resurfacing Socialism: Resisting the Appeals of Tribalism and Localism," *Social Text* 44, vol. 13, no. 3 (fall/winter 1995): 97–118. Here, Martin suggests that one has to try to think about the interconnectedness and scale of what techniques of state have wrought, and to admit the possibility that they could be put to different uses.

18. Michael Hardt, "The Withering of Civil Society," *Social Text* 45, vol. 14, no. 4 (winter 1995): 27–44.

19. Toby Miller, *Technologies of Truth: Cultural Citizenship and the Popular Media* (Minneapolis: University of Minnesota Press, 1998). Miller says he does not want to count expenditures or behavior in the popular media but comprehend population imageries in order to mix a critical political economy that asks "who gets to speak to whom and what forms these symbolic encounters take in the major spaces of public culture with how discourse and imagery are organized in complex and shifting patterns of meaning and how these meanings are reproduced, negotiated, and struggled over in the flow and flux of everyday life" (226).

20. I do not think it is any accident that this is state work. Miller notes that popular culture, like madness before it for Foucault, can be characterized as the opposite of work (*Technologies of Truth,* 266). But in these imageries of state workers there is perhaps an example of the boldness of the circuitry of social production, of capital leaving behind class relations, in the cultural constitution of citizen and subject. Such imageries show work as culture, as the social, without fear of class, and yet it is clearly state work and thus obvious that fearlessness must be in part bravado.

21. Félix Guattari and Toni Negri, *Communists Like Us* (New York: Semiotexte, 1990).

22. See Alisa Del Re, "Women and Welfare: Where is Jocasta?" in *Radical Thought in Italy: A Potential Politics,* ed. Paolo Virno and Michael Hardt (Minneapolis: University of Minnesota Press, 1996), 98–112.

23. I am indebted to Tony Tinker for this insightful observation about the series.

24. The popularity of the series in Canada and Australia would permit an extension of this reading into a kind of neocolonial dimension in which not only do state workers in general represent the labor of advanced association among producers but especially state workers in the most intricate systems of power in the most involved imperializing nation.

25. There is a growing literature on conspiracy, with both rightist and leftist impulses. As

an example of the rightest view, see Daniel Pipes, *Conspiracy: How the Paranoid Style Flourishes and Where It Comes From* (New York: Free Press, 1998). For an enthusiasm for the antiauthoritarian attitude in conspiracy—an attitude that Pipes would find irresponsible for the intellectual to encourage—see Jodi Dean, *Aliens in America: Conspiracy Cultures from Outerspace to Cyberspace* (Ithaca, N.Y.: Cornell University Press, 1997).

26. See Paolo Virno, "Virtuosity and Revolution: The Political Theory of Exodus," in *Radical Thought in Italy: A Potential Politics,* ed. Paolo Virno and Michael Hardt (Minneapolis: University of Minnesota Press, 1996), 189–210.

27. Al Gore and the Executive Office of the President, *From Red Tape to Results: Creating a Government That Works Better and Costs Less* (Washington, D.C.: U.S. Government Printing Office, 1993), *Putting Customers First: Standards for Serving the American People* (Washington, D.C.: U.S. Government Printing Office, 1994), *Common Sense Government: Works Better and Costs Less* (Washington, D.C.: U.S. Government Printing Office, 1995), and *The Blair House Papers* (Washington, D.C.: U.S. Government Printing Office, 1997).

28. Jacques Derrida, *Spectres of Marx: The State of the Debt, the Work of Mourning, and the New International* (London: Routledge, 1994).

29. See Anne Showstack Sassoon, *Gramsci's Politics* (London: Hutchinson, 1987).

30. Gilles Deleuze and Félix Guattari, *A Thousand Plateaus: Capitalism and Schizophrenia* (Minneapolis: University of Minnesota Press, 1987), 130.

31. Quoted in Showstack Sassoon, *Gramsci's Politics,* 268–69.

32. Ernesto Laclau, "The Specificity of the Political," in *Politics and Ideology in Marxist Theory* (London: Verso, 1979), 51–79.

33. Hardt and Negri, *Labor of Dionysus,* 226.

34. Hardt, "The Withering of Civil Society."

35. The *Economist* speaks of e-citizenship and seems to concede that such a citizenship will be not only more intimate with government but also the source of much of its labor. See "Government and the Internet: The Next Revolution," *Economist,* 24 June 2000, 3–34.

36. David Osborne and Ted Gaebler, *Reinventing Government: How the Entrepreneurial Spirit is Transforming the Public Sector from the Schoolhouse to the Statehouse, City Hall to the Pentagon* (Reading, Mass.: Addison-Wesley, 1992).

37. See Peter Dunleavy and Charles Hood, "From Old Public Administration to New Public Management," *Public Money and Management* (July/September 1994): 9–16.

38. Michael Hammer, "Reengineering Work: Don't Automate, Obliterate," *Harvard Business Review* (July–August 1990): 104–12.

39. See Deleuze and Guattari, *A Thousand Plateaus,* 454–55.

40. Richard Nixon's commission represented a facile attempt to introduce business practices into government following the destruction of the Great Society state project. Gore's project, by contrast, represents an attempt to assist in the realization of the

axiomatic through new techniques—for instance, by mixing ambitious social goals with strict budgets pushing state labor down through the levels of government and eventually out into the labor of publics.

41. Donald F. Kettl and John Dilulio Jr., eds., *Inside the Reinvention Machine: Appraising Governmental Reform* (Washington, D.C.: Brookings Institute, 1995); and B. Guy Peters, "Models of Governance for the 1990s," in *The State of Public Management*, ed. Donald F. Kettl and H. Brinton Milward (Baltimore, Md.: Johns Hopkins University Press, 1996), 15–44.

42. Michael Barzelay and Babak J. Armajani, *Breaking through Bureaucracy: A New Vision for Managing Government* (Berkeley: University of California Press, 1992).

43. This debate in public administration can be traced to Frank Goodnow, *Politics and Administration: A Study in Government* (New York: Russell and Russell, 1900), and continues today with network theories' insistence on the almost completely porous bodies of administration and politics.

44. Deleuze and Guattari, *A Thousand Plateaus,* 130.

45. Michel Foucault, *Discipline and Punish* (London: Harmondsworth, 1979); and Claus Offe, *Contradictions of the Welfare State* (Cambridge: MIT Press, 1984). For an account of the way Foucault refined his ideas of discipline in later lectures, see Colin Gordon, "Governmental Rationality: An Introduction," in *The Foucault Effect: Studies in Governmentality*, ed. Graham Burchell, Colin Gordon, and Peter Miller (Chicago: University of Chicago Press, 1991).

46. This is certainly a conclusion that could be drawn from the spectacle of citizenship in Miller, *Technologies of Truth.*

47. Mary Parker Follet, "The Giving of Orders," in *Classics of Public Administration*, ed. Jay M. Shafritz and Albert C. Hyde, 4th ed. (Fort Worth, Tex.: Harcourt Brace, 1997), 53–60.

48. See Frank Fischer, "Organizational Expertise and Bureaucratic Control: Behavioral Science as Managerial Ideology," in *Critical Studies in Organization and Bureaucracy*, ed. Frank Fischer and Carmen Sirianni (Philadelphia, Pa.: Temple University Press, 1994), 174–95.

49. Louis Bronlow, Charles E. Merriam, and Luther Gulick, "Report of the President's Committee on Administrative Management," in *Classics of Public Administration*, ed. Jay M. Shafritz and Albert C. Hyde, 4th ed. (Fort Worth, Tex.: Harcourt Brace, 1997), 90–94.

50. Charles Lindblom, "The Science of Muddling Through," in *Classics of Public Administration*, ed. Jay M. Shafritz and Albert C. Hyde, 4th ed. (Fort Worth, Tex.: Harcourt Brace, 1997), 198–208. More recently, this line of flight has been understood by Ralph Hummel in "Stories Managers Tell: Why They are as Valid as Science," in *Research in Public Administration: Reflections on Theory and Practice*, ed. Jay D. White and Guy B. Adams (Thousand Oaks, Calif.: Sage, 1994).

51. Michael Hardt and Antonio Negri, *Empire* (Cambridge: Harvard University Press,

2000). For a discussion of what they call the third imperative of empire, see Stefano Harney, *Neocolonial Management* (New York: Routledge, forthcoming).

52. Gore, *Blair House Papers*, 1.

53. Hindy Lauer Schachter, *Frederick Taylor and the Public Administration Community: A Reevaluation* (Albany, N.Y.: State University of New York Press, 1989).

54. Michael Burawoy, *Manufacturing Consent: Changes in the Labor Process under Monopoly Capitalism* (Chicago: University of Chicago Press, 1979). I take up the labor process literature as it might apply to the state elsewhere in this book.

55. James O'Connor, *The Fiscal Crisis of the State* (New York: St. Martin's, 1973); and Antonio Negri, "The State and Public Spending," in *Labor of Dionysus: A Critique of the State-Form*, Michael Hardt and Antonio Negri (Minneapolis: University of Minnesota Press, 1994), 180–213.

56. See Jane Slaughter, *The Concept of Teams* (Boston: South End Press, 1988).

57. Gore, *Blair House Papers*, 7.

58. Robin Murray, "Life After Henry," *Marxism Today* (October 1988): 24–29.

59. Gore, *Blair House Papers*, 11.

60. See David Gordon, *Fat and Mean: The Corporate Squeeze of Working America and the Managerial Myth of "Downsizing"* (New York: Free Press, 1996).

61. Gore, *Blair House Papers*, 12.

62. Ibid., 3–4.

63. Ibid., 12.

64. Of course, as Keith Grant and Steve Woolgar point out in *The Machine at Work: Technology, Work, and Organization* (Cambridge, U.K.: Polity, 1997), capitalism includes a general rationalization process, one that is both at work and promoted in the state labor process. But despite Max Weber, state workers have continually thought about their work as having goals other than rationalization, and even today many public administrators and theorists write of helping U.S. workers to be more competitive as a goal and not a means to something else.

65. See William D. Richardson, *Democracy, Bureaucracy, and Character: Founding Thoughts* (Kansas City: University of Kansas Press), 1997.

66. See Hindy Lauer Schachter, *Reinventing Government or Reinventing Ourselves: The Role of Citizen-Owners in Making a Better Government* (Albany: State University of New York Press, 1997).

67. Gore, *Blair House Papers*, 2.

68. See Michael Lipsky, *Street-Level Bureaucracy: Dilemmas of the Individual in the Public Services* (New York: Russell Sage, 1980).

69. Gore, *Blair House Papers*, 10.

70. Ibid., 5.

71. Lauren Berlant, *The Queen of America Goes to Washington City* (Durham, N.C.: Duke University Press, 1997), 230.

72. Antonio Negri, "Twenty Theses on Marx," in *Marxism beyond Marxism*, ed. Saree Makdisi, Cesare Cesarino, and Rebecca E. Karl (New York: Routledge, 1996), 149–80.

73. Tom Peters, 3.

74. Philip K. Howard, 7.

75. See Donna Haraway, "A Cyborg Manifesto," in *Simians, Cyborgs, and Women: The Reinvention of Nature* (New York: Routledge, 1991).

4. GENERALIZING SOCIAL TERROR: PUBLIC MANAGEMENT AND PERFORMANCE BY OBJECTIVES

1. For extended discussions of this notion of the state effect, see Graham Burchell, Colin Gordon, and Peter Miller, eds., *The Foucault Effect: Studies in Governmentality* (Chicago: University of Chicago Press, 1991).

2. Michael Denning, *The Cultural Front: The Laboring of American Culture in the Twentieth Century* (New York: Verso, 1997).

3. Philip Corrigan and Derek Sayer, *The Great Arch: English State Formation and Cultural Revolution* (Oxford: Blackwell, 1991).

4. Antonio Negri, "Twenty Theses on Marxism," in *Marxism beyond Marxism,* ed. Saree Makdisi, Cesare Cesarino, and Rebecca E. Karl (New York: Routledge, 1996), 149–80; Paolo Virno, "Virtuosity and Revolution: The Political Theory of Exodus," in *Radical Thought in Italy: A Potential Politics,* ed. Paolo Virno and Michael Hardt (Minneapolis: University of Minnesota Press, 1996), 189–212.

5. Tony Tinker, *Paper Prophets: A Social Critique of Accounting* (New York: Praeger, 1985).

6. "The prime directive of management is to look after the system," says Nicholas Henry in the seventh edition of his widely used textbook, *Public Administration and Public Affairs* (Upper Saddle River, N.J.: Prentice Hall, 1999), 472.

7. Here one might note Judith Butler's belated observation in *The Psychic Life of Power: Theories in Subjection* (Stanford, Calif.: Stanford University Press, 1997) that Foucault understood identities as "formed within contemporary political arrangements in relation to certain requirements of the liberal state. . . . The more specific identities become, the more totalized an identity becomes by that very specificity" (83).

8. Paolo Virno views immaterial labor as work defined by "cultural, informational, or knowledge components or by qualities of service and care." Paolo Virno and Michael Hardt, eds., *Radical Thought in Italy: A Potential Politics* (Minneapolis: University of Minnesota Press, 1996), 262. It is more difficult to separate labor time from time outside work in immaterial labor, and also more difficult to administer this labor.

9. Donald F. Kettl, introduction to *The State of Public Management,* ed. Donald. F. Kettl and H. Brinton Milward (Baltimore, Md.: Johns Hopkins University Press, 1996), 8.

10. For an example of the first critique, see H. George Frederickson, *The Spirit of Public Administration* (San Francisco, Calif.: Jossey-Bass, 1997). For an example of the latter critique, see John Clarke and Janet Newman, *The Managerial State: Power, Politics, and Ideology in the Remaking of Social Welfare* (Thousand Oaks, Calif.: Sage, 1997).

11. For an example of the public administrationist critique, see "Symposium: Leadership, Democracy, and the New Public Management," *Public Administration Review* 58, no. 3

(May/June 1998): 189–231. For an example of the social democratic critique see Robert Reich, *The Wealth of Nations* (New York: Alfred Knopf, 1991).

12. Barry Bozeman, ed., *Public Management: The State of the Art* (San Francisco, Calif.: Jossey-Bass, 1993); and Donald F. Kettl and H. Brinton Milward, eds., *The State of Public Management* (Baltimore, Md.: Johns Hopkins University Press, 1996).

13. Kettl, introduction, 11.

14. Donald F. Kettl and John Dilulio Jr., *Inside the Reinvention Machine: Appraising Governmental Reform* (Washington, D.C.: Brookings Institute, 1995).

15. Jürgen Habermas, *Legitimization Crisis*. Boston: Beacon Books, 1975.

16. Kettl, introduction, 6.

17. Jeffrey Pressman and Aaron Wildavsky, *Implementation: How Great Expectations in Washington are Dashed in Oakland or, Why It's Amazing That Federal Programs Work at All, This Being the Saga of the Economic Development Administration* (Berkeley: University of California Press, 1973).

18. For an account of the critical turn in U.S. social sciences, see Michael E. Brown and Randy Martin, "Socialism in Transition: Documents and Discussion; An Essay on Rethinking the Crisis in Socialism," *Socialism and Democracy* 7, no. 3 (1991): 9–56.

19. For an example of this case being laid at the feet of implementationists and public managerialists, see Peter G. Brown, "The Legitimacy Crisis and the New Progressivism," *Public Administration Review* 58, no. 4 (July/August 1998): 290–92. As Brown writes, "My thesis is that those of us who educate for public service have, through the best of intentions, played an important role in this crisis" (290).

20. Kettl, introduction, 4.

21. Laurence E. Lynn Jr., "The New Public Management: How to Transform a Theme into a Legacy," *Public Administration Review* 58, no. 3 (May/June 1998): 231–38; and B. Guy Peters, "Models of Governance for the 1990s," in *The State of Public Management,* ed. Donald F. Kettl and H. Brinton Milward (Baltimore, Md.: Johns Hopkins University Press, 1996), 15–46.

22. Tony Cutler and Barbara Waine, *Managing the Welfare State: The Politics of Public Sector Management* (London: Berg, 1994), 26.

23. See Organization for Economic Cooperation and Development, *Governance in Transition: Public Management Reforms in OECD Countries* (Paris: Organization for Economic Cooperation and Development, 1995). See also Jan-Erik Lane, ed., *Public Sector Reform: Rationale, Trends, and Problems* (London: Sage, 1997).

24. Mark Turner and David Hulme, *Governance, Administration, and Development: Making the State Work* (West Hartford, Conn.: Kumarian, 1997), 240.

25. David Osborne and Ted Gaebler, *Reinventing Government: How the Entrepreneurial Spirit is Transforming the Public Sector from the Schoolhouse to the Statehouse, City Hall to the Pentagon* (Reading, Mass.: Addison-Wesley, 1992).

26. H. Brinton Milward, "Conclusion: What is Public Management?" in *The State of*

Public Management, ed. Donald F. Kettl and H. Brinton Milward (Baltimore, Md.: Johns Hopkins University Press, 1996), 310.

27. Some typical examples of this distributionist critique can be found in Ronald Aronson, "A Question of Values," *Nation,* 1998; Michael Walzer, "Pluralism and Social Democracy," *Dissent,* 1998; Mitchell Cohen, "Why I Am Still 'Left,'" *Dissent,* 1998; and Ulrick Beck, "Capitalism without Work," *Dissent,* 1998.

28. Of course, the United States is notorious for not having an organized social democratic party, but a look at the disorganized social democratic impulses in this country reveal precisely this program. See, for instance, the party platforms of the New Party, Green Party–New York, and newly formed Labor Party. See especially Juliet Schor's platform piece for the New Party, *A Sustainable Economy for the Twenty-first Century* (Westfield, N.J.: Open Media, 1995).

29. Theodor W. Adorno, "The Sociology of Knowledge and Its Consciousness," in *The Essential Frankfurt School Reader,* ed. Andrew Arato and Eike Gebhardt (New York: Continuum, 1994), 453.

30. For a clear exposition on this ideology of exchange, see Bertell Ollman, "Market Mystification in Capitalist and Market Socialist Societies," in *Market Socialism: The Debate among Socialists,* ed. Bertell Ollman (New York: Routledge, 1998), 81–121.

31. This insistence on the role that public management plays in dismantling the social welfare state does not preclude a view of the crisis as partly brought on by the success of labor and other social movements, but it is remarkable how often this insistence comes to overshadow other causalities.

32. Robert Reich, for instance, originally advocated investment in human capital instead of the search for immediate profitability, but published *Public Management in a Democratic Society* (Englewood, N.J.: Prentice Hall, 1990), in which he tried to reconcile the two approaches. Advocates of the second approach, gathered in David Trend, ed., *Radical Democracy: Citizenship, Identity, and State* (New York: Routledge, 1997), have argued the efficiency case for cooperative and grassroots power, as the New Public Administration did in the late 1960s and early 1970s before its eclipse by a certain kind of implementation studies.

33. Linda Kaboolian, "The New Public Management: Challenging the Boundaries of the Management vs. Administration Debate," *Public Administration Review* 58, no. 3 (May/June 1998): 189.

34. See William D. Richardson, *Democracy, Bureaucracy, and Character: Founding Thought* (Kansas City: University of Kansas Press, 1997); and Brian J. Cook, *Bureaucracy and Self-Government: Reconsidering the Role of Public Administration in American Politics* (Baltimore, Md.: Johns Hopkins University Press, 1996).

35. See Hindy Lauer Schachter, *Reinventing Government or Reinventing Ourselves: The Role of Citizen-Owners in Making a Better Government* (Albany: State University of New York, 1997); and Rita Mae Kelly and Georgia Duerst-Lahti, eds., *Gender Power, Leadership, and Governance* (Ann Arbor: University of Michigan Press, 1995).

36. Laurence E. Lynn Jr., "Public Management Research: The Triumph of Art over Science," *Journal of Policy Analysis and Management* 13, no. 2 (1994): 231–59.

37. See O. C. McSwite, *Legitimacy in Public Administration: A Discourse Analysis* (Thousand Oaks, Calif.: Sage, 1997).

38. See Henry D. Kass and Bayard Catron, eds., *Images and Identities in Public Administration* (Thousand Oaks, Calif.: Sage, 1990); and Jay D. White and Guy B. Adams, eds., *Research in Public Administration: Reflections on Theory and Practice* (Thousand Oaks, Calif.: Sage, 1994).

39. Ewan Ferlie et al., *The New Public Management in Action* (Oxford: Oxford University Press, 1996), argues that performance can be relegated to one category of the New Public Management, "efficiency drives." This is inconsistent with the managerialist literature from which the New Public Management derives so many of the "concepts" boxed by the Ferlie et al. book. Performance is a central goal in all these "themes and concepts" (except the "public service orientation" category) in all managerialist literature, and implicitly in the New Public Management literature Ferlie et al. are reviewing.

40. For the sake of clarity, I am using the terms private sector and public sector in the way they appear in the literature, although obviously they are relationally constitutive.

41. Peters, "Models of Governance," 22.

42. See David J. Teece, Gary Pisano, and Amy Shuen, "Dynamic Capabilities and Strategic Management," *Strategic Management Journal* 18, no. 7 (1997): 509.

43. On getting managers to work hard, see Vicki Smith, *Managing in the Corporate Interest: Control and Resistance in an American Bank* (Berkeley: University of California Press, 1990).

44. A good review of the firm literature is Bengt Holmstrom and John Roberts, "The Boundaries of the Firm Revisited," *Journal of Economic Perspectives* 12, no. 4 (fall 1998): 73–94.

45. See Stanley Aronowitz, "Marx, Braverman, and the Logic of Capital," in *The Politics of Identity: Class, Culture, and Social Movements* (New York: Routledge, 1992).

46. Michael E. Brown, *The Production of Society: A Marxian Foundation for Social Theory* (Totowa, N.J.: Rowman and Littlefield, 1986), 118.

47. Ibid., 118.

48. Peggy Phelan, "Introduction: The Ends of Performance," in *The Ends of Performance*, ed. Peggy Phelan and Jill Lane (New York: New York University Press, 1998), 3.

49. Peggy Phelan, *Unmarked: The Politics of Performance* (New York: Routledge, 1993).

50. Victor Turner, *The Forest of Symbols* (Ithaca, N.Y.: Cornell University Press, 1970); and Richard Schechner, *Between Theatre and Anthropology* (Philadelphia: University of Pennsylvania Press, 1985).

51. See especially Judith Butler's last essay on the political implications of her work, "Implicit Censorship and Discursive Agency," in *Excitable Speech: A Politics of the Performative* (New York: Routledge, 1997), *Bodies That Matter: On the Discursive Limits of "Sex"* (New York: Routledge, 1993), and *Gender Trouble: Feminism and the Subversion*

of Identity (New York: Routledge, 1990). But see also Jon McKenzie, "Genre Trouble: (The) Butler Did It," in *The Ends of Performance,* ed. Peggy Phelan and Jill Lane (New York: New York University Press, 1998), 217–35.

52. Randy Martin, "Staging Crisis: Twin Tales in Moving Politics," in *The Ends of Performance,* ed. Peggy Phelan and Jill Lane (New York: New York University Press, 1998), and *Socialist Ensembles* (Minneapolis: University of Minnesota Press, 1994).

53. Fred Moten, introduction to *Women and Performance: A Journal of Feminist Theory* 18, vol. 9, no. 2 (1997): 1–2. See also Moten's "The Dark Lady and the Sexual Cut: Sonnet Record Frame/Shakespeare Jones Eisenstein," in the same issue (143–57). Moten extends his search for an organization moment when he says that "sonnet, record, frame are their own improvisations; this is to say that something held within these forms also exceeds them. . . . [T]his ephemeral and paradoxical generativity, this expressive procreativity," hints at "the possibility of a totality, to which we must remain devoted" (155–57).

54. I am using statelike to preserve some of the uncertainty of boundaries any post-Foucauldian analysis should respect. I also use it to emphasize that quality of social return that despite the public choice literature, cannot be reduced to pure profit seeking at its source.

55. See William Andrews, "The New NYPD," *Spring 3100,* at http://www.ci.nyc.ny.us/html/nypd/html/3100/newnypd.html.

56. I discuss the state labor process elsewhere in my work on public administration.

57. Kaboolian, "New Public Management," 190.

58. See Michael K. Brown, *Working the Street: Police Discretion and the Dilemma of Reform* (New York: Russell Sage, 1981).

59. See, for instance, Barbara Koremos and Laurence E. Lynn Jr., "Leadership of a State Agency," in *The State of Public Management,* ed. Donald F. Kettl and H. Brinton Milward (Baltimore, Md.: Johns Hopkins University Press, 1996). This advocacy of a return to managerial authority to act, and away from the influences, however real, of quality-of-life circles and team-based approaches, is an important development in the managerialist literature, authorized especially by the reengineering discourse in the 1980s.

60. See Dennis Rosenbaum, ed., *The Challenge of Community Policing: Testing the Promises* (Thousand Oaks, Calif.: Sage, 1994).

61. See Steve Herbert, "Police Subculture Reconsidered," *Criminology* 36, no. 2 (May 1998): 343–69. Herbert argues for a more complex source of brutality, but acknowledges social distance as a prime source.

62. For instance, in an end-of-the-year interview, Police Chief Howard Safir attributed continuing downward trends in violent crimes to his not giving in to the "bullying" of community activists who wanted a return to community policing (see Mike Kelly, "Crime Lowest since 1964," *New York Times,* 24 December 1998, 1).

63. See Chris Mitchell, "The Brutal Truth," *City Limits Magazine* (December 1997): 16–21.

64. Paul Chevigny, *Edge of the Knife: Police Violence in the Americas* (New York: New Press, 1995).

65. Angela Davis, "Masked Racism: Reflections on the Prison-Industrial Complex," in *Colorlines: Race, Culture, Action* 1, no. 2 (fall 1998): 11–12.

66. See Paul Wright, "Captive Labor: U.S. Business Goes to Jail," *Covert Action Quarterly Magazine* (spring 1997): 26–31.

67. See George Kelling and Catherine Coles, *Fixing Broken Windows: Restoring Order and Reducing Crime in Our Communities* (New York: Free Press, 1996).

68. See Annette Fuentes, "The Crackdown on Kids," *Nation*, 15/22 June 1998, 20–24.

69. See Jennifer Gonnerman, "New York's Drug Law Debacle," *Village Voice*, 12 May 1998, 38–40.

70. Antonio Gramsci, "Americanism and Fordism" in *Selections from the Prison Notebooks*. The emphasis on surveillance—as in the cover story by Mark Boal, "Surveillance City: From the Stores to the Streets, Cameras Watch Your Every Move," *Village Voice*, 6 October 1998, 38–44—tends to stress control over a more insidious process: a managed care of the self as corporate consumer and worker.

71. John Dilulio Jr., "Help Wanted: Economics, Crime, and Public Policy," *Journal of Economic Perspectives* 10, no. 1 (winter 1998): 3–24. Here, Dilulio links obsessions with black crime and public management.

72. See Mimi Abramovitz, *Under Attack, Fighting Back*, 2d ed. (New York: Monthly Review Press, 1999).

73. See Vaughan S. Radcliffe, "Knowing Efficiency: The Enactment of Efficiency in Efficiency Auditing," *Accounting, Organizations, and Society* 24 (1999): 333–62.

74. Claus Offe, *Contradictions of the Welfare State* (Cambridge: MIT Press, 1984).

75. Pasquale Pasquino, "Theatrum Politicum: The Genealogy of Capital; Police and the State of Prosperity," in *The Foucault Effect: Studies in Governmentality*, ed. Graham Burchell, Colin Gordon, and Peter Miller (Chicago: University of Chicago Press, 1991), 116.

76. Paolo Virno, "Notes on the General Intellect," in *Marxism beyond Marxism*, ed. Saree Makdisi, Cesare Cesarino, and Rebecca E. Karl (New York: Routledge, 1996), 265–72.

5. THE ADMINISTRATION OF MOTIVATION: ANY COOK CAN NETWORK

1. Andrew Zimbalist, introduction to *Case Studies on the Labor Process*, ed. Andrew Zimbalist (New York: Monthly Review Press, 1979), xv.

2. I will be drawing particularly on the labor process as understood by Michael Burawoy in *Manufacturing Consent: Changes in the Labor Process under Monopoly Capitalism* (Chicago: University of Chicago Press, 1979). He, in turn, is drawing on Harry Braverman, *Labor and Monopoly Capital: The Degradation of Work in the Twentieth Century* (New York: Monthly Review Press, 1974).

3. See David Knights and Hugh Willmott, eds., *Labor Process Theory* (London: Macmillan, 1990).

4. There has been an attempt to talk about a state labor process in Australia; see John Alford, "Who Said Production Was Simple: Delineating the Public Production Process," *Australian Journal of Public Administration* 55, no. 4 (December 1996): 157–63. The term in this book is closer to its origins in this marxist line of inquiry.

5. An admirable attempt to break from this instrumentalism can be observed in Gary L. Wamsley and James F. Wolf, eds., *Refounding Democratic Public Administration: Modern Paradoxes, Postmodern Challenges* (Thousand Oaks, Calif.: Sage, 1996). Although they make some interesting observations about public administration labor through the lens of postmodernism, their solutions tend to be ethical.

6. In fact, considerable social scientific effort has been devoted to understanding public worker motivation from a strictly instrumentalist perspective. For a good review, see Carole Jurkiewicz, Tom Massey, and Roger Brown, "Motivation in Public and Private Organizations: A Comparative Study," *Public Productivity and Management Review* 21, no. 3 (March 1998): 230–50.

7. "Curious as it may seem today, bureaucrats in the '30s were regarded by many as heroes in the struggles for better social order" (Herbert Kaufman, "Administrative Decentralization and Political Power," in *Classics of Public Administration,* ed. Jay M. Shafritz and Albert C. Hyde, 4th ed. [Fort Worth, Tex.: Harcourt Brace, 1997], 121).

8. Burawoy, *Manufacturing Consent.*

9. Jacques Taminiaux, *Dialectic and Difference: Modern Thought and the Sense of Human Limits* (Atlantic Highlands, N.J.: Humanities Press, 1990), 52.

10. Randy Martin's reading of the commodity fetish against the grain of the standard marxist interpretation suggests Marx understood more of the Nietzschean antihumanist moment than has commonly been credited ("On Your Mark," a talk at the Rethinking Marxism conference on "Teaching Capital." Amherst, Mass., 9 December 1996).

11. See Robert Kangel, *The One Best Way: Frederick Winslow Taylor and the Enigma of Efficiency* (New York: Penguin, 1997).

12. Luther Gulick and Leon Urwick, *Papers on the Science of Administration* (New York: Institute of Public Administration, 1937).

13. Quoted in Stephen P. Waring, *Taylorism Transformed: Scientific Management Theory since 1945* (Chapel Hill: University of North Carolina Press, 1991), 15. Waring's business history, although more theoretically informed than most, maintains the fiction of the divide between scientific management and human relations discussed below. Although he quotes Burawoy late in the book, he cannot quite bring himself to say that the recourse to the irrational that occurs when rational management fails is a product of the contradictions of forcing people to do something that is not in their interest—that is, work for wages.

14. See Keith Grant and Steve Woolgar, *The Machine at Work: Technology, Work, and Organization* (Cambridge, U.K.: Polity, 1997).

15. Waring, *Taylorism Transformed*, 18.

16. The best single introduction to public administrationist discursive history is Jan-Erik Lane, ed., *Public Sector Reform: Rationale, Trends, and Problems* (London: Sage, 1997).

17. Indeed, without the marxist politics, critical organizational theorists, especially in England, have understood the organizational narrative in just this way. See, for instance, Michael Reed and Michael Hughes, eds., *Rethinking Organization: New Directions in Organization Theory and Analysis* (London: Sage, 1992).

18. Chris Smith and Paul Thompson, "Reevaluating the Labor Process Debate," in *Rethinking the Labor Process*, ed. Mark Wardell, Thomas L. Steiger, and Peter Meiksins (Albany: State University of New York, 1999), 214–15.

19. Andrew Sturdy, David Knights, and Hugh Willmott, eds., *Skill and Consent: Contemporary Studies in the Labour Process* (London: Routledge, 1992), 18. By contrast, I try to use subjectivity here as a figure of social relations.

20. David Knights and Theo Vurdubakis, "Foucault, Power, Resistance, and All That," in *Resistance and Power in Organizations*, ed. John M. Jermiet, David Knights, and Walter R. Nord (London: Routledge, 1994), 167–98.

21. Avery Gordon, "The Work of Corporate Culture: Diversity Management," *Social Text* 44 (fall/winter 1995): 3–30; and Christopher Newfield, "Corporate Pleasures for a Corporate Planet," *Social Text* 44 (fall/winter 1995): 31–44.

22. Newfield, "Corporate Pleasures," 40.

23. Ibid., 39.

24. I will be using the phrase alien ethical state as the notion of an alien politics is initially situated in a good historical account by Paul Thomas in his *Alien Politics: Marxist State Theory* (New York: Routledge, 1994).

25. Ralph Miliband, *The State in Capitalist Society* (London: Quartet Books, 1984).

26. Graham T. Allison, "Public and Private Management: Are They Fundamentally Alike in All Unimportant Respects?" in *Classics of Public Administration*, ed. Jay M. Shafritz and Albert C. Hyde, 4th ed. (Fort Worth, Tex.: Harcourt Brace, 1997), 383–400.

27. Toby Miller, *Technologies of Truth: Cultural Citizenship and the Popular Media* (Minneapolis: University of Minnesota Press, 1998), 96–97.

28. Edward Pendleton Herring, *Public Administration and the Public Interest* (New York: McGraw Hill, 1936).

29. James L. Nolan, *The Therapeutic State: Justifying Government at Century's End* (New York: New York University Press, 1998).

30. Judith Butler, *The Psychic Life of Power: Theories in Subjection* (Stanford, Calif.: Stanford University Press, 1997), 128. In *Conscience Doth Make Subjects of Us All: Althusser's Subjection*, she first seems to reject, then accept an idealist understanding of ethics, perhaps misreading Giorgio Agamben's notion about the social and material imperative to be something. She locates a deeper being beyond interpellation in self rather than in pleasures of representing a society of producers.

31. Philip Selznick, "The Cooptating Mechanism" in Jay M. Shafritz and Albert C. Hyde,

eds. *Classics of Public Administration*, 4th ed. (Fort Worth, Tex.: Harcourt Brace, 1997), 147–53.

32. Louis Althusser, *For Marx* (London: Verso, 1965), 230.

33. Michael Hardt and Antonio Negri, *Labor of Dionysus: A Critique of the State-Form* (Minneapolis: University of Minnesota Press, 1994), 140.

34. Claus Offe, *Contradictions of the Welfare State* (Cambridge: MIT Press, 1984); see especially the interview titled "Reflections on a Welfare State," in which he summarizes his theory of de-commodification and suggests that capitalism's ability to organize social life is being reduced by the modern welfare state.

35. Burawoy, *Manufacturing Consent*, 202.

36. Stanley Aronowitz, *The Politics of Identity: Class, Culture, and Social Movements* (New York: Routledge, 1992), 76–124.

37. See Michael Burawoy's *The Politics of Production* (London: Verso, 1985), where in an essay on Braverman, Burawoy lays out his critique.

38. Luther H. Martin, Huck Gutman, and Patrick H. Hutton, eds., *Technologies of the Self: A Seminar with Michel Foucault* (Amherst: University of Massachusetts Press, 1988).

39. Michael E. Brown, *The Production of Society: A Marxian Foundation for Social Theory* (Totowa, N.J.: Rowman and Littlefield, 1986), 76.

40. See Nicholas Abercrombie, Stephen Hill, and Bryan S. Turner, *Dominant Ideologies* (London: Unwin Hyman, 1990).

41. Antonio Gramsci, "Americanism and Fordism," in *Selections from the Prison Notebooks of Antonio Gramsci*, ed. Quentin Hoare and Geoffrey Nowell Smith (New York: International Publishers, 1971).

42. The literature on "trust" is similarly unable to acknowledge that the freedom to calculate is based on the historical development of forms of trust that may then be naturalized back into human nature and the economy. Oliver Williamson, Herbert Blau, and even Harold Garfinkel lack this historical perspective in various ways in their considerations of trust—a historical perspective requiring not just historicizing but antihumanizing to uncover the construction called trust, just as one would want to uncover the humanist conception of skill in Braverman's work. For a summary of this "trust" literature, see Craig Thomas, "Maintaining and Restoring Public Trust in Government Agencies and Their Employees," *Administration and Society* 30, no. 2 (May 1998): 166–93.

43. Alan McKinlay and Ken Starkey, "Afterword: Deconstructing Organization—Discipline and Desire," in *Foucault, Management, and Organization Theory: From Panopticon to Technologies of Self*, ed. Alan McKinlay and Ken Starkey (Thousand Oaks, Calif.: Sage, 1998), 238.

44. See Randy Martin, *Critical Moves: Dance Studies in Theory and Politics* (Durham, N.C.: Duke University Press, 1998).

45. I borrow the term underlife from Michael E. Brown in his discussion of the infraprocesses of class struggle. He actually uses the phrase "underlife of protest" (*The*

Production of Society: A Marxian Foundation for Social Theory [Totowa, N.J.: Rowman and Littlefield, 1986], 98).

46. Toby Miller, *The Well-Tempered Self: Citizenship, Culture, and the Postmodern Subject* (Baltimore, Md.: Johns Hopkins University Press, 1993).

47. Michel Foucault, *Remarks on Marx* (New York: Semiotexte, 1991), 64. On academic laborers, see Stefano Harney and Fred Moten, "Doing Academic Labor," in *Chalk Lines: The Politics of Labor in the Managed University,* ed. Randy Martin (Durham, N.C.: Duke University Press, 1998).

48. Mark R. Rutgers, "Beyond Woodrow Wilson: The Identity of the Study of Public Administration in Historical Perspective," *Administration and Society* 29, no. 3 (July 1997): 296.

49. See Toby Miller, review of *Postmodern Public Administration: Towards Discourse,* by Charles J. Fox and Hugh T. Miller, *Australian Journal of Public Administration* 55, no. 4 (December 1996): 178–79. See also Linda F. Dennard, "The Democratic Potential in the Transition of Postmodernism," *American Behavioral Scientist* 41, no. 1 (September 1997): 148–62.

50. Frank Goodnow, *Politics and Administration: A Study in Government* (New York: Russell and Russell, 1900), 17.

51. Leonard D. White, *Introduction to the Study of Public Administration* (Upper Saddle River, N.J.: Prentice Hall, 1926), 3.

52. R. A. W. Rhodes, "The New Governance: Governing without Government," *Political Studies* 44 (1996): 656. See also Peter Bogason and Theo A. J. Toonen, "Introduction: Networks in Public Administration," *Public Administration* (76, summer 1998): 205–27. And in sociology, see Manuel Castells's trilogy, *The Information Age: Economy, Society, and Culture* (Oxford: Blackwell, 1996, 1997, 1998).

53. Game theory and rational choice models abound in the managerialist literature on networks.

54. See Joshua Cohen and Joel Rogers, *Associations and Democracy,* ed. Erik Olin Wright (London: Verso, 1995).

55. Indeed, *Managing Complex Networks: Strategies for the Public Sector,* ed. Walter J. M. Kickert, E. Hans Klijn and Joop F. M. Koppenjan (London: Sage, 1997), speaks of networks as the reality public management must learn to manipulate.

56. Samuel R. Delany, *Times Square Red, Times Square Blue* (New York: New York University Press, 1999).

57. Maurizio Lazzarato, "Immaterial Labor," in *Radical Thought in Italy: A Potential Politics,* ed. Paolo Virno and Michael Hardt (Minneapolis: University of Minnesota Press, 1996), 146.

SELECT BIBLIOGRAPHY

Abercrombie, Nicholas, Stephen Hill, and Bryan S. Turner, eds. *Dominant Ideologies*. London: Unwin Hyman, 1990.

Abramovitz, Mimi. *Under Attack, Fighting Back*. 2d ed. New York: Monthly Review Press, 1999.

Aglietta, Michel. *A Theory of Capitalist Regulation*. London: Verso, 1979.

Albo, Gregory. "Democratic Citizenship and the Future of Public Management." In *A Different Kind of State? Popular Power and Democratic Administration*, edited by Gregory Albo, David Langille, and Leo Panitch. Toronto: Oxford University Press, 1993.

Alford, John. "Who Said Production Was Simple: Delineating the Public Production Process." *Australian Journal of Public Administration* 55, no. 4 (December 1996): 157–63.

Althusser, Louis, and Etienne Balibar. *Reading Capital*. London: Verso, 1986.

Aronowitz, Stanley. *The Politics of Identity: Class, Culture, and Social Movements*. New York: Routledge, 1992.

———. *The Death and Rebirth of American Radicalism*. London: Routledge, 1996.

Balibar, Etienne, and Immanual Wallerstein. *Race, Class, Nation*. London: Verso, 1991.

Barzelay, Michael, and Babak J. Armajani. *Breaking through Bureaucracy: A New Vision for Managing Government*. Berkeley: University of California Press, 1992.

Berlant, Lauren. *The Queen of America Goes to Washington City*. Durham, N.C.: Duke University Press, 1997.

Bonefeld, Werner, and John Holloway, eds. *Post-Fordism and Social Form: A Marxist Debate on the Post-Fordist State*. London: Macmillan, 1991.

Bourdieu, Pierre. *Acts of Resistance: Against the Tyrannies of the Market*. New York: New Press, 1998.

Bozeman, Barry, ed. *Public Management: The State of the Art*. San Francisco, Calif.: Jossey-Bass, 1993.

Brandt, Deborah. *Naming the Moment: Political Analysis for Action*. Toronto: Jesuit Centre for Social Faith and Justice, 1989.

Braverman, Harry. *Labor and Monopoly Capital: The Degradation of Work in the Twentieth Century*. New York: Monthly Review Press, 1974.

Brown, Michael E. *The Production of Society: A Marxian Foundation for Social Theory*. Totowa, N.J.: Rowman and Littlefield, 1986.

Brown, Michael E., and Randy Martin. "Socialism in Transition: Documents and Discussion; An Essay on Rethinking the Crisis in Socialism." *Socialism and Democracy* 7, no. 3 (1991): 9–56.

———. "Left Futures." *Socialism and Democracy* 9, no. 1 (spring 1995): 59–89.

Brown, Michael E., et al., eds. *New Studies in the Politics and Culture of U.S. Communism*. New York: Monthly Review Press, 1993.

Brown, Michael K. *Working the Street: Police Discretion and the Dilemma of Reform*. New York: Russell Sage, 1981.

Brown, Wendy. *States of Injury: Power and Freedom in Late Modernity*. Princeton, N.J.: Princeton University Press, 1995.

Burawoy, Michael. *Manufacturing Consent: Changes in the Labor Process under Monopoly Capitalism*. Chicago: University of Chicago Press, 1979.

———. *The Politics of Production*. London: Verso, 1985.

Burchell, Graham, Colin Gordon, and Peter Miller, eds. *The Foucault Effect: Studies in Governmentality*. Chicago: University of Chicago Press, 1991.

Burrows, Roger, and Brian Loader, eds. *Towards a Post-Fordist Welfare State*. London: Routledge, 1994.

Butler, Judith. *Gender Trouble: Feminism and the Subversion of Identity*. New York: Routledge, 1990.

———. *Bodies That Matter: On the Discursive Limits of "Sex."* New York: Routledge, 1993.

———. "Implicit Censorship and Discursive Agency." In *Excitable Speech: A Politics of the Performative*. New York: Routledge, 1997.

———. *The Psychic Life of Power: Theories in Subjection*. Stanford, Calif.: Stanford University Press, 1997.

Castells, Manuel. *The Information Age: Economy, Society, and Culture*. Oxford: Blackwell, 1996, 1997, 1998.

Chevigny, Paul. *Edge of the Knife: Police Violence in the Americas*. New York: New Press, 1995.

Clarke, John, and Janet Newman. *The Managerial State: Power, Politics, and Ideology in the Remaking of Social Welfare*. Thousand Oaks, Calif.: Sage, 1997.

Clarke, Simon, ed. *The State Debate*. New York: St. Martin's, 1991.

Cohen, Joshua, and Joel Rogers. *Associations and Democracy*. Edited by Erik Olin Wright. London: Verso, 1995.

Cook, Brian J. *Bureaucracy and Self-Government: Reconsidering the Role of Public Administration in American Politics*. Baltimore, Md.: Johns Hopkins University Press, 1996.

Corrigan, Philip, and Derek Sayer. *The Great Arch: English State Formation and Cultural Revolution*. Oxford: Blackwell, 1991.

Cutler, Tony, and Barbara Waine. *Managing the Welfare State: The Politics of Public Sector Management*. London: Berg, 1994.

Davis, Jim, et al., eds. *Cutting Edge: Technology, Information, Capitalism, and Social Revolution*. London: Verso, 1997.

Dean, Jodi. *Aliens in America: Conspiracy Cultures from Outerspace to Cyberspace*. Ithaca, N.Y.: Cornell University Press, 1997.

Delany, Samuel R. *Times Square Red, Times Square Blue*. New York: New York University Press, 1999.

Deleuze, Gilles, and Félix Guattari. *A Thousand Plateaus: Capitalism and Schizophrenia*. Minneapolis: University of Minnesota Press, 1987.

Denning, Michael. *The Cultural Front: The Laboring of American Culture in the Twentieth Century*. New York: Verso, 1997.

Derrida, Jacques. *Spectres of Marx: The State of the Debt, the Work of Mourning, and the New International*. London: Routledge, 1994.

Dobuzinskis, Laurent, Michael Howlett, and David Laycock, eds. *Policy Studies in Canada: The State of the Art*. Toronto: University of Toronto Press, 1996.

Doray, Bernard. *From Taylorism to Fordism: A Rational Madness*. London: Free Association Books, 1988.

Fairbrother, Peter. *Politics and the State as Employer*. London: Mansell, 1994.

Feigenbaum, Harvey B., and Jeffrey R. Henig. *Shrinking the State: The Political Underpinnings of Privatization*. Cambridge: Cambridge University Press, 1998.

Ferlie, Ewan, et al. *The New Public Management in Action*. Oxford: Oxford University Press, 1996.

Fischer, Frank. "Organizational Expertise and Bureaucratic Control: Behavioral Science as Managerial Ideology." In *Critical Studies in Organization and Bureaucracy*, edited by Frank Fischer and Carmen Sirianni. Philadelphia, Pa.: Temple University Press, 1994.

Foucault, Michel. *Discipline and Punish*. London: Harmondsworth, 1979.

——. *Remarks on Marx*. New York: Semiotexte, 1991.

Frederickson, H. George. *The Spirit of Public Administration*. San Francisco, Calif.: Jossey-Bass, 1997.

Fuentes, Annette. "The Crackdown on Kids." *Nation*, 15/22 June 1998, 20–24.

Gonnerman, Jennifer. "New York's Drug Law Debacle." *Village Voice*, 12 May 1998, 38–40.

Goodnow, Frank. *Politics and Administration: A Study in Government*. New York: Russell and Russell, 1900.

Gordon, Avery, and Christopher Newfield, eds. *Mapping Multiculturalism*. Minneapolis: University of Minnesota Press, 1996.

Gordon, David. *Fat and Mean: The Corporate Squeeze of Working America and the Managerial Myth of "Downsizing."* New York: Free Press, 1996.

Gore, Al, and the Executive Office of the President. *From Red Tape to Results: Creating a*

Government That Works Better and Costs Less. Washington, D.C.: U.S. Government Printing Office, 1993.

Gramsci, Antonio. *Selections from the Prison Notebooks of Antonio Gramsci.* Edited by Quentin Hoare and Geoffrey Nowell Smith. New York: International Publishers, 1971.

Grant, Keith, and Steve Woolgar. *The Machine at Work: Technology, Work, and Organization.* Cambridge, U.K.: Polity, 1997.

Guattari, Félix, and Toni Negri. *Communists Like Us.* New York: Semiotexte, 1990.

Gulick, Luther, and Leon Urwick. *Papers on the Science of Administration.* New York: Institute of Public Administration, 1937.

Habermas, Jürgen. *Legitimization Crisis.* Boston: Beacon Books, 1975.

Haines, Charles G., and Marshall E. Dimock, eds. *Essays on the Law and Practice of Governmental Administration: A Volume in Honor of Frank Johnson Goodnow.* Baltimore, Md.: Johns Hopkins University Press, 1935.

Hall, Stuart, and Martin Jacques, eds. *New Times.* London: Lawrence and Wishart, 1989.

Haraway, Donna, *Simians, Cyborgs, and Women: The Reinvention of Nature.* New York: Routledge, 1991.

Hardt, Michael. "The Withering of Civil Society." *Social Text* 45, vol. 14, no. 4 (winter 1995): 27–44.

Hardt, Michael, and Antonio Negri. *The Labor of Dionysus: A Critique of the State-Form.* Minneapolis: University of Minnesota Press, 1994.

——. *Empire.* Cambridge: Harvard University Press, 2000.

Harney, Robert F. "So Great a Heritage as Ours." *Daedalus.*

Harney, Stefano. *Neocolonial Management.* New York: Routledge, forthcoming.

Hassard, John. *Sociology and Organization Theory: Positivism, Paradigms, and Postmodernity.* Cambridge: Cambridge University Press, 1995.

Hawkesworth, M. E. *Theoretical Issues in Policy Analysis.* Albany: State University of New York Press, 1988.

Henry, Nicholas. *Public Administration and Public Affairs.* 7th ed. Upper Saddle River, N.J.: Prentice Hall, 1999.

Herbert, Steve. "Police Subculture Reconsidered." *Criminology* 36, no. 2 (May 1998): 343–69.

Herring, Edward Pendleton. *Public Administration and the Public Interest.* New York: McGraw Hill, 1936.

Holden, Matthew. *Continuity and Disruption: Essays in Public Administration.* Pittsburgh, Pa.: University of Pittsburgh Press, 1996.

Holzer, Marc, and Kathe Callahan. *Government at Work: Best Practices and Model Programs.* Thousand Oaks, Calif.: Sage, 1998.

Hummel, Ralph P. *The Bureaucratic Experience.* New York: St. Martin's, 1987.

Ibbitson, John. *Promised Land: Inside the Mike Harris Revolution.* Toronto: Prentice Hall, 1989.

Ignatieff, Noel, ed. *Race Traitor.* New York: Routledge, 1998.

James, C. L. R. *Every Cook Can Govern: A Study of Democracy in Ancient Greece*. Detroit, Mich.: Bewick, 1992.

Jameson, Fredric. *The Geopolitical Aesthetic: Cinema and Space in the World System*. Bloomington: University of Indiana Press, 1992.

Jermier, John M., David Knights, and Walter R. Nord, eds. *Resistance and Power in Organizations*. London: Routledge, 1994.

Kangel, Robert. *The One Best Way: Frederick Winslow Taylor and the Enigma of Efficiency*. New York: Penguin, 1997.

Kass, Henry D., and Bayard Catron, eds. *Images and Identities in Public Administration*. Newbury Park, Calif.: Sage, 1990.

Kelling, George, and Catherine Coles. *Fixing Broken Windows: Restoring Order and Reducing Crime in Our Communities*. New York: Free Press, 1996.

Kelly, Rita Mae, and Georgia Duerst-Lahti, eds. *Gender Power, Leadership, and Governance*. Ann Arbor: University of Michigan Press, 1995.

Kettl, Donald F., and John Dilulio Jr., eds. *Inside the Reinvention Machine: Appraising Governmental Reform*. Washington, D.C.: Brookings Institute, 1995.

Kettl, Donald F., and H. Brinton Milward, eds. *The State of Public Management*. Baltimore, Md.: Johns Hopkins University Press, 1996.

Knights, David, and Hugh Willmott, eds. *Gender and the Labour Process*. Aldershot, England: Gower, 1986.

——. *Labor Process Theory*. London: Macmillan, 1990.

Knights, David, and Theo Vurdubakis, "Foucault, Power, Resistance, and All That." In *Resistance and Power in Organizations*, edited by John M. Jermiet, David Knights, and Walter R. Nord. London: Routledge, 1994.

Laclau, Ernesto. *Politics and Ideology in Marxist Theory*. London: Verso, 1979.

Laclau, Ernesto, and Chantal Mouffe. *Hegemony and Socialist Strategy*. London: Verso, 1985.

Lane, Jan-Erik, ed. *Public Sector Reform: Rationale, Trends, and Problems*. London: Sage, 1997.

Lipsky, Michael. *Street-Level Bureaucracy: Dilemmas of the Individual in the Public Services*. New York: Russell Sage, 1980.

Low, Donald M. *The Body in Late-Capitalist USA*. Durham, N.C.: Duke University Press, 1995.

Lyotard, Jean-François. *The Postmodern Condition: A Report on Knowledge*. Minneapolis: University of Minnesota Press, 1984.

Marini, Frank, ed. *Toward a New Public Administration: The Minnowbrook Perspective*. Scranton, Pa.: Chandler, 1971.

Martin, Luther H., Huck Gutman, and Patrick H. Hutton, eds. *Technologies of the Self: A Seminar with Michel Foucault*. Amherst: University of Massachusetts Press, 1988.

Martin, Randy. *Socialist Ensembles.* Minneapolis: University of Minnesota Press, 1994.

——. "Fragmentation and Fetishism: The Postmodern in Marx." *Critical Perspectives on Accounting* 9 (1998): 77–93.

——. *Critical Moves: Dance Studies in Theory and Politics*. Durham, N.C.: Duke University Press, 1999.

Marx, Karl. *Grundrisse: Introduction to the Critique of Political Economy*. New York: Vintage, 1973.

McKinlay, Alan, and Ken Starkey, eds. *Foucault, Management, and Organization Theory: From Panopticon to Technologies of Self*. Thousand Oaks, Calif.: Sage, 1998.

McKinnon, Catherine. *Toward a Feminist Theory of the State*. Cambridge: Harvard University Press, 1991.

McSwite, O. C. *Legitimacy in Public Administration: A Discourse Analysis*. Newbury Park, Calif.: Sage, 1997.

Miliband, Ralph. *The State in Capitalist Society*. London: Quartet Books, 1984.

Miller, Toby. *The Well-Tempered Self: Citizenship, Culture, and the Postmodern Subject*. Baltimore, Md.: Johns Hopkins University Press, 1993.

——. *The Avengers*. London: British Film Institute, 1997.

——. *Technologies of Truth: Cultural Citizenship and the Popular Media*. Minneapolis: University of Minnesota Press, 1998.

Mitchell, Chris. "The Brutal Truth." *City Limits Magazine* (December 1997): 16–21.

Moore, Mark H. *Creating Public Value: Strategic Management in Government*. Cambridge: Harvard University Press, 1997.

Munoz, Jose Esteban. *Disidentifications*. Minneapolis: University of Minnesota Press, 1999.

Murray, Robin. *Breaking with Bureaucracy: Ownership, Control, and Nationalisation*. Manchester, England: Centre for Local Economic Strategy, 1987.

——. *Exil*. Paris: Editions Mille et Un Nuits, 1998.

——. *Insurgencies: Constituent Power and the Modern State*. Minneapolis: University of Minnesota Press, 1999.

Negt, Oskar, and Alexander Kluge. *The Public Sphere and Experience: Toward an Analysis of the Bourgeois and Proletarian Public Sphere*. Minneapolis: University of Minnesota Press, 1993.

Nelson, Cary, and Lawrence Grossberg, eds. *Marxism and the Interpretation of Culture*. Urbana: University of Illinois Press, 1988.

——. *Cultural Studies*. New York: Routledge, 1991.

Nolan, James L. *The Therapeutic State: Justifying Government at Century's End*. New York: New York University Press, 1998.

O'Connor, James. *The Fiscal Crisis of the State*. New York: St. Martin's, 1973.

Offe, Claus. *Contradictions of the Welfare State*. Cambridge: MIT Press, 1984.

Ollman, Bertell, ed. *Market Socialism: The Debate among Socialists*. New York: Routledge, 1998.

Ontario Antiracism Secretariat. *On Anti-Racism and the Ontario Anti-Racism Secretariat*. Toronto: Government of Ontario, 1993.

——. *A Guide to Key Anti-Racism Terms and Concepts*. Toronto: Government of Ontario, 1993.

Organization for Economic Cooperation and Development. *Governance in Transition: Public*

Management Reforms in OECD Countries. Paris: Organization for Economic Cooperation and Development, 1995.

Osborne, David, and Ted Gaebler. *Reinventing Government: How the Entrepreneurial Spirit is Transforming the Public Sector from the Schoolhouse to the Statehouse, City Hall to the Pentagon.* Reading, Mass.: Addison-Wesley, 1992.

Phelan, Peggy. *Unmarked: The Politics of Performance.* New York: Routledge, 1993.

Phelan, Peggy, and Jill Lane, eds. *The Ends of Performance.* New York: New York University Press, 1998.

Piore, Michael J., and Charles F. Sabel. *The Second Industrial Divide: Possibilities for Prosperity.* New York: Basic Books, 1984.

Pipes, Daniel. *Conspiracy: How the Paranoid Style Flourishes and Where It Comes From.* New York: Free Press, 1998.

Pollert, Anna, ed. *Farewell to Flexibility?* Oxford: Blackwell, 1991.

Poulantzas, Nicos. *Political Power and Social Classes.* London: New Left Books, 1973.

———. *State, Power, and Socialism.* London: New Left Books, 1978.

———. *Classes in Contemporary Capitalism.* London: Verso, 1979.

Pressman, Jeffrey, and Aaron Wildavsky. *Implementation: How Great Expectations in Washington are Dashed in Oakland, or Why It's Amazing That Federal Programs Work at All, This Being the Saga of the Economic Development Administration.* Berkeley: University of California Press, 1973.

———. *From Protest to Power.* Toronto: Viking, 1996.

Reed, Michael, and Michael Hughes, eds. *Rethinking Organization: New Directions in Organization Theory and Analysis.* London: Sage, 1992.

Reich, Robert. *Public Management in a Democratic Society.* Englewood, N.J.: Prentice Hall, 1990.

Richardson, William D. *Democracy, Bureaucracy, and Character: Founding Thoughts.* Kansas City: University of Kansas Press, 1997.

———, ed. *The Phantom Public Sphere.* Minneapolis: University of Minnesota Press, 1993.

Rosenbaum, Dennis, ed. *The Challenge of Community Policing: Testing the Promises.* Thousand Oaks, Calif.: Sage, 1994.

Schachter, Hindy Lauer. *Frederick Taylor and the Public Administration Community: A Reevaluation.* Albany, N.Y.: State University of New York Press, 1989.

———. *Reinventing Government or Reinventing Ourselves: The Role of Citizen-Owners in Making a Better Government.* Albany: State University of New York Press, 1997.

Schechner, Richard. *Between Theatre and Anthropology.* Philadelphia: University of Pennsylvania Press, 1985.

Schor, Juliet. *A Sustainable Economy for the Twenty-first Century.* Westfield, N.J.: Open Media, 1995.

Scott, James C. *Seeing like a State: How Certain Schemes to Improve the Human Condition Have Failed.* New Haven, Conn.: Yale University Press, 1998.

Shafritz, Jay M., and Albert C. Hyde, eds. *Classics of Public Administration.* 4th ed. Fort Worth, Tex.: Harcourt Brace, 1997.

Showstack Sassoon, Anne. *Gramsci's Politics*. London: Hutchinson, 1987.

Slaughter, Jane. *The Concept of Teams*. Boston: South End Press, 1988.

Slaughter, Sheila, and Larry L. Leslie. *Academic Capitalism: Politics, Policies, and the Entrepreneurial University*. Baltimore, Md.: Johns Hopkins University Press, 1997.

Smith, Chris, David Knights, and Hugh Willmott, eds. *White Collar Work: The Non-Manual Labour Process*. Basingstoke, England: Macmillan, 1991.

Smith, Vicki. *Managing in the Corporate Interest: Control and Resistance in an American Bank*. Berkeley: University of California Press, 1990.

Sturdy, Andrew, David Knights, and Hugh Willmott, eds. *Skill and Consent: Contemporary Studies in the Labour Process*. London: Routledge, 1992.

Taminiaux, Jacques. *Dialectic and Difference: Modern Thought and the Sense of Human Limits*. Atlantic Highlands, N.J.: Humanities Press, 1990.

Theakston, Kevin. *The Civil Service since 1945*. Oxford: Basil Blackwell, 1995.

Thomas, Paul. *Alien Politics: Marxist State Theory*. New York: Routledge, 1994.

Tinker, Tony. *Paper Prophets: A Social Critique of Accounting*. New York: Praeger, 1985.

——. "Braverman's Return: A Reexamination of the British Labor Process Critiques." 9 June 2000. Paper.

Trend, David, ed. *Radical Democracy: Citizenship, Identity, and State*. New York: Routledge, 1997.

Turner, Mark, and David Hulme. *Governance, Administration, and Development: Making the State Work*. West Hartford, Conn.: Kumarian, 1997.

Turner, Victor. *The Forest of Symbols*. Ithaca, N.Y.: Cornell University Press, 1970.

Virno, Paolo, and Michael Hardt, ed. *Radical Thought in Italy: A Potential Politics*. Minneapolis: University of Minnesota Press, 1996.

Walby, Sheila. *Patriarchy at Work*. Cambridge, England: Polity Press, 1986.

Waldo, Dwight. *The Administrative State: A Study of the Political Theory of American Public Administration*. 2d ed. New York: Holmes and Meier, 1984.

Wamsley, Gary L., and James F. Wolf, eds. *Refounding Democratic Public Administration: Modern Paradoxes, Postmodern Challenges*. Thousand Oaks, Calif.: Sage, 1996.

Waring, Stephen P. *Taylorism Transformed: Scientific Management Theory since 1945*. Chapel Hill: University of North Carolina Press, 1991.

Weeks, Kathi. *Constituting Feminist Subjects*. Ithaca, N.Y.: Cornell University Press, 1998.

White, Jay D., and Guy B. Adams. *Research in Public Administration: Reflections on Theory and Practice*. Newbury Park, Calif.: Sage, 1994.

Wilson, James Q. *Bureaucracy: What Government Agencies Do and Why They Do It*. New York: Basic Books, 1989.

Woolgar, Steve, *Science: The Very Idea*. New York: Routledge, 1993.

Wright, Paul. "Captive Labor: U.S. Business Goes to Jail." *Covert Action Quarterly Magazine* (spring 1997): 26–31.

Zimbalist, Andrew, ed. *Case Studies on the Labor Process*. New York: Monthly Review Press, 1979.

INDEX

Stefano Harney is Assistant Professor of Sociology, City University of New York, College of Staten Island. He is author of *Nationalism and Identity: Culture and the Imagination in a Caribbean Diaspora* (Zed Books, 1996) and of a forthcoming study on neocolonial management (Routledge).

Library of Congress Cataloging-in-Publication Data
Harney, Stefano.
State work : public administration and mass
intellectuality / Stefano Harney.
Includes bibliographical references and index.
ISBN 0-8223-2880-1 (cloth : alk. paper) —
ISBN 0-8223-2895-x (pbk. : alk. paper)
1. Bureaucracy. 2. Public administration.
3. Popular culture. 4. Popular culture—Study and teaching. I.
Title.
JF1501 .H37 2002   306.2—dc21   2001007739